GENETICS AND THE POLITICS OF SECURITY

Presenting a social science perspective on the contemporary gaze on the body of the suspect, this book considers how definitions of criminality, offenses, individual rights, and the concepts of identity and difference have been altered by changes in the biological status of the human.

Spurred by rapid developments in genetics and information technology, a number of countries, including France, the United States, the United Kingdom, China, and the Netherlands, have considerably expanded their genetic databases used by the police and the criminal justice system. Whilst this makes it possible to compare DNA left at the scene of a crime with that of an individual known to the police, helping to identify individuals for the purposes of court proceedings, these innovations also raise a number of important questions, such as how the relationship between respect for the rights of individuals and the security of populations is discussed, as well as for how long this data should be retained. Genetic analysis also raises concerns related to phenotyping and "biogeographical origin" that could lead to the stigmatization of targeted groups.

Offering a comprehensively argued view on how DNA acts not only as a tracker of suspicion but also as a marker of contemporary social developments, *Genetics and the Politics of Security* will appeal to students and scholars, judiciary personnel, lawyers, police officers, and people with an interest in criminology and the use of genetics in the criminal justice process.

Joëlle Vailly is a French sociologist, anthropologist, and biologist. She is Director of Research at the French Scientific Research National Center (CNRS) and a member of the Institute for Interdisciplinary Research into Social Issues, IRIS, France.

Routledge Frontiers of Criminal Justice

European Perspectives on Pre-Trial Detention
A Means of Last Resort
Christine Morgenstern, Walter Hammerschick and Mary Rogan

War as Protection and Punishment
Armed Military Interventions at the 'End of History'
Teresa Degenhardt

Criminalising Coercive Control
Challenges for the Implementation of Northern Ireland's Domestic Abuse Offence
Edited by Vanessa Bettinson and Ronagh McQuigg

Restorative Justice at a Crossroads
Dilemmas of Institutionalisation
Edited by Giuseppe Maglione, Ian D. Marder and Brunhilda Pali

The Lived Experiences of Claiming Wrongful Conviction in Prison
Maintaining Innocence
Emma Burtt

Sexual Offences Against Children in India
Understanding the Criminal Justice Responses
Sonali Swetapadma and Paromita Chattoraj

Prison Recipes and Prison Cookbooks
A.E. Stearns

Genetics and the Politics of Security
A Social Science Perspective
Joëlle Vailly

For more information about this series, please visit: www.routledge.com/Routledge-Frontiers-of-Criminal-Justice/book-series/RFCJ

GENETICS AND THE POLITICS OF SECURITY

A Social Science Perspective

Joëlle Vailly

Translated by Rachel Gomme

Routledge
Taylor & Francis Group
LONDON AND NEW YORK

Designed cover image: gettyimages.com

First published in English 2024
by Routledge
4 Park Square, Milton Park, Abingdon, Oxon OX14 4RN

and by Routledge
605 Third Avenue, New York, NY 10158

Routledge is an imprint of the Taylor & Francis Group, an informa business

Translated by Rachel Gomme

British Library Cataloguing-in-Publication Data
A catalogue record for this book is available from the British Library

ISBN: 978-1-032-59747-8 (hbk)
ISBN: 978-1-032-58888-9 (pbk)
ISBN: 978-1-003-45605-6 (ebk)

DOI: 10.4324/9781003456056

Typeset in Sabon
by Taylor & Francis Books

CONTENTS

ACKNOWLEDGMENTS

This book is the result of a long process that would not have been possible without the help and support of many individuals. My thanks go first to the research team on the "Genetic Databases and Witnesses. Genealogy, Social issues, Circulation" project, which culminated in this book: Pascal Beauvais, Florence Bellivier, Élisabeth Fortis, Christine Noiville, Florence Paterson, and Vololona Rabeharisoa, and most especially to the project's post-doctoral researchers Gaëlle Krikorian and Yasmine Bouagga for their assistance in gathering field data.

The Institut de recherche interdisciplinaire sur les enjeux sociaux (Institute for Interdisciplinary Research into Social Issues, IRIS) offered me a stimulating and supportive working environment throughout the process of this research. The Institute for Advanced Study in Princeton provided me with an exceptional context for preparing this book.

I would like to express my profound gratitude to Didier Fassin for his always attentive support and his helpful and constructive advice. Heartfelt thanks also to Jean-Pierre Hassoun, Benjamin Lemoine, Helena Machado, Amade M'charek, Susana Narotzky, Alondra Nelson, and Peter Wade, for the conversations we have had at various points during this research.

I am deeply grateful to Medha Malaviya, senior editorial assistant, for her helpfulness and the welcome she extended to my manuscript, and to the editorial staff at Routledge.

My thanks go also to all the individuals we interviewed and who were willing to answer our questions, helping to bring clarity to our work. This gratitude extends to all those who agreed to share their experience and their opinions with us.

Many thanks too to Rachel Gomme for her meticulous, precise, and efficient work translating the text into English. I am grateful to Anne-Claire Baratault for her help with documentation, to Helena Devillers for managing the administrative side of the project, to Estelle Girard for her assistance in promoting and supporting our research, and to Émilie Jacquemot for her help in putting the project together.

Last but not least, my heartfelt thanks to the close people who have accompanied me through the various episodes of this scientific saga.

This study was made possible by a grant from the Agence nationale de la recherche (contract ANR-14-CE29–0014). The translation into English was funded by the LabEx Tepsis (Transformation of State, Politization in Society, Social Institution) and by IRIS.

INTRODUCTION

Identity and profiling in the 21st century

Renewing digital identity documents, submitting our fingerprints or leaving the image of our iris on a scanner when crossing a border; passing in front of a CCTV camera or using facial recognition on a mobile phone; leaving a DNA trace that could be used in a criminal or civil investigation; learning that exiles drowned in the Mediterranean or the Channel have been identified on the basis of DNA; witnessing the exhumation of the as yet unidentified body of a victim of dictatorship in Latin America or elsewhere: all of these methods of identification are part of our lives, or feature in our near or more distant environments. Increasingly common, they are employed both in everyday state administration and in situations of crime or disaster. These biometric methods, which consist of automatically recognizing an individual on the basis of their physical or biological characteristics, have become part of our identity and lived experience. The fact that they are rooted in the body enables long-term identification from which it is difficult to escape. They may also be applied without the knowledge of the individual concerned, on the basis of traces left involuntarily, rendering them especially accessible, provided that the technical and legal conditions are met. Today, moreover, they are present throughout the world, all the more so in a global space characterized by the circulation of people and technologies (Ong and Collier, 2005). Questions about excessive, unforeseen, or wasteful use of the associated data may therefore arise in situations where these methods are insufficiently regulated. In short, on the positive side they enjoy a high degree of scientific legitimacy and offer the power to resolve and elucidate problematic situations or crimes. On the negative side, they give rise to concerns about civil liberties in political contexts that vary and evolve over time. As they continue to develop rapidly, there is an urgent need for reflection on the knowledges they make possible to produce, the professional and institutional rationales behind them, and their social and political implications, in order to address questions both of theory and of civil rights.

DOI: 10.4324/9781003456056-1

Starting from this consideration, this study is located at the point where some of these new biometric practices intersect with police and court databases. First, because the biometric techniques that are used in criminal law merit particular study, given that the police and judicial administrations form a significant facet of the political regulation of societies (De Maillard and Roché, 2009). What is sometimes known as the "scientification" of police work (Johnson et al., 2003) – in other words the growing use of scientific techniques in police practice – creates expectations about the use of databases in preventing and detecting crime. Second, police databases (which, we should bear in mind, are not comprised entirely of biometric data) facilitate the identification of suspects in serious crimes or of unidentified cadavers, help to exonerate those wrongly accused, and provide evidence in trials. Indeed, over the last twenty years there has been a rapid rise in the use of records and databases by the police and justice system. Moreover, given that infinitesimal traces (a hair, a few cells, a CCTV image) are now sufficient to serve as evidence in a criminal investigation, it is worth asking whether the possibility of being erroneously categorized as a suspect for a period of time is increasing as the potential for being entered into a police database grows. Just as there are two sides to biometrics, in terms of the legitimacy it conveys and the debate it gives rise to, police records are at once indispensable to police services in ensuring the safety of the public and conducting investigations, and based on sometimes dubious criteria of suspicion and risk that raise questions about how individuals are categorized.

That said, the incorporation of proof and evidence within suspects – in other words the idea that identity and danger can be detected in the body – is not new. In 19^{th}century criminology and physical anthropology, the body of the criminal, an object of medical and subsequently biomedical knowledge, was already being harnessed in the search for scientific and legal evidence of guilt (About and Denis, 2010). Alphonse Bertillon, a French criminologist working in the second half of the 19th century, developed a method that consisted of taking a series of measurements of an individual's body, together with photography and physical description (scars, tattoos, etc.), in order to identify recidivists. This method, which marked the beginning of biometrics, spread throughout Europe and the United States before it was definitively supplanted by the fingerprint technique, developed by British statistician Francis Galton.[1] Furthermore, the exchange and accumulation of police reports was established in France from the late 19th century. The foundations of biometrics and records were thus placed, particularly in France, which played an important early role in these changes. Nevertheless, while they made it possible to identify repeat offenders, the data collected operated on vastly smaller scales than today, and were less easy to consult than contemporary databases, since they were not presented in simple, transferable digital form.

The DNA databases and genetic analysis techniques used by the police and judicial system, emblematic of these developments in terms of both biometrics and records, are the subject of this book. Although it may capture public attention in high-profile court cases, as a whole this practice is subject to little public debate, and is almost unknown in its routine forms. The media and TV series highlight the genetic tests used in this context without the reader or viewer knowing exactly what is involved, beyond the fact that the genetic analyses most often used in criminal cases make it possible to compare the DNA left at a crime scene with that of an individual known to the police.

Despite being thus invisible, or only partially visible, genetic databases have grown exponentially in many countries since the 1990s (Hindmarsh and Prainsack, 2010). In 2019 Interpol, the international criminal police organization, found that 70 countries around the world, in Africa, North and South America, Asia, and Europe, had a genetic database, 31 had a specialist database on missing persons, and 89 used DNA profiles in police investigations.[2] In France, the National Automated DNA Database (Fichier national automatisé des empreintes génétiques, FNAEG) has expanded considerably since it was set up in 1998: as of 2020 it contained over 3.3 million records of individuals, and an additional 660,000 unidentified records derived from traces taken at crime scenes or from unidentified cadavers.[3] As I discuss below, three quarters of the records in the database are from suspects who have not been convicted, and this already offers a glimpse of some of the changes taking place in relation to the contemporary suspect. France has the second largest database of this kind in Europe after the United Kingdom; at the end of 2020 the latter contained around 6.7 million DNA profiles.[4] A number of other examples from around the world reveal similar expansion, which may extend beyond criminal cases. I shall come back to the case of the United States, but it is worth noting at this point that in 2019 the US government under President Donald Trump was planning to collect and store genetic data from all migrants detained after entering the United States illegally,[5] indicating that these people would become suspects on the same basis as criminal suspects. More broadly, population-wide databases are distinguished from police databases in not being based (or claiming not to be based) on prior differentiation of those who represent a threat. In 2019 the Kenyan government moved from one of these two types of databases to the other, launching a vast program to collect genetic and fingerprint data, as well as iris scans, from all the country's citizens. However, while the Kenyan High Court approved the system of digital identification, it rejected generalized collection of DNA by the public authorities.[6] Similarly, in 2015 the Kuwaiti government passed a law enabling the Ministry of the Interior to collect and store the genetic profiles of all its citizens and residents, independent of any criminal investigation. However, two years later the constitutional court challenged the law on grounds of the breach of privacy entailed, and the project was abandoned. China, which is well known to conduct iris capture and analysis, as well as the extensive facial recognition that has become part of people's daily lives, now appears to be the only country in the world where the police take mass DNA samples outside of the context of criminal investigations. In 2020 *The New York Times* reported that according to state media China had the largest genetic database in the world, with 80 million profiles, notably from minority ethnic groups such as the Uighurs, taken on the pretext of compulsory medical examinations in order to reinforce surveillance of them.[7] The organization Human Rights Watch, drawing on several municipal reports from various Tibetan towns under Chinese control, reports mass collection of DNA samples without consent from residents, including from children over the age of five.[8] What might be called the geopolitical irony of this story is that in 2017 the scientific journal *Nature* reported that in China sequencing was carried out mainly using scientific equipment supplied by Thermo Fisher, a US giant in the sector.[9] Following the controversy these revelations aroused in the United States, the company announced two years later that it was ending its involvement in DNA profiling of the Uighurs. In China, the national DNA collection program is meeting unwonted opposition, and the authorities fear that the public may react negatively to a huge database containing what they consider to be private genetic information and family relationships. That the expansion of databases is a more complex issue than first appears is thus already apparent, since genetic data clearly raise sensitive questions in the arenas of both law and public policy.

Most of those with knowledge of these questions are aware that DNA can play an important role in the conduct of a criminal investigation, helping to incriminate or exonerate a suspect, and I shall cite a number of examples. The aim of this book is not to show that these uses are entirely good or bad, particularly since they have not been evaluated in detail. It is rather to present a social science study of the contemporary suspect, at a time when a new kind of scientific expertise has been developed, capable of identifying allegedly deviant individuals on the basis of their DNA, and preserving a trace of those who are deemed dangerous to society. More specifically, this book aims to analyze the social meaning of this reality that constitutes the subject and her/his body as objects of scientific knowledge, as material evidence and proof, and as a site of securitarian government. It seeks to grasp the issues arising from technologies designed to render human difference and, potentially, human dangerousness decipherable. In this it aligns with a current of interest in the body as site of evidence and index of legal truths detected from within the molecular depths and from the surfaces of bodies, while at the same time seeking to interrogate that interest. The book raises questions about how definitions of criminality, of offenses, and of individual rights, and notions of identity and difference, are altered by changes in the biological status of the human being. More concretely, it seeks not only to examine the construction of suspects enabled by legislation and public policy, but also and above all to grasp the reasoning behind this process of construction, its forms and its effects, through the discourses and practices of agents of the state, heads of biotechnology companies, and of the individuals to whom these methods are applied. But this study can also be read as a contribution to the social science of issues around evidence, identity, and privacy, since these developments can offer a lens through which to analyze more general questions. While I focus particularly on the situation in France, I also draw examples from other countries including the United States, the United Kingdom, and the Netherlands, which, like France, are spearheading these developments. Indeed, while the models may be diverse, what is under discussion here has a value applicable to contexts beyond France.

I am interested in these uses of genetics by the police and the judicial system particularly because they sit at the heart of major contemporary shifts, for which they act as both mirror and catalyst: rapid changes in science and technology, the increased place of security issues in public debate, and the articulation of the body in public policy. Each of these areas merits extended discussion which is beyond the scope of this study. I shall note only a few features that help to place my thesis in its context.

At the intersection of major changes

On the technical and scientific level, these practices initially gained impetus from the power of scientific authority and from rapid developments in genetics. Globally, there has been a boom in knowledge, technologies, funding, and research in genetics: the (genetic) "variants" of Covid-19 and the famous "PCR" test (standing for Polymerase Chain Reaction, a technique for amplifying genetic sequences) that became the focus of daily media attention from the start of the recent pandemic offer merely one dramatic example. Health and social issues, from chronic and infectious diseases to disabilities, social problems, family relationships and quality of life, are increasingly understood from the point of view of genetics, although more complex tendencies are at play at a time when clinical practice is reasserting itself to some extent (Nelkin and Lindee, 1994; Atkinson et al., 2009; Vailly 2013). Thus while it incorporates increasing levels of complexity, the molecularization of life continues, and DNA is still a significant focus of attention in scientific research. We are also witnessing the extension of biomedical research into social worlds beyond health and science – into the police and judicial sectors but also into genealogy, with genetic tests sold online, into parenthood and family in cases where paternity is contested, and into immigration policy, with countries such as Finland, the United States, and Germany requiring DNA tests when exiles seek to reunite their families (Lee and Voigt, 2020). At the same time, knowledge of genetics is spreading – only partially, of course – through societies, and fueling people's imaginations. It is not uncommon to hear the cliché that such and such a characteristic is "in our DNA." Private companies are not lagging behind. In a context of international circulation of ideas, knowledges, methods, and biological materials, investments in biotechnology companies are increasing in both rich and "emergent" economies (Bourgain et al., 2021). To sum up, biologists, their funders, the economy of biotechnology companies, the media, political authorities, and many other actors are part and parcel of a way of thinking that is tending to find explanatory causes and solutions for social and health issues that are oriented towards genetics.

These developments sometimes generate utopian or dystopian fantasies, ranging from hopes for technological solutions to fears of manipulation by science. For this reason, as I have explained elsewhere (Vailly, 2013), it is helpful to analyze not only what science and technology *could do* but also what they are doing today. From this point of view, genetics has a certain tendency to generate analyses that are either overenthusiastic about it or highly alarmist in relation to its current or potential uses, or else that focus on issues at the center of a range of public debates around bioethics. The study on which this book is based differs in both its approach and its type of subject. It focuses on a type of practice that is developing very rapidly and, as noted above, is not widely debated. In other words, this book attempts to give an account of the routine practices and discourses of genetics in the early 21st century, and what these tell us about the contemporary suspect.

Another powerful social dynamic that is bound up with the issue of profiling is that of the use of digital technologies, since like many of our everyday activities (Flichy and Parasie, 2013; Lupton, 2014), the records are today largely digitized. Whereas historically only targeted analysis was possible through comparison of individual records, automation allows for mass processing of data over an entire population. In this context it should be noted that in France the 1978 Law on Information Technology and Civil Liberties stated that records relating to public safety, defense, and state security could only be created by decree of the Council of State, following approval by the National Committee for Information Technology and Civil Liberties (Commission Nationale de l'Informatique et des Libertés, CNIL). However, the procedure involving approval by the CNIL was abolished in 2004, and the committee, which now has a merely consultative role, thus lost the power of joint decision making over creation of the most sensitive records.[10] Although there was some opposition to this weakening of the regulatory framework, particularly among academics connected with the Center for Studies in Citizenship, Computerization and Civil Liberties (Centre d'études citoyenneté, informatisation et libertés, CECIL),[11] we may hypothesize that this change was possible because most citizens believed that digital technology helps to resolve social problems and provides them with services without any disadvantage to them. This hypothesis would suggest that concern about potential abuse of the use of data for security purposes disappears, thanks in part to the perception that these data do not relate to law-abiding citizens and only concern criminals, and in part to the idea that identification is an efficient means of maintaining public safety (Nelkin and Andrews, 1999). Similarly, appeals have been made to the Council of State condemning certain police databases as illegal,[12] but overall the number of databases continues to rise: in October 2018, a National Assembly information commission published a report noting 106 databases available to the security forces (police and gendarmerie),[13] 36 more than in 2011 (and 48 more than in 2009, 61 more than in 2008, and 70 more than in 2007).[14] More generally, Pierre Favre (2009) points out that, in a context where violence takes many forms, some of which are on the rise while others fall or change, the reduction in the public's tolerance of violence leads to a parallel increase in calls for police intervention. After the controversy stirred up by the revelations of Edward Snowden, a former contractor with the US National Security Agency, in 2013 regarding the practices of intelligence services in the English-speaking world, it is assumed that everyone is aware of the mass collection of personal data in the name of the fight against terrorism, using new digital technologies.[15] Ten years after this global scandal, the subject seems to have been relegated to the background of the concerns of politicians, journalists, and the public. The problem is that it is more difficult to object to the collection of data for police databases when we ourselves supply a huge amount of personal data online, on social media networks or elsewhere, and usually do it happily in order to meet our needs or desires for goods (buying an object), services (booking a train ticket), or social relations (keeping in touch with loved ones). The new digital technologies record our interests when we use a search engine, remember our credit card or public transportation use, gather data on our tastes, our social relationships and our photos on social networks, store commercial data when we make purchases online, collect our image on CCTV cameras in public places, all in a way that transforms our conceptions of privacy. It is as if the idea of maintaining the sanctity of private life, which not so long ago was considered essential, has become completely obsolete. Or as if anonymity and confidentiality were old-fashioned notions. In his book on what he calls the "expository society," Bernard Harcourt (2015) argues that most citizens seem resigned to this state of affairs, uninterested or unaware of it, even if some attempt to resist. We might add that many appear to approve of it when public safety is at stake. While some may believe there is no link between social media and police activity, we should remember that the New York police, for example, consider Facebook an excellent informer. According to *The New York Times*, their strategy is to use Facebook posts by suspected gang members and their digital connections to build files on entire groups of associated wrongdoers that otherwise would require years of laborious undercover work to penetrate.[16] According to the American Civil Liberties Union (ACLU), Twitter, Instagram, and Facebook are tools used by 500 US police forces, and they spied on the comings and goings of people demonstrating against police violence in a number of cities in 2014 and 2015.[17] More specifically, the police bought surveillance services from the Geofeedia corporation, which has access to data from these social networks. All of this illustrates the point to which digital technologies and their hold over private life have become run-of-the-mill for most people, helping to explain the context in which genetic databases are being developed throughout the world.

Finally, the development of police and court databases, particularly biometric databases, can clearly only be understood in the broader context of a rapid rise in securitarian legislation, evident not only in France (to quote just the most recent, the laws on "global security" and on "separatism") but also in other countries including Germany, the United Kingdom, and the United States

(Favre, 2009). Robert Castel (2003) considers the paradox inherent in the fact that the feeling of social insecurity is strongest in the societies with the highest level of security measures. Without pretending to an exhaustive literature review, it is worth noting that various explanations for this have been put forward. First, Castel distinguishes civil protection, which is designed to protect the safety of goods and persons under the rule of law, from social protection that focuses on protecting people against social adversity (sickness, accident, unemployment, etc.). He explains the paradox in terms of social instability, which sharpens a feeling of insecurity that extends to a range of different areas (health, fear of others, etc.). More specifically, he suggests that an individual in a situation of precarity, who does not know how to get through tomorrow, without a future or out of work, in a context where social protections are being eroded, comes to experience the outside as a threat. Castel also explains the paradox (which, it should be noted, is not limited to those living in precarity) in terms of the emergence of a new generation of risks – industrial, technological, health, and environmental – which increase the sense of insecurity. Other authors place contemporary developments in the long-term context, analyzing shifts in the meaning of the term "security." Frédéric Gros (2019 [2012]) identifies four key meanings of the concept. The first is the sense of serenity or peace of mind, promoted in antiquity particularly by Greek and Roman philosophy. The second relates to an objective situation marked by the absence of danger or the disappearance of threats, a sense prevalent in the Middle Ages when it stemmed from millenarian beliefs. The remaining two senses are of particular interest here, since they are more prominent in the present day, although Gros points out that all may coexist today in updated forms. The third meaning, which emerged in the 17th century through the founding texts of Hobbes, Locke, and Rousseau in particular, is that of fundamental rights, the preservation of goods and persons, and of public order, guaranteed by the state. In this sense of the term, security is the purpose, goal, and primary function of the state, which in turn draws its legitimacy from this function. Three aspects of the state are apparent here. First, the rule of law defines a contract according to which I declare myself subject to the laws laid down by the state on condition that they give me security, even at the cost of equality and liberty (legal dimension). Second, public force is designed to preserve goods and persons, to maintain public order, and to monitor and regulate circulation of all kinds (policing dimension). Finally, external power is concerned with relations with other states and especially with questions of sovereignty (military dimension). The fourth sense of the concept of security, more contemporary, relates to what Gros calls biosecurity as the control of flows, which is apparent in discourse around food safety, health security, and emotional and human security. Here security takes the sense of continuity of the life process: as a protection rather than a guarantee (of the type provided by the modern state), it relates to the individual recognized as biologically finite and also includes techniques of identification via the body. This analysis of these various meanings helps to reveal the developments, articulations, principles, and above all the important place of these concepts of security up to the present day: lower tolerance of risk, and fear, encourage pursuit of the goal of a secure society, and indeed foster the dream of a crime-free world. Lastly, other authors highlight the magnifying effects produced by media avid for sensational stories, in a context of intense competition for a scandal-hungry audience, and of escalation in political discourse. According to these authors, this leads people in France to demand or approve of increasingly securitarian policies. To sum up, the use of genetic analysis in criminal law is fed by (and feeds) the increasing prevalence of security in government action, and the growing attention focused by the authorities, particularly since 2001, on issues of terrorism (Robert and Pottier, 2004). Ultimately, the practice is located at the junction between two independent processes: on the one hand the development of genetic and digital knowledge that have risen to the top of the scientific hierarchy, and on the other the foregrounding of security issues in the political arena in Western societies.

Analytical framework

Before entering into the heart of the subject of genetic analysis, I shall begin by outlining my analytical methodology. A number of social science studies focusing on biometric and digital technologies, and on police profiling, draw on the concepts of surveillance or "social control," which have been seen since the 1960s as primarily a tool of repression (Linhardt, 2005). For a long time, the idea conveyed was often that of measures imposed from above, implemented by state powers in alliance with the private sector, and applied to populations who submitted or occasionally resisted them. These studies thus remained centered on the idea of dominance, manipulation, and coercion. Some of them drew on Michel Foucault's early works on surveillance, control, and punishment as practiced in the eighteenth and nineteenth centuries (Foucault, 1977).[18] In the 1990s, Philip Agre (1994) explained that the surveillance model has five components: 1) visual metaphors, as in Orwell's "Big Brother is watching you"; 2) the assumption that this surveillance is nondisruptive and surreptitious; 3) territorial metaphors, as in the "invasion" of a "private" personal space marked out by "rights" and the opposition between "coercion" and "consent"; 4) centralized orchestration by means of a bureaucracy with a unified set of "files"; 5) identification with the state, and in particular with consciously planned-out malevolent aims of a specifically political nature. Over time, what has become known as surveillance studies has offered a whole host of concepts, including dataveillance (Clarke, 1988), the society of control (Deleuze, 1992), the panopticon (Bentham, 1995 [1791]), securitization (Buzan et al. 1998), liquid modernity (Bauman, 2000), the surveillant assemblage (Haggerty and Ericson, 2000), the surveillance society (Marx, 2015), the culture of surveillance (Lyon, 2018), genetic surveillance (Machado and Granja, 2022), and many others. In more recent years, however, some authors like Gary Marx (2015; see also Boyne, 2000; Lianos, 2003; Lyon, 2018) have argued that surveillance is not solely, or necessarily, hierarchical, "from above," and is not designed purely to put the subject at a disadvantage. Marx points out that the current softening of "new" surveillance, which he describes as "surveillance creep," is characterized by minimal invasiveness, which renders it less visible, and that manipulation and persuasion are replacing traditional coercion. A shift in the focus of research studies, moving away from the security issue toward recent developments in online tools and the use of social networks, and the active participation of internet users in these developments, played an important part in this change of direction. These studies are useful in identifying general trends, alerting us to dangers and describing developments, particularly in terms of the invisibilization of surveillance, which gets forgotten because it has become a routine part of everyday life. But because of their sometimes still global viewpoint, they do not always allow for fine analysis of the shifts that emerge when we focus on the latest technological developments, or help to explain the varied uses of these tools, to analyze how they are received by individuals and populations, or to compare social contexts. In order to fully grasp what is at stake, I argue here that we need not overlook the essential factors that *make possible* the large-scale use of these tools and which, ultimately, lead them to be, if not desirable, at least tolerable to citizens, including in the arena of criminal justice. The arguments around efficiency of institutional services, put forward by professionals and those who promote these tools, need to be analyzed; the influence of new practices in relation to social networks and gaming would benefit from being put in perspective; and field studies based on interviews and observation would provide first-hand data.

In this sense, Foucault's analytical framework offers some useful tools. First, because they reveal how life and the living being entered into political strategies, Foucault's theories can provide analytical keys for studying the questions discussed here: the study of DNA is undoubtedly an example of the entry of the living being into political strategies. Foucault's concept of biopower refers to the emergence in the 17th century of a "power over life" that was deployed at the individual and, sometime later, collective level (Foucault, 1979). Individual because this power was centered on the body, with the aim of training it and increasing its strength, freeing it of bodily, sexual, and social habits that might be harmful to health; collective because it sought to control the species, which became a stake in political strategies to ensure reproduction and longevity, on the basis of demographics and epidemiology. These two aspects, which Foucault called the "anatomopolitics of the human body" and "biopolitics of the population," constituted two axes of development that could also find points of convergence. In short, from the 18th century, the former societies of sovereignty, in which the aim was to levy production rather than to organize it, and to decree death rather than manage life, were succeeded by "disciplinary societies." In his book "*The will to knowledge*", Foucault notes an "explosion of numerous and diverse techniques for achieving the subjugation of bodies and the control of populations, marking the beginning of an era of 'biopower' in the 18th century" (Foucault, 1979, p. 140). Foucault, who died in 1984, did not have the opportunity to take recent technological revolutions, both in genetics and in information technology, into account. Gilles Deleuze, extending Foucault's thesis, argued in 1990 that "societies of control are in the process of replacing disciplinary societies," using the tools of information technology:

> The old societies of sovereignty made use of simple machines – levers, pulleys, clocks; but the recent disciplinary societies equipped themselves with machines involving energy, with the passive danger of entropy and the active danger of sabotage; the societies of control operate with machines of a third type, computers, whose passive danger is jamming and whose active one is piracy and the introduction of viruses.
>
> *(Deleuze, 1992, p. 6)*

But to return to Foucault's line of analysis, the historical movement he studies might seem somewhat linear, and once again somewhat of an overview. The strength of the Foucauldian analytical framework is that, by demonstrating how politics becomes inscribed in bodies, it allows divergent interests to be integrated into ways of thinking, interests that can moderate this general movement of the entry of life and the living being into public policy. Indeed, later on, Foucault introduced the concept of "government," decentering and transforming theories of power, partly in response to criticism that he had not made space for resistance to a power that was seen as too omnipotent. Indeed, with its concepts of control, surveillance, and fabrication of a docile and submissive body, the first version of his theory of biopower laid itself open to this criticism. What Foucault subsequently added more clearly was an element of freedom. This term immediately calls for two remarks. First, crucially, the freedom in question is *internal* to power, for not only does power include it in its own techniques, but it can only endure with the support of this freedom. What provides this power with stability is that it neither represses nor forbids – hence the metaphor of the bee that rules without using its sting – but rather incites and produces. Secondly, more than a power or powers, what Foucault analyzes is *relations* of power that are exercised over another, recognized and maintained to the end as a subject of action. Foucault (2007) therefore defines government as the set of modes of more or less considered and calculated actions intended to act on the possibilities of action of other individuals. In this sense, government refers not only to political structures and the administration of states but to a way of structuring the possible field of action of others, "the conduct of conducts." Since this conception of power no longer situates it solely "at the top," this analytical framework includes a "microphysics" of power made up of all the apparently minor processes of power that are diffused through the fabric of society. It is therefore important for the researcher to grasp not only the strategies and instruments of government as previously defined, but also power in its extremities, where it becomes capillary, present at the level of each individual.

The centrality of the body in the "government" of individuals and populations, and in the development of knowledges, finds both new sources and new fields of application in the genetics used by the police and legal system. Foucault's exposition of power not in terms of biopower but in terms of government is particularly interesting with respect to the points made earlier, that most citizens have few expectations of privacy, and accept the collection of personal data in numerous arenas. My argument here is that the situation is more complex than that of imposed social control: practices of recording and collecting data are also becoming an everyday fact of life. We may also hypothesize that a level of tolerance has developed with regard to them, owing either to indifference or to assent from a large proportion of the public, particularly in the context of terrorist risks. As with other techniques of intrusion into private life (social networks, CCTV in public spaces, etc.), they seem to be used with the passive agreement of the majority of the population. It would appear that the routinization of these practices on the one hand, and security issues on the other, render these developments imperceptible and indeed acceptable to the majority of citizens. However, I shall argue here that their invisibility and the way they appear to go without saying ultimately makes them more problematic because they conceal everyday practices and block debate. These practices represent a particular type of securitarian "government" that operates through biological techniques in an attempt to resolve social and political problems. New subjects of law appear to be constituted – public, individuals questioned about or convicted of misdemeanors or felonies – and these need to be described.

The birth of a genetics policy

I now turn to the heart of the matter: the genetic analysis techniques used by the police and judicial system. The first point of note is that they emerged out of scientific and technical developments that led to the birth of genetic profiling in 1984. A team of biologists at the University of Leicester in the United Kingdom, led by Alec Jeffreys, showed that human DNA contains sequences (base pairs) that are repeated, and specifically that the number of repetitions varies from one individual to another, making it possible to identify them.[19] Applying this study to an immigration dispute between a family of exiles and the British Home Office, Jeffreys confirmed that a young man living in Ghana was indeed the biological son of a woman, and brother of her three children all living in the UK, as she claimed. Jeffreys described his method to the media as the science that had saved the young man from deportation (Aronson, 2005). The public image of the technique, associated with a story that ended with a happy family reunited, appeared extremely positive. This first use of the technique for the purpose of human identification in the context of immigration law was soon extended to criminal law (and to family law, which I shall not be discussing here). In 1986 the British police asked Jeffreys if he could confirm that a suspect who had confessed to the rape and murder of two young girls was indeed the person who had left a trace of semen at the scene of the crime. Biological analysis exonerated him, showing that he was not the culprit. The police then embarked on large-scale collection of over 4,000 DNA samples from local men aged between 17 and 34, to compare them to the trace. At this point a man told a woman in a pub that he had helped a friend to escape testing by attending in his place. The woman reported his remarks to the police, who then showed, with the help of the team of biologists, that the DNA of the man who had been replaced matched that of the trace, and arrested him. The man confessed to the two murders and was convicted. Jeffreys later admitted that the reliability of the technique used, known as RFLP (Restriction Fragment Length Polymorphism) was at that time unconfirmed (Aronson, 2005). It was the indirect pressure exerted on the murderer by the existence of DNA evidence, and the legitimacy it enjoyed, that did the work as much as the scientific reliability of a technique that was still in its infancy. The story excited a great deal of interest in the United Kingdom and elsewhere, and use of the method gradually increased. Initially, given that it was a lengthy and painstaking process, that it involved having large quantities of DNA available and that the information produced was not easily converted into numerical data, its use was limited to isolated comparisons of traces with the profile of suspects created through traditional investigations (Williams and Johnson, 2005). The aim at this point was to *confirm* that such suspects, including those among a small population local to the site of a crime, had indeed left their bodily traces at the scene.

From 1990 onwards, the now famous PCR (Polymerase Chain Reaction) technique made it possible both to secure a genetic profile rapidly and to extract it from small amounts of DNA. Above all, rather than transforming "words into numbers" it made it possible to "measure" (Desrosières, 2008) the number of repetitions at various points in the genome, and thus to present the results in digital form: in a purely imaginary example, TCTATCTATCTATCTA corresponds to the number four.[20] This meant that the technical conditions were in place to create large computer databases that could easily be consulted to compare profiles of individuals or traces from crime scenes. An expert in forensics testified to this development at a conference in France:

> I change an image [the RFLP] into an alphanumerical value. I move from an image that cannot be compared to an alphanumeric value that will be compared and that's it, the switch that made it possible to create databases. Now you can send the numbers by fax, by email, from one lab to another, the data can be stored, Interpol can have them, you can have databases.
>
> *(Legal expert 1)*

Genetic databases take the form of figures corresponding to the number of repetitions of small DNA sequences of very varying size, measured at several sites (known as loci) on the genome. They therefore do not contain information on the entire genome of individuals, and the "genetic markers" (small sequences) that may be analyzed by genetic profiling, of which there is now a permitted maximum of twenty-one in France, are specified by decree.[21] This approach has now become routine in criminal investigations; increasingly automated, it is based on "kits" sold by companies throughout the world to analyze several loci in a single test. In concrete terms, when a sample is taken at a police station, for example, the officer, wearing gloves and a mask, uses a small stick to rub over the mucous membranes in the mouth of the individual whose DNA is to be analyzed. The sample is sent to laboratories, which, in France, are either public or private and licensed by the state.[22] The DNA is extracted, "amplified" by PCR; its fragments are then sorted by size by passing them through a capillary tube subjected to an electric current, and the results are analyzed by forensic experts. DNA from a trace left by an unknown individual can be extracted from various types of tissue (hair, skin, semen, blood, bone, etc.) and subjected to the same kind of analysis, but the quality is sometimes not as good, and there is less of it, which can complicate interpretation of the results. In short, while PCR was not a scientific revolution, in that it did not provide a solution to theoretical problems, it generated a huge change in scientific and technical practices in the life sciences (Rabinow, 1996). At a time when genetics has become one of the flagship disciplines of the sciences (Fox Keller, 2000), this approach has come to provide a form of "primary identity" that is robust, non-modifiable and embodied (Jenkins, 2000, p. 14) – here based on genetic markers.

These innovations in the use of genetics by the police and judicial system raise a number of important questions. The first concerns how the relationship between respect for individual rights and the safety of populations is discussed, and how the resulting decisions are implemented. I use the term "relationship" rather than the commonly used "balance" here because less freedom does not necessarily mean greater security. I shall take France's National Automated DNA Database (FNAEG) as a central case for responding to these questions. What are the methods of comparison of genetic profiles, the procedures for entering data into the FNAEG, and the conditions for accessing it? How useful is the genetic database to professionals, and how are these innovations received by the public? How do they alter categories of identification? Thus these policies and practices raise key issues of category definition (boundaries and content), of legitimacy, and of the effects of the FNAEG. The first task will be to describe the emergence of new categories of suspects that are located at the interface between the perpetrator of an offense, the potential perpetrator or, as I shall show, the individual who is a biological relative of a perpetrator or a suspect.

Secondly, alongside the development of DNA databases, another new technique known as phenotyping makes it possible to infer certain physical characteristics (such as skin, eye and hair color) or, to use the term used by the professionals, continental "biogeographical origin" (Europe, Asia, sub-Saharan Africa, America, Oceania) on the basis of suspects' DNA, and thus to guide police and judicial investigations in the absence of other avenues of inquiry. In France these approaches have raised further questions about protection of privacy and fears that targeted groups would be stigmatized. But following a series of rapes that caused great alarm in the city of Lyon, these techniques, which are designed to predict the appearance of suspects, were authorized in 2014 by a ruling of the Court of Cassation and are today being developed without raising any substantial objection. How are they used, regulated, and debated (or not debated)? How do they fundamentally differ from traditional oral testimony about the appearance of a suspect? What effect do they have on conceptions of the relationship between biology and categories of origin? More specifically, in France, in contrast to English-speaking countries, little or no data is collected as to the origin of individuals, because French law upholds values of equality and universalism that prohibit such collection. For this reason, the way this specifically French restriction is circumvented through the routinization of analysis of suspects' origins merits considered attention. These innovations feed biological conceptions of human difference, and thus raise questions around identity, the place of the biological in the definition and interpretation of identity, and about the social and political implications of a marking associated with a particular group. As I shall point out, the genetic tools used in phenotyping are different from those of the FNAEG, and they are governed by a separate regulatory framework (the results they provide are not called genetic profiles and are not entered into the FNAEG). I shall also discuss current forensic research that attempts to link biometric facial measurements to DNA, so far without significant results. In this sense, biometrics is present in intention, even if these approaches do not currently make it possible to *identify* individuals but rather limit the group of individuals potentially sought or to be identified.

Thirdly, new evidentiary tools are being developed. Automatic comparison of the genetic profiles contained in the national databases of participating European countries – and where two profiles match, circulation of information on suspects among European police and judicial services – have been permitted since 2008, under what is known as the Prüm Decision.[23] This ruling was made to facilitate circulation of information on an unprecedented level, since it involved opening secure databases relating to persons from third countries not on a case-by-case basis but automatically, on a continent-wide scale. Indeed, the Prüm system encourages co-operation between countries that have different regulations on the collection and storage of information. This illustrates how these technologies, whether genetic or of other kinds, today provide answers about the biological identity of individuals that can be communicated much more easily than before. What is the precise nature of the information exchanged, given that co-operation between European police services existed before these measures were introduced? What do these exchanges tell us about the relations of power between the police and the judicial system? What guarantees are given in exchange for this information? In a context where there are plans for the exchange of other biometric information (facial recognition) in Europe, this raises the question of how such information is circulated, and of the relationship between individual state sovereignty and the prerogatives of the European Union. The issue here is how the local, national, and transnational levels are articulated, and the effects of these policies, including how police powers are being extended at the cost of those of the courts, as well as representations of deviant alterity coming from other countries.

Outline of the study

The approach taken in this book to the investigation of these questions is to analyze the everyday practices of professionals working with these new techniques of genetic analysis, the debates and challenges they provoke (or the absence of them), and the underlying shifts they reveal. Moving from forensic laboratories to courts and police stations, the aim is to shed light on the role DNA and population-wide profiling plays in establishing judicial truths, and to observe how security practices are inscribed in the body through the use of these tools. This opens the way to fine-grained study of the identities produced, the power relations at play, and the thinking that is being put into practice. Notwithstanding these changes, and the importance of grasping what is at stake in them socially, there has been little social science research into the uses of DNA in the work of the police and courts in France. In short, the focus here is on policies as they are enacted and not as they are articulated in legislation or the media. Moreover, with respect to the relationship between DNA and criminality, this book is not concerned with behavioral genetics that claim to at least partially explain certain criminal behaviors, such as violence, in terms of an individual's genetic inheritance, as these relatively uncommon and scientifically contested approaches are applied predominantly in the United States and the United Kingdom (Larregue, 2020).

In this interdisciplinary study, I draw predominantly upon work in sociology, anthropology, and occasionally philosophy. The point is to integrate my thinking into a current of thought whose purpose is to "do social science": in other words, to bring together the various social sciences in a synthetic approach. This approach relies in particular on a type of anthropology that includes power relations and social relations in its scope – phenomena traditionally emphasized more in sociology. The aim of this interdisciplinary approach is to combine explanations in terms of political and social context, social dynamics, and historically situated processes with attention to what can be learned from observation, and with a world of more general investigations and questioning. The approach is rooted in the conviction that not only can it remain coherent despite disciplinary differences, but it can also offer particular analytical and methodological advantages.

This book is derived from research conducted primarily in France, over a period of eight years. Following an exploratory study on the technique known as phenotyping, conducted between 2012 and 2014, most of the research was undertaken as part of a collective project funded by the French National Research Agency (Agence nationale de recherche) between 2015 and 2019 (Vailly et al., 2016; Vailly, 2021).[24] Drawing on criminal cases as case studies, the project focused both on genetic profiling and the uses of DNA evidence and on the technique known as phenotyping, and police and court practices in the context of the Prüm system. My research incorporated 112 in-depth interviews, observation of around a dozen trials, and study of court case files. Nine of the interviews were conducted collectively with the team of sociologists and legal scholars involved in the project. Most of the interviews with professionals were conducted at their workplace (FNAEG management services, police stations, courts, forensic laboratories, ministries, etc.). Some interviewees were chosen because they held direct responsibility in the management of the FNAEG, within the National Gendarmerie Institute of Criminal Research (Institut de recherche criminelle de la gendarmerie nationale, IRCGN), or in the department in charge of the Prüm system, while others were information officers in large police stations, or trade union representatives within the police (national police and gendarmerie; 46 interviews). A further group consisted of specialists with the forensic police or heads of biotechnology laboratories (geneticists, biologists; 17 interviews). Some interviewees were chosen because they oppose current uses of the FNAEG (trade unionists, human rights activists, activists from the alternative left or environmentalists, lawyers, etc.; 18 interviews), many of them approached during observations of court cases involving individuals charged with refusing to provide a DNA sample. Another set of interviewees were chosen because of their experience of regulating the FNAEG and phenotyping through their work with the Ministry of Justice, the FNAEG Monitoring Committee, the Committee responsible for certifying persons authorized to conduct DNA identification, or the CNIL (judges, senior civil servants, officers of the CNIL; 31 interviews). Finally, many documents gathered with the help of interviewees were analyzed: legal and regulatory texts, reports on genetic profile matches, ministerial reports, press articles, "grey" literature (documents, etc.), and academic forensic science articles.

The book comprises six chapters that relate microsocial (everyday practice, case studies, etc.) to macrosocial levels (public policy, contemporary social tendencies, etc.). These chapters are grouped into three sections: police rationales and the public attitude toward genetic databases; predicting the appearance of suspects; and what can be called the "new frontiers" of genetic suspects. Examples of cases are presented to illustrate the role of DNA in various situations.

The first part of the book comprises two symmetrical chapters examining the viewpoints of first police officers and gendarmes, and then opponents of current uses of the FNAEG. The first chapter, drawing on the point of view expressed by police officers in interviews, focuses on the police rationales behind genetic databases. I show that rationales of action and organization prevail, facilitating a porosity between the categories of perpetrator, suspect, and what can be described as a "reliable" suspect, thus altering the "bioidentity" of individuals, in other words their identity in relation to biological techniques. Despite the fact that DNA sometimes exonerates suspects, these rationales are interwoven and converge in a process that extends and perpetuates suspicion. In counterpoint to the positions of the police, the following chapter focuses on public contestation of the uses of the FNAEG with regard to what is sometimes seen as the "intimacy" of DNA. On the basis of particular cases and observations of trials for refusal to provide a DNA sample, this chapter presents the arguments of those who oppose extension of the database to include new groups regardless of the seriousness of the offense committed. The second part of the book focuses on genetic tests designed to provide indications as to the appearance or the geographical origin of suspects, and on the questions these raise. The third chapter traces how DNA tests seeking to predict the geographical origin of suspects aroused brief but heated debate in France in the late 2000s, driven particularly by members of the Judges' Union. Concerned about the politically explosive combination of DNA, crime, and origin, the Ministry of Justice temporarily banned these tests in 2011, putting them on the back burner for a while. This chapter explains how the controversy sheds light on contemporary changes in the concept of origin. Continuing from the preceding chapter, the fourth chapter considers practices currently being developed in various countries including France, relating to the appearance of suspects derived from DNA. The Court of Cassation eventually authorized these tests of "appearance" in 2014 and did not exclude data on origin. In short, by focusing attention on the visible, these new technologies make it possible for tests combining crime, origin, and DNA to be rendered acceptable by routinizing and depoliticizing them. In the third and final part of the book, I focus on developments resulting from new DNA evidence techniques, and from the relatively recent introduction of exchange of information on genetic suspects across Europe. The fifth chapter therefore examines the probative weight of genetic evidence and the interaction between science and law. The question is addressed first from the point of view of how DNA evidence forms a piece of the puzzle that the investigator must put together in order to arrive at judicial truths. Other new techniques are described, such as kinship analysis to identify a suspect within the biological family of individuals contained in the database, or police use of family data derived from clients of commercial or genealogical genetic analysis websites, without their knowledge. These approaches illustrate how the imperatives of judicial truth are articulated with the protection of interests other than that of evidence. The final chapter draws on a series of criminal cases described by police officers who were responsible for investigating them to consider the circulation of genetic data and individuals in Europe. It describes how the police have been given a much greater role than the courts, and that despite conflicting approaches due to the disparity of national norms, this favors the movement of information and the extension of suspicion to a continent-wide arena. The conclusion presents an analysis of this government of security through DNA that also takes into account the tensions at play. These developments are set within a context where the possibilities opened up by science and technology (biometrics, facial recognition, etc.) will continue to support not only targeted identification of individuals but also profiling of population groups that transforms the concept of suspect.

Notes

1 It is often pointed out that Galton was Charles Darwin's cousin, but it is sometimes forgotten that he was also the founder of eugenics in the United Kingdom.

2 Interpol 2019, Global DNA profiling survey results. See https://www.interpol.int/How-we-work/Forensics/DNA (accessed January 7 2020).
3 "Replicates," or individuals recorded under more than one name, have been subtracted from these figures. Assemblée Nationale: Rapport d'information sur les fichiers mis à la disposition des forces de sécurité, présenté par les députés Didier Paris et Pierre Morel-À-L'Huissier, October 17 2018, and Biet, G. (2020, May 18). Il y a 20 ans, le fichier national des empreintes génétiques révolutionnait les enquêtes! *Europe 1.*
4 This figure is approximate because the British authorities estimate that around 15% of the profiles are "replicates," and therefore profiles from the same person under different identities: see https://www.gov.uk/government/statistics/national-dna-database-statistics (accessed January 8 2021).
5 Dickerson, C. (2019, October 2). US government plans to collect DNA from detained immigrants. *The New York Times.*
6 Niba, W. (2019, May 17). Focus on Africa: Kenya sets up controversial DNA database. *Radio-France International*, and Malalo, H., & Mohammed, O. (2020, January 31). Court orders safeguards for Kenyan digital IDs, bans DNA collecting. *Reuters.*
7 Defranous, L. (2019, February 22). Fichage génétique en Chine: l'Amérique se réveille. *Libération*; Wee, S.-L. (2020, June 17). China is collecting DNA from tens of millions of men and boys, using U.S. gear. *The New York Times*; Dika, E., & Leibold, J. (2020, July 24). China is harvesting the DNA of its people: Is this the future of policing? *The New York Times.*
8 Human Rights Watch (2022). China: New evidence of mass DNA collection in Tibet, https://www.hrw.org/news/2022/09/05/china-new-evidence-mass-dna-collection-tibet (accessed September 19 2022).
9 Defranous, L. (2019, February 22). Fichage génétique en Chine: l'Amérique se réveille. *Libération.*
10 Law no. 2004–801 of August 6 2004 on the protection of physical persons in relation to the processing of personal data.
11 CECIL (2008). Il faut restaurer l'autorité de la Cnil. *Terminal*, 102.
12 Strong opposition was voiced particularly against the Edvige database (Exploitation documentaire et valorisation de l'information Générale/Documentary Use and Best Use of General Information), but also to the Christine database (Centralisation du renseignement intérieur pour la sécurité du territoire et les intérêts nationaux/Centralization of internal information for the security of homeland and national interests) and the Eloi database (which aimed to facilitate removal of undocumented foreigners) (Piazza, 2009).
13 In France policing is the responsibility of two organizations: the civilian *police nationale*, who are responsible to the Ministry of the Interior, and the *gendarmerie*, a branch of the military responsible for local policing. Both can conduct criminal investigations [translator].
14 Rapport d'information sur les fichiers mis à la disposition des forces de sécurité, présenté par les députés Didier Paris et Pierre Morel-À-l'Huissier, Assemblée Nationale, October 17 2018.
15 Gidda, M. (2013, August 21). Edward Snowden and the NSA files. *The Guardian.*
16 Goldstein, J., & Goodman, J. D. (2013, September 18). Frisking tactic yields to a focus on youth gangs. *The New York Times.*
17 Seibt, S. (2016, October 13). Facebook, Twitter et Instagram ont permis à la police américaine d'espionner les activistes. *France 24.*
18 "Delinquency, with the secret agents that it procures, but also with the generalized policing that it authorizes, constitutes a means of perpetual surveillance of the population: an apparatus that makes it possible to supervise, through the delinquents themselves, the whole social field," writes Foucault (1977, p. 281). For a review of surveillance studies, see Olivier Aïm's synthesis (2020).
19 Jeffreys, A. J., Wilson, V., & Thein, S. L. (1985). Hypervariable "minisatellite" regions in human DNA. *Nature, 314*, 67–73.

20 These repetitions are known as Short Tandem Repeats (STR). They are distinct from other genetic markers of the SNP (Single Nucleotide Polymorphism) type, studied in scientific research and other police approaches in order to provide evidence of whether the suspect belongs to one or more population groups.
21 Article A38 of the French Code of Penal Procedure (CPP), amended by the ruling of August 10 2015.
22 The five public forensic laboratories are located in Paris, Lyon, Marseille, Lille, and Toulouse. The Institut national de la police scientifique (National Forensic Police Institute), replaced in 2021 by the Service national de la police scientifique (National Forensic Police Service), is the umbrella body for these laboratories and was set up under the 2001 law on "everyday security." The Gendarmerie Nationale's Service Central d'Analyses Génétiques (National Gendarmerie's Central Genetic Analysis Department) is located in Pontoise.
23 European Council Decision No. 2008/615/JHA of June 23 2008.
24 Project "Fichiers et témoins génétiques: généalogie, enjeux sociaux, circulation" ("Genetic Databases and Witnesses: Genealogy, Social issues, Circulation," FiTeGe, contract ANR-14-CE29–0014, director Joëlle Vailly).

References

About, I., & Denis, V. (2010). *Histoire de l'identification des personnes*. La Découverte.

Agre, P. E. (1994). Surveillance and capture: Two models of privacy. *Information Society*, 10 (2), 101–127. doi:10.1080/01972243.1994.9960162.

Aïm, O. (2020). *Les théories de la surveillance: Du panoptique aux* Surveillance Studies. Armand Colin.

Aronson, J. D. (2005). DNA fingerprinting on trial: The dramatic early history of a new forensic technique. *Endeavour*, 29(3), 126–131. doi:10.1016/j.endeavour.2005.04.006.

Atkinson, P., Glasner, P., & Lock, M. (Eds.). (2009). *Handbook of genetics and society: Mapping the new genomic era*. Routledge.

Bauman, Z. (2000). *Liquid modernity*. Polity.

Bentham, J. (1995 [1791]). Panopticon letters. In M. Bozonic (Ed.), *The panopticon writings* (pp. 29–96). Verso.

Bourgain, C., Cassier, M., Gaudillière, J.-P., & Juven, P.-A. (2021). Les félicités du capital en santé: Épanouissement, épreuves et tensions critiques des industries pharmaceutiques aux Nords et aux Suds. *Revue française de socio-économie*, 26(1), 127–147. doi:10.3917/rfse.026.0127.

Boyne, R. (2000). Post-panopticism. *Economy & Society*, 29(2), 285–307. doi:10.1080/030851400360505.

Buzan, B., Wæver, O., & de Wilde, J. (1998). *Security: A new framework for analysis*. Lynne Reiner.

Castel, R. (2003). *L'insécurité sociale: Qu'est-ce qu'être protégé?* Seuil.

Clarke, R. A. (1988). Information technology and dataveillance. *Communications of the ACM*, 31(5), 498–512. doi:10.1145/42411.42413.

Deleuze, G. (1992). Postscript on the societies of control, trans. Martin Joughin. *October*, 59, 3–7.

De Maillard, J., & Roché, S. (2009). Les chantiers de réforme de la police dans les États occidentaux. *Revue française de science politique*, 59(6), 1093–1095. doi:10.3917/rfsp.596.1093.

Desrosières, A. (2008). *Pour une sociologie historique de la quantification: L'argument statistique I*. Presses des Mines.

Favre, P. (2009). Quand la police fabrique l'ordre social: Un *en deçà* des politiques de la police? *Revue française de science politique*, 59(6), 1231–1248. doi:10.3917/rfsp.596.1231.

Flichy, P., & Parasie, S. (Eds.). (2013). *Réseaux: Sociologie des bases de données*, 2–3 (178–179). https://www.cairn.info/revue-reseaux-2013-2.htm.
Foucault, M. (1977). *Discipline and punish: The birth of the prison*, trans. Alan Sheridan. Penguin.
Foucault, M. (1979). *The history of sexuality, Vol. 1: The will to knowledge*, trans. Robert Hurley. Allen Lane.
Foucault, M. (2007). *Security, territory, population: Lectures at the Collège de France 1977–78*, trans. Graham Burchell. Palgrave Macmillan.
Fox Keller, E. (2000). *The century of the gene*. Harvard University Press.
Gros, F. (2019 [2012]). *The security principle: From serenity to regulation*, trans. David Broder. Verso.
Haggerty, K. D., & Ericson, R. V. (2000). The surveillant assemblage. *British journal of sociology*, 51(4), 605–622. doi:10.1080/00071310020015280.
Harcourt, B. (2015). *Exposed: Desire and disobedience in the digital age*. Harvard University Press.
Hindmarsh, R., & Prainsack, B. (Eds.). (2010). *Genetic suspects: Global governance of forensic DNA profiling and databasing*. Cambridge University Press.
Jenkins, R. (2000). Categorization: Identity, social process and epistemology. *Current Sociology*, 48(3), 7–25. doi:10.1177/0011392100048003003.
Johnson, P., Williams, R., & Martin, P. (2003). Genetics and forensics: Making the National DNA Database. *Science Studies*, 16(2), 22–37. doi:10.23987/sts.55153.
Larregue, J. (2020). *Héréditaire: L'éternel retour des théories biologiques du crime*. Seuil.
Lee, C., & Voigt, T. H. (2020). DNA testing for family reunification and the limits of biological truth. *Science, Technology & Human Values*, 45(3), 430–454. doi:10.1177/0162243919862870.
Lianos, M. (2003). Le contrôle social après Foucault. *Surveillance & Society*, 1(3), 431–448.
Linhardt, D. (2005). La "question informationnelle": Éléments pour une sociologie politique des fichiers de police et de population en Allemagne et en France (années 1970 et 1980). *Déviance et Sociétés*, 29(3), 259–272.
Lupton, D. (2014). *Digital sociology*. Routledge.
Lyon, D. (2018). *The culture of surveillance*. Polity.
Machado, H., & Granja, R. (2022). *Genetic surveillance and crime control: Social, cultural and political perspectives*. Routledge.
Marx, G. T. (2015). Surveillance studies. *International Encyclopedia of the Social & Behavioral Sciences*, 23, 733–741. doi:10.1016/B978-0-08-097086-8.64025-4.
Nelkin, D., & Andrews, L. (1999). DNA identification and surveillance creep. *Sociology of Health & Illness*, 21(5), 689–706. doi:10.1111/1467-9566.00179.
Nelkin, D., & Lindee, S. (1994). *The DNA mystique: The gene as cultural icon*. W. H. Freeman & Co Ltd.
Ong, A., & Collier, S. J. (2005). *Global assemblages: Technology, politics, and ethics as anthropological problems*. Blackwell Publishing.
Piazza, P. (2009). Edvige et les résistances au fichage policier. *Hermès, La Revue*, 53, 75–78. doi:10.4267/2042/31479.
Rabinow, P. (1996). *Making PCR: A story of biotechnology*. The University of Chicago Press.
Robert, P., & Pottier, M.-L. (2004). Les préoccupations sécuritaires: Une mutation? *Revue française de sociologie*, 45(2), 211–241. doi:10.3917/rfs.452.0211.
Vailly, J. (2013). *The birth of a genetics policy: Social issues of newborn screening*. Routledge.

Vailly, J. (Ed.). (2021). *Sur la trace des suspects: L'incorporation de la preuve et de l'indice à l'ère de la génétique*. Éditions de la Maison des sciences de l'homme.

Vailly, J., Bellivier, F., Noiville, C., & Rabeharisoa, V. (2016). Les fichiers d'empreintes génétiques et les analyses d'ADN en droit pénal sous le regard du droit et de la sociologie. *Cahiers Droits, Sciences & Technologies*, 6, 43–53. doi:10.4000/cdst.476.

Williams, R., & Johnson, P. (2005). Inclusiveness, effectiveness and intrusiveness: Issues in the developing uses of DNA profiling in support of criminal investigations. *The Journal of Law, Medical & Ethics*, 33(3), 545–558. doi:10.1111/j.1748-720X.2005.tb00517.x.

PART 1

Police rationales and attitudes toward genetic databases

1

GENETIC PROFILING AS THE EXTENSION OF SUSPICION

In recent years, the question of identity in its relation to biology has been the focus of growing interest in the social sciences. In a celebrated study, anthropologist Paul Rabinow (1996) predicted the likely formation of new identities and individual and collective practices based on genetic knowledge. He analyzed how groups of patients formed around collective identities of susceptibility to a genetic disease – identities that he described as "bioidentities." Today these predictions are coming true, with the formation of groups of patients and their families, or genealogical groups, constituted on the basis of genetic tests offered by private companies or public bodies (Dimond et al., 2015). Clearly, although the techniques employed may be similar, the genetic tests associated with medical practices are different from those used to help determine guilt or innocence, in terms of the issues of relationship and belonging they entail: being "predisposed" to a disease in one case, and being identified during a criminal investigation in the other (Schramm et al., 2012). Here we move from a medical bioidentity to another, less expected one, from that of a person affected by a disease to that of a suspect, or even perpetrator (Keck, 2010).

One point needs to be clarified because on close consideration the term "bioidentity" offers a range of meanings, depending on whether it is restricted to the bioidentification of an individual or whether the field of application is broadened. Paul Ricœur (1992) distinguishes two important senses of the term "identity," which can be understood as the equivalent of either the Latin *idem* or *ipse*. The first sense, which he calls "sameness," is used in the context of *comparison* (for example, in the phrase "two molecules are identical"); the second, which he calls "selfhood," is used in the context of *characterization* of the human subject (for example, in the expression "this person has multiple identities"). However, while Ricœur focuses on the identity of the "self" as reflexive, speaking subject, as she/he considers her/himself from the inside, here

DOI: 10.4324/9781003456056-3

the focus is on the "Other," as she/he is classified and experienced from the outside. Unlike Ricœur, and indeed Rabinow, what interests me here is not "I" or "we" (the speaking subject, the patient) but "she/he" or "they" (the perpetrator, the suspect): in other words, to follow Richard Jenkins (2000), not the "group" of belonging recognized by its own members but the "category" attributed to the Other that emerges in social practices linked to a knowledge/power.

As I shall show, these concepts are useful in understanding what is at stake in genetic databases. The questions posed here may be formulated as follows: what role do social practices of genetics play in the police and judicial context, in the production of identities attributed to perpetrators and suspects? On what power relations and rationales is this process based? In short, the aim is to grasp how scientific data alter social categories. In order to address these questions, in this chapter I focus on the practices and discourses of police officers and gendarmes in France. Here, then, the focus is on an intermediate level of social actors located between the decision-makers (who determined to set up the French National Automated DNA Database, FNAEG, and introduced modifications through legislation) and the governed (the individuals recorded in the FNAEG, victims of crime from whom DNA samples are taken, etc.). The aim is not only to examine how legislative texts and public policy enable the construction of suspects but also to grasp their effects in the discourses and practices of state agents (Harrits and Moller, 2011).

New technologies, new legislation

The sociotechnological developments highlighted in the introduction in their turn paved the way for new legislation and judicial procedures. In France the FNAEG was set up in 1998, in the wake of the arrest earlier that year of Guy Georges, who had committed seven rapes and murders in eastern Paris and was identified following the manual examination of 3,500 records held in laboratory archives, which had been ordered by the examining magistrate in charge of the case.[1] Supporters of a centralized database argued that at least two of the murders could have been prevented if a national database had existed at the time.

Following the creation of the FNAEG, which was originally limited to sex offenders, the 2001 law on "everyday security" (known as the Vaillant law), passed two months after the September 11 attacks, extended genetic profiling to all crimes against persons. The "interior security" law (or Sarkozy law) passed in 2003 broadened the database's field of application still further, opening it to the perpetrators of crimes and attacks on property. Henceforth, it covered voluntary attacks on the life of another person, torture and cruelty, voluntary violence, theft, extortion, fraud, criminal damage, threats of damage to property, etc. – in other words, most of the offenses listed in the Penal Code apart from those under the law on foreigners, and involuntary offenses against persons (involuntary homicide or bodily harm).[2] Some parliamentary representatives even sought at the time to extend profiling to the entire French population.

In debates in the National Assembly in 2003, Jean-Christophe Lagarde, a representative from the center-right UDF (Union pour la Démocratie Française) party, stated:

> Originally the UDF wanted to propose an amendment that would extend the FNAEG to the entirety of the population. [...] However, we decided not to propose this amendment because we currently lack the necessary financial and other resources. But I would like the government to consider this for the future.[3]

Continuing in this spirit of extending profiling, in 2008 the Interior Minister declared her intention to create a "Forensic Police Plan" (Plan police technique et scientifique, PTS) focused on genetic and physical fingerprints. This initiative moved the project onto a mass scale: the activity of the PTS doubled between 2011 and 2015, and it is estimated that today three quarters of the cases examined in French courts may involve genetic profiling.[4] But there are still some restrictions on this extension of the field of the FNAEG, as certain forms of economic and financial crime are not included (insider trading, tax fraud, misuse of corporate assets, etc.), although aggravated fraud, money laundering, and receiving stolen goods are. The operation of a system that enshrines "differentiations determined by the law or by traditions of status and privilege" between types of crime, in other words a "system of differentiations" of illegalisms that derives from power relations, is in evidence here (Foucault, 1983, p. 223).

The expansion in the number of offenses included was compounded by the fact that the database incorporates not only those convicted but also people who were simply questioned, in other words suspects who, under French law, are presumed innocent.[5] Indeed, according to the Interior Ministry's official and reiterated statistics, individuals questioned (suspects) account for around 75% of the profiles entered in the database.[6] According to one senior official at the Ministry of Justice, these figures need to be put in perspective, as individuals are entered into the database as suspects, but their records are not always updated when they are convicted. Nevertheless, the vast majority of those included are not convicted offenders. Moreover, the laws on "everyday security" and "interior security" introduced penalties for refusing to provide a DNA sample.[7]

In addition to these important considerations, there is the issue of the period of retention of data in the FNAEG. Until October 2021, this was 25 years for suspects and 40 years for convicted offenders, traces, missing persons, and unidentified cadavers. It should be emphasized that these periods of retention applied to all those included (minors over the age of 13 and adults), regardless of the seriousness of the offense. These were the regulations in force when I undertook my field study. In 2010, however, an appeal to the Constitutional Council by an anti-GMO activist resulted in the Council expressing a reservation with regard to the FNAEG, though it did not rule it unconstitutional. The Council called for the introduction of criteria of proportionality between the seriousness of offenses and the period of retention of data, and adjustment to take into account the specific circumstances of juvenile crime.[8] In the same spirit, in 2017, when a farmer convicted of refusing to provide a DNA sample after being arrested at a union demonstration lodged a complaint with the European Court of Human Rights (ECHR), the Court ruled against France in the matter of the FNAEG, for reasons I discuss in Chapter 2.[9] This situation placed France in a judicially uncertain position, continually at risk of further ECHR rulings against it. Nevertheless, it was not until October 2021, after more than ten years of preparation, hesitation, and exchanges between the Ministries of the Interior and Justice (as I was told by senior civil servants interviewed at the time), and a detailed, comprehensively argued opinion from the Commission Nationale de l'Informatique et des Libertés (National Committee for Information Technology and Civil Liberties, CNIL), that the French state published a decree modifying the period of retention of data in certain circumstances.[10] This decree introduced a distinction based on the seriousness of the offense and the age of the individuals concerned.[11] The periods for adults were set at 25 years (for an offense deemed serious) or 15 years (offense deemed less serious) for suspects, and 40 or 25 years respectively for convicted perpetrators. For minors they were reduced to 15 or 10 years respectively for suspects, and 25 or 15 years for convicted perpetrators; the period of retention of biological traces was set at 25 or 40 years, depending on the seriousness of the offense. The offenses to which the maximum periods of retention apply include crimes against persons or property (voluntary violence, rape and sexual assault, drug dealing, kidnapping and false imprisonment, hijacking of public transport, pimping, robbery with violence, criminal damage and vandalism causing a danger to others, etc.). The CNIL issued an overall favorable opinion on these new periods of retention, while noting that some categories of offense, such as robbery and criminal damage, cover actions of varying seriousness. It considered that for this type of offense, in less serious cases a period of 25 years might be disproportionate. The CNIL also called for the new periods to be applied to the entirety of the data already included in the FNAEG, not merely any new profiles entered.[12] It is still too early to know whether this point of view has shifted, and equally to infer the ECHR's position on the new measures stipulated by the decree. Under the 2003 law, DNA samples from individuals identified must be destroyed, although the laboratory retains a record of the person's file for potential future checks.[13]

Overall, then, the level of use of the genetic database is relatively high in France compared with other countries (Lazer, 2004; Hindmarsh and Prainsack, 2010; Toom et al., 2023): the database includes both individuals questioned but not convicted (suspects) and minors, and it covers a wide range of offenses. On the one hand, the FNAEG is used routinely on a mass scale, both in terms of the number of genetic profiles held and the type of offense for which profiles or traces are recorded (not only the relatively infrequent serious crimes but also burglaries, thefts, criminal damage, and so on, which are much more common);

on the other, the period of data retention remains long, including for suspects, whether the suspected offense is serious or not (25 or 15 years). In addition to the legislative framework, it is also worth mentioning the not-for-profit organization Aide aux Parents d'Enfants Victimes (Help for Parents of Child Victims, APEV). The organization first called for a national genetic database of sex offenders to be set up in 1995, and in 2001 it began demanding that the genetic profile of anyone questioned be included in it.[14] In their analysis, Lene Koch and Dirk Stemerding (1994) propose the term "regime" to describe the set of technological, organizational, and societal practices that result from prior processes of attunement, which incorporate technological possibilities, professional demands, and social acceptability. In France, as in other countries like the United States and United Kingdom, the established regime of profiling sex offenders facilitated legislation for, and acceptance of, wider-ranging profiling based on the same type of technical organization and social interaction. Furthermore, it is worth pointing out that these policies and practices once again raise the question of the articulation between individual and collective, since they are both individualizing (identifying suspects or anonymous cadavers) and totalizing (profiling entire populations).

Finally, some aspects of the regulatory framework for the FNAEG contribute to its acceptability by insuring, at least on paper, a degree of neutrality. First, French law states that the DNA tests used for genetic profiling must be based on "non-coding" DNA markers.[15] By definition, non-coding DNA, which makes up about 95% of human DNA, is not directly involved in coding proteins and, like physical fingerprints, should give no information other than the identity of the individuals. This provision, which aims to protect the privacy of those concerned, helped to win acceptance for the FNAEG in parliamentary debates when it was being set up (Krikorian, 2021). This is a norm of genetic profiling widely shared across many countries, although as I shall show, the situation is more complex given the development of scientific knowledge. Secondly, access to FNAEG data is restricted to authorized staff within the Subdirectorate of the Forensic Police (PTS), persons assigned to the Central Department for the Storage of Biological Samples, and agents authorized under the conditions stipulated in the Prüm system.[16] Officers and representatives of the Judicial Police[17] may ask if a person has a profile but may not have access to the individual's full record. The aim of the legislation is to place certain limits on the powers of the police to access data, although as I shall show, overall their prerogatives in the domain of genetic profiling are expanding.

The changes in legislation noted here, combined with the technological developments described earlier, have altered the identifying categories that emerge in the practices and discourses of state agents. In the following three sections, I present three types of category: that of *perpetrators of offenses*, whose genetic profiles are entered into in the FNAEG, whether they have been identified through DNA or by other means; that of *suspects*, whose genetic profiles are entered into the FNAEG; and that of *suspects who can be described as reliable*, identified on the basis of a match between their DNA and that found at a crime scene.

Between perpetrator and suspect, a porosity of categories

Perpetrators and lasting suspicion

As is to be expected, one category of actors that is strongly present in police discourse around the FNAEG is that of the *perpetrator of an offense*. As one PTS officer summed it up in an interview, "the aim of the database is to help identify perpetrators of offenses" (Police Officer 1). However, the rationale is not simply to identify criminals in the manner of Alphonse Bertillon or Francis Galton, the 19th-century precursors of biometrics in France and Great Britain, who sought to thwart criminals (using manually created profiles), rather than to prevent crimes (Noiriel, 2007). Today the underlying rationale, evident in the discourse of many police officers, is to profile those who are following "criminal paths," resonating with Howard Becker's concept of criminal "careers" (2018 [1963]). More precisely, as the Director of the Judicial Police stated in a newspaper article: "It is very rare that serial rapists or murderers are not known to the police for lesser offenses (thefts, petty arson, cruelty to animals, etc.)."[18] Or, as a gendarme at the National Gendarmerie Institute of Criminal Research (IRCGN) put it in an interview: "Anyone who commits a misdemeanor commits a felony, and vice versa" (Gendarme 1). This idea of the criminal career that progresses from minor offenses to burglary and then to serious crime is similarly the rationale behind the inclusion of profiles of offenders at the beginning of their career in other countries, such as the United Kingdom (Lynch and McNally, 2009). In this simultaneously "retrospective" and "prospective" spirit (Cole and Lynch, 2006), the overall rationale is based on the idea that criminality is characteristically repetitive and recidivist, and that the boundary between these different forms of criminality is fluid. This is how the *perpetrator* judged guilty also becomes a *suspect* in other offenses, past or future, with a porosity between the two categories.

The media occasionally report cases that illuminate this point of view. One example was that of a firefighter, who in 2003 fought with security guards after they had caught him without a parking ticket. Convicted of aggravated assault and battery, he received a suspended three-month prison sentence and was required to take a DNA test for the FNAEG, whose remit covers this type of crime. He initially refused to take the test but complied a few months later after several summons. The results were clear: his DNA showed a strong match with semen found in the body of a 16-year-old high school student who had been raped and murdered in 1987. During the period between this crime and the arrest of the suspect in 2006, the young woman's mother, supported by two examining magistrates, had done everything she could to prevent the case being closed. In fact, the file should have been closed ten years after the event, but her insistence had prevented this (since that time the statute of limitations for this type of crime has been extended to 20 years). The suspect was sentenced to life imprisonment at the Gard département criminal court. According to the mother's attorney:

"This is the first time a man has been sentenced in this way for a crime committed twenty years earlier, except for crimes against humanity."[19] This is typically the kind of case cited by professionals to justify a large-scale database and long-term retention of data.

The police reasoning in terms of repetition and recidivism that is illustrated by this case brings in a temporal dimension, since it articulates the idea of clearing past cases (after the offense) and preventing future crimes (before the offense). There is a connection here to the length of time for which data on convicted individuals is retained in the database (40 years during the time of my study, 25 or 40 years for adults as of late 2021): it is thanks to this long period of retention that the ideas of clearance after the event, and prevention, can be articulated. Clearance of past cases is facilitated by forensic approaches, since the PCR technique makes it possible to study even partially degraded DNA from older cases dating from the period of early genetic analysis when the DNA had to be fresh and intact. Prevention comes into play with the entry of perpetrators into the database; they thus become potential suspects, as early as possible in their career, in order to dissuade them from committing further offenses, and to solve the crimes if they do. In this spirit, Michèle Alliot-Marie, the Interior Minister, told the press in 2008: "[The forensic police] are an essential element of deterrence: I am convinced that the greater the risk you will be found, the more likely you are to hesitate before committing an offense."[20] Although it is not really corroborated, since it is difficult to measure the impact of genetic databases on the absence of offenses, this point of view is evident in other countries, as suggested, for example, by New York's criminal justice coordinator: "[collecting a large number of DNA samples] will prevent future crimes."[21]

Taking a broader view, in Europe the European Court of Human Rights (ECHR) drew up a report on the practices of member countries of the Council of Europe regarding the length of retention of genetic data in the case of minor offenses. It revealed that eleven states retained profiles for minor offenses for long periods, even after the individuals concerned had died:

> Concerning the retention of DNA profiles following a conviction for a minor criminal offence four out of thirty one Council of Europe member States surveyed (Cyprus, Ireland, North Macedonia and Montenegro) have indefinite retention periods. Twenty States (including France) have retention periods limited in time.[22] [...] Of those twenty, seven have a defined retention period [...] linked to the date of death of the convicted person (Bosnia and Herzegovina, Denmark, Finland, the Republic of Moldova, the Netherlands, Norway and Switzerland). Of those seven, the legislation of the Netherlands specifies the longest retention period of twenty years from the date of death for serious offences, with decreasing periods for less serious offences.[23]

This internationally shared desire for early profiling, including for minor crimes, can be compared to practices in medical genetics that are rooted in the medical obsession with early diagnosis and "aiming to take control of the future" (Dew et al., 2016, p. 203; Grimes and Schulz, 2002). However, while in both cases the aim is to anticipate future events, the temporality in question is clearly not the same. In the medical model put forward by Rabinow (1996), individuals carry a genetic modification that *directly contributes* to the onset of a disease. However, here the "non-coding" DNA is merely a *tracer* that is theoretically neutral, in the same way as physical fingerprints. In this sense, the relationship between biological life and social life (Vailly et al., 2011), which constitutes bioidentity, is not of the same order: in the first case it is explanatory (the "mutation" indicates a predisposition to a disease), in the second it is correlative (the "marker" acts as an identity tracer).

Moreover, these genetic markers can provide standardized and precise scientific data, articulating traditional categories (perpetrators, suspects, etc.). Nevertheless, it should be noted that in France they do so in a different way to the United Kingdom. In a study of the UK's genetic database, David Skinner (2011) revealed a policy centered on the construction and use of racialized data. Indeed, in the United Kingdom the use of what are known as ethnic or racial categories is perennially debated, in a way that it is not in France. There is no doubt that in France the combination of criminality, genetics, profiling, and so-called ethnic origin would render the database both illegal and highly controversial.[24] It is, then, easy to understand why traditional categories (perpetrators, suspects) come to be mixed (or not, in the case of origin in France) with other more recent data (genetic markers, which are merely a tracer). To return to our theoretical framework, it is also clear that the bioidentity of individuals derived from this mix is marked by a correlation between perpetrators and suspects that alters these categories, rendering them mutually porous. More precisely, it is bioidentity as selfhood that is principally at stake, since these perpetrators are included in a category that describes their actions and characterizes them. Regarding the question of temporalities, Ricœur (1992) argues that selfhood does not imply any assertion concerning some unchanging core of personality, unlike sameness, which indicates permanence in time. Similarly in this case, the selfhood of perpetrators and suspects varies (depending on the professional interviewed, they move from one category to the other), but their sameness (genetic markers) does not change.

Profiled suspects: an intermediate category

As I have noted, convicted perpetrators do not represent the largest proportion of the records in the FNAEG (making up around 14%). The largest category is therefore that of profiled *suspects*, who are distinguished from the general population in that their genetic profile is systematically compared for every offense involving DNA in France – in other words routinely, in the same way as that of convicted offenders (Williams and Johnson, 2005). They thus remain latent suspects for 15 or 25 years, the length of time their data are retained in the database, or until a match arises. One gendarme's hypothetical burglary scenario gives an idea of what this means:

> [The] detective goes to the scene and says: if there are five cigarette ends, it means the guy was watching, he must have spent a long time smoking before the people left, so I'm going to take those cigarette ends because they must be linked to the burglary. Which is just his interpretation, because there might have been someone who was meeting his girlfriend the day before or a few hours before who smoked a lot, who has nothing to do with the burglary, and if he has the misfortune to be someone who is already known, I think that gentleman is in for a lot of trouble, unless he can prove categorically he wasn't there.
>
> *(Gendarme 2)*

This example shows that having one's genetic data included in the database as a suspect is not as neutral as it seems, even if one has "done nothing wrong," as the popular phrase has it: if these data happen to correspond to a trace collected at the scene of a crime, the person will be in "trouble" or will have to "prove categorically" that he or she was elsewhere. It could be countered that, notwithstanding the FNAEG, there is nothing new in the fact that some individuals are called on to justify themselves more often than others, since sociology has shown that certain groups are frequently stopped by the police on the basis of their appearance (Jobard et al., 2012). What is different about genetic profiling is that the situation persists over time, and that once the individual is entered into the database, her/his data are systematically compared. Moreover, there are specific aspects of DNA traces compared with physical fingerprints, particularly in terms of family connections, to which I return below.

The French police officers we met offered various arguments for the creation of this category. The first argument concerns the efficacy of the FNAEG, and thus the stated objective of solving cases, given that the majority of matches between DNA found at a crime scene and that of an individual involve suspects (76%) rather than convicted offenders (22%).[25] An officer in a senior management post at the FNAEG told me:

> We argued for the FNAEG to be extended to other offenses and also to all individuals who are questioned under caution. Of course we did. Because what that means is that we have more possibilities of solving cases than we had before.
>
> *(Police officer 2)*

This establishes a close relationship between the inclusion of individuals' data in the categories of offenders and suspects and the clearance of investigations (the aim is to "have more possibilities of solving cases"). Moreover – and this is a significant point – DNA is used not only as evidence against a criminal but also as a tool for police inquiries and criminal investigations. I shall return to this below.

The second argument police officers put forward in favor of retaining this category of suspects in the FNAEG relates to prevention. A gendarme explained that several years may elapse between the arrest of an individual and her/his potential conviction, during which she/he may be arrested again. Like the "patients-in-waiting" who await the possible diagnosis of a disease (Timmermans and Buchbinder, 2010), these "suspects-in-waiting" (awaiting trial) then prove to be the perpetrators of new offenses.

The third argument makes a distinction within the categorization of the suspect, depending on the judicial outcome. An officer with the Judicial Police responsible for training in genetic testing at the police academy, and employed by one of the police unions, confirmed that permanent suspicion remains on individuals who are not convicted when a case is dismissed:

> Just because a case is dismissed, it doesn't mean the person isn't guilty. It might also [mean] that we haven't got enough evidence, or it can mean that the offense hasn't been clearly described. Not convicted does not necessarily mean innocent. Judged innocent in court,[26] but is that really the case? There are some cases where you might wonder.
>
> *(Police officer 3)*

In other words, this officer challenges the act of dismissal and what she interprets by extrapolation as a legal category of "innocent" because she considers that the person is liable to move back into the category of perpetrators. This shows a degree of "category malleability" (Jenkins, 2000), related to the circumstances in which the case was dismissed, with an implicit movement from "not convicted" to "suspect." In general, as Geoffrey C. Bowker and Susan Leigh Star (1999) note, categories are not always mutually exclusive, particularly when there is disagreement or ambiguity around a case, as there is here regarding the categorization of the person when a case is dismissed.

To conclude this section, on the one hand the FNAEG can be described as a database that supports investigation, enabling matches to be made between DNA profiles, and thus contributes to solving crimes and providing evidence for trials. On the other, it can also be described as the producer of a majority category that forms an intermediate group between the innocent and the convicted: individuals who have been questioned but not convicted. The fact that this category makes up 75% of the data in the database reinforces Cole and Lynch's argument (2006) that the concept of a *suspect individual*, as it was previously understood in criminal cases, is changing, becoming that of a *suspect population*. This broad category stems first and foremost from profiling independent of the judicial outcome of the offense, since most of the individuals included in the FNAEG have not been convicted, in contrast to the situation in other countries (in Portugal, for example, suspects are not included in the database). It also stems from systematic comparison: once people have been entered into the database, their profile is systematically compared to new traces, in the same way as that of convicted criminals (Williams and Johnson, 2005; Tutton and Levitt, 2010; Skinner, 2011). Thus there emerges a porosity not only between perpetrator and suspect, as described above, but also between suspect in a single case and long-term suspect. Once in the database, the two categories of perpetrators and profiled suspects together make up the category of latent suspects, in a sort of "electronic trawl" (Lynch et al., 2008). In effect, their "bioidentity" and their "selfhood" come together in the database, as each becomes that of long-term suspects. They differ from suspects identified through traditional investigations, as they have long been understood, but their situation also differs from that of the general population. This reinforces the idea that what is at stake here is not just the management of neutral genetic markers, known as tracers, but also the porosity and transformation of categories, and more generally the formation of bioidentities of long-term suspects. There seems to be a runaway development of the measure initially designed in the late 1990s for sex offenders.

Reliable suspects who have to "explain themselves"

The matching of genetic profiles in order to identify a potential perpetrator falls into the sphere of sameness. And indeed, in some cases – as is the objective – the DNA of a suspect (in the traditional sense), an offender, or a profiled suspect matches that found at the scene of a new offense. It can also happen that the DNA does not match, helping to exonerate the suspect and therefore to remove her/him from the potential perpetrator category. If the DNA trace of an individual is found at a crime scene without a clear reason, the individual will have to give an account of her/his movements and, as the police officers we spoke with put it, "explain her/himself" to the investigator. I discuss below the repercussions of this when evidence is being constituted for the purpose of establishing judicial truth. Whatever the case, the suspect who has to explain her/himself because of a DNA match becomes a suspect who could be described as "reliable" and comes a little closer to the category of perpetrators, without being incorporated into it until she/he is judged guilty.

A more detailed description of this category is called for. There are some variants within it: the potential perpetrator may be *confirmed* by her/his DNA, when it is added to a collection of evidence previously furnished by a traditional investigation, or she/he can be *exposed* by her/his DNA. One area where this latter practice particularly applies is burglary, and all forms of breaking and entering. Thanks to PCR techniques, genetic analysis of small quantities of DNA allows for the study of minute traces left at burglary scenes. Official data suggest that burglary is a crime with a high level of repeat offending and a low clearance rate (around 9% in 2019), while most of the time investigators are unable to identify suspects using traditional investigation methods.[27] An officer responsible for DNA matching at the FNAEG, who had previously been a detective, explained:

> The FNAEG makes it possible to conduct investigations where we couldn't before. [...] More generally, if we didn't have the forensic police on these offenses [in the case of burglary], [colleagues on the ground] would be quite helpless because they're not offenses where you're likely to have [...] testimony from the victim who's going to be able to describe the suspect. In general burglary happens when the house is empty, no one's ever seen anything and there's no specific line of inquiry except for traces.
>
> *(Police officer 4)*

Thus the actions that may lead to a police intervention are continually evolving, and the idea that unless caught in the act a theft will not result in any police action (Favre, 2009) should perhaps now be reconsidered in the light of forensic police work. Contrary to the widespread media image of DNA being used as a "genetic witness" (Aronson, 2007) only in serious crimes, the distribution of types of offense in relation to the number of matches between a DNA trace and an individual, or between DNA traces, reveals the proportion of thefts and property crime in these matches. Thus the percentages are, by type of offense: 53% for aggravated theft, 11.5% for simple theft, 10.8% for crimes against property, 7% for armed robbery, 5.4% for sexual offenses and 12.3% for others.[28] In other words, thefts and property crimes represented the vast majority of matches using the FNAEG.

According to some police officers, while the clearance rate for burglaries is low, the small proportion of cases that are solved are usually done so thanks to genetic analysis. This claim is difficult to verify, since it is impossible to know whether the matches relate to different cases or the same case, or to know the outcome of cases where matches were made (conviction, acquittal, etc.). Nor is it possible to find out the proportion of matches involving individuals who were not suspects already identified at the time of the investigation, and hence clearance that can genuinely be ascribed to the FNAEG. More generally, in claims about the efficacy of genetic databases, the statistics most often quoted are those for the number of matches between an unknown trace and a recorded profile (or between two traces). But these data are too embryonic to evaluate the precise role of DNA in the conduct of an investigation. To paraphrase Alain Desrosières (2008), who distinguishes the use of statistics as a "tool of government" (to direct the action of others) from their use as a "tool of proof" (to persuade), the use of figures as a tool of proof of efficacy has its limitations. All the same, it is worth noting that in the international context, a report by the British Commissioner for the Retention and Use of Biometric Material states that "DNA plays an important role in contemporary policing, yet in only 0.3%

of recorded crime was DNA involved in the resulting case outcome" (I shall return to this point in Chapter 6)[29]. The report notes that the rate was highest for homicides (8.4%), followed a long way behind by burglaries (1.4%), vehicle theft (0.9%), and rape (0.6%). A study by legal scholars cites various reasons for these low figures in the United Kingdom: the small proportion of offenses where DNA evidence is applicable, suspects who are already identified by other means, budget and policing priorities, and others (Amankwaa and McCartney, 2021).

Thus today, owing to the respective frequency of the offenses, the FNAEG is used more for burglaries than for serious crimes, although this was not its initial purpose. Moreover, in the case of burglaries and, more broadly, offenses where evidence from traditional investigation is lacking, investigators turn to DNA and sometimes seem to use it as a primary line of investigation. Ultimately, when a match is found between an individual's profile and a trace, what we are seeing are changes of category, between suspect and suspect required to "explain her/himself", and of bioidentity, from suspect to suspect "reliable."

Another important aspect of this category relates to the information provided (or not provided) by genetic markers. As noted above, French law states that genetic profiles stored in the FNAEG may only be extracted from segments of non-coding DNA. Indeed, it goes further because it specifies the genetic markers that are to be used to establish profiles incorporated into the database.[30] As noted in the introduction, these markers are short repeated sequences of DNA known as Short Tandem Repeats (STR). However, the situation is more complex today because recent research shows that, in general and regardless of the genetic profiles used in criminal law, some information can now be recovered from non-coding DNA. The situation has evolved considerably since the 1990s, when many scientists called non-coding DNA "junk DNA," as many published works have demonstrated the role of this non-coding DNA in control and regulation (Bourgain and Darlu, 2013). National police officers and gendarmes, who depending on their positions (detective working at a local police station, police forensic analyst, head of genetic profile training, etc.) may be more or less familiar with this idea, express a variety of opinions on the subject.

One point of view is that the situation is relatively simple, since the genetic markers used in the FNAEG do not provide any information about individuals except that required to identify them when profiles are compared, on the basis of their sameness. As one police officer explained at a public meeting, "non-coding DNA does not give us information on the physical characteristics of an individual. Neither geographical origin nor physical characteristics" (Police officer 5). Another officer went further in an interview:

> Here we're studying regions of DNA that aren't coding, so they won't be linked to visible markers, the visible characteristics of the individual. [...] Non-coding [material], biologically, it's evolutionary trash.
>
> *(Police officer 4)*

According to another opinion, the situation is slightly more complex because the law lags behind developments in scientific knowledge that show that non-coding DNA can provide some information on individuals' characteristics. One gendarme interviewed said:

> This distinction between coding and non-coding DNA is theoretical. It's theoretical, we're well aware today that it's much more complex than that. [...] In my view, [the distinction between] coding and non-coding DNA is ridiculous, because there's information in both of them.
>
> *(Gendarme 3)*

One police officer gave the specific example of a non-coding marker known as FGA, which is included in the FNAEG and a variant of which is over-represented among Tahitian populations. This means that an investigator who observed the presence of this variant might infer that the person suspected was probably of Tahitian origin. However, this officer added that the level of information about individuals' origin provided by the markers in the FNAEG was low because these markers were not selected for this purpose. More precisely, he explained that they were chosen to be those of *one single individual* rather than those of *a group of individuals*. This correlates with the fact that STRs are associated with high levels of modification of the genome that generate diversity within each generation. It is clear how high levels of genetic diversity provide a good amount of information on individuals but less on populations, which are understood to retain more homogeneity within them. Furthermore, there is no demand on the part of the police to authorize use of the medical information provided by genetics for the purpose of investigations. Overall, notwithstanding some differences, these police officers reiterate the spirit of the legislation, arguing for a sort of "genomic minimalism," in other words that minimal information is provided by the FNAEG's markers (Williams and Johnson, 2004). According to them, no phenotypical information (on diseases, physical appearance, origin, etc.) can be derived from the genetic profiles contained in the FNAEG, or the data are too fragmentary to be used in this way.

Another observation that sheds light on their perspective is that some police officers make reference less to science than to the law. Taking up the regulations governing the FNAEG, a senior national representative of the PTS remarked in the press:

> There is a conflation of the technical possibilities of DNA and the database that contains it. [...] As demarcated by the law, the FNAEG does not authorize this type of [ethnic or medical] profiling. Technically it is possible but the CNIL forbids it and it is officially prohibited to use the FNAEG to find out any information other than the sex of the individual.[31]

As I shall show, this distinction between what is *technically possible* and what is *legally authorized* feeds the arguments of those who oppose current uses of the FNAEG. To sum up, the boundary between coding and non-coding DNA has been shattered, but under French law the genetic markers in the FNAEG must be "non-coding." In effect, professionals in the field have to shape their own ethical norms in order to keep up with this evolution (Krikorian, 2021). This helps to explain how norms are adapted when biological constructions assumed to be natural are thrown into question by advances in knowledge about non-coding DNA. It also emphasizes how for most police officers and gendarmes genetic profiling allows them to remain within the register of *comparison* (sameness) without straying into *characterization* (without selfhood). This position allows them to see genetic profiles as routine, and to retain the analogy with physical fingerprints that has been maintained since these practices emerged.

Table 1.1 summarizes the data derived from the three categories I have discussed. It reveals the porosity between categories (from perpetrator to long-term suspect, from suspect in one case to long-term suspect, from suspect to "reliable" suspect). DNA can be used to exonerate individuals, and this may be crucial for those involved and for the police investigation: I cited one example in the introduction and return to this situation below in my analysis of the Innocence Project in the United States. Nevertheless, striking as they are, such cases are vanishingly rare compared with those where the individual's status as suspect is maintained. Except where comparison of genetic profiles shows no DNA match, in general the linkage of genetic markers with traditional categories (perpetrators, suspects) favors the formation of bioidentities that tend to *reinforce the suspect nature of the person.* I term these bioidentities "suspect by recidivism," "suspect by extension," and "reliable suspect by matching."

TABLE 1.1 Categories of identification, porosity and changes of category, and bioidentities

Category of identification	*What does the FNAEG or DNA produce?*	*Porosity and change of category*	*Bioidentity*
Perpetrator of an offense included in the FNAEG field of application	Data retained for 25 or 40 years (15 or 25 years for minors)	From perpetrator to long-term suspect	Suspect by recidivism following conviction
Suspect of an offense included in the FNAEG field of application	Data retained for 15 or 25 years (10 or 15 years for minors)	From suspect of a single offense to long-term suspect	Suspect by extension
Suspect (or innocent person) by DNA comparison	Match (or no match)	From suspect to suspect who must "explain her/himself" (or from suspect to innocent)	Reliable suspect by matching (or innocent by absence of match)

Having presented these three categories, the shifts between them, and their effects, I now seek to better understand the grounds on which these shifts are based and the logics underlying them.

Police rationales and institutional configurations

Probabilistic rationales around solving cases

Although many of the professionals I met with were sorry that financial crime does not fall within the database's field of application, and hence did not subscribe to this particular form of differential treatment of illegalisms discussed above, all the police officers and gendarmes expressed their satisfaction regarding the broadening of the scope of the FNAEG. They believe that the presentation of a "reliable" suspect through DNA matching helps to move forward an investigation that might not have been resolved had there been no name to cite in the case file. And taking a probabilistic point of view, they frequently suggest that a massive abundance of data in the database will increase the chances of a DNA match. One police chief and former detective at a large precinct, for example, said during a group interview:

> The bigger the database, the more useful it is. I have to say that's just my opinion.
>
> [Interviewer:] Because it enables you to identify perpetrators?
>
> Yes.
>
> [Interviewer:] And you've seen that in your work?
>
> I do know it worked.
>
> *(Police officer 6)*

Similarly, one crime squad gendarme said in the press: "The more information there is in the database, the more DNA identifications there are."[32] Among the police officers and gendarmes I interviewed, not only was the FNAEG unanimously seen as an essential tool assisting investigation, but they also took the view that the category of "reliable" suspects would be larger if the other two (perpetrators and suspects) were.

Furthermore, as if echoing the remarks of the Justice Minister, who supported the development of the PTS (Forensic Police), to the effect that the aim was to "bring justice for the victim by finding those who have harmed her/him,"[33] a union representative of the PTS stated in an interview:

> Someone who's a victim of crime, we should morally have the right to give them an answer and go digging to do all that we can to try to solve – or at any rate to help – the investigator to solve the case. [...] Someone whose

> car has been stolen, someone who's been burgled, when we give them an answer saying that we've identified the perpetrator of their burglary, [...] we're giving them a social response that is also helpful for people who are victims; to be sure, victims of less serious harm but victims all the same.
>
> *(Police officer 4)*

The focus is on demonstrating to victims of all kinds that they are heard, that their point of view is taken seriously using all available means, including scientific methods, and avoiding releasing suspects for lack of evidence. In other words, the approach in question is not merely a matter of police or judicial procedure: it also involves a form of duty to take an interest in victims, a duty that is characterized by an ethos and sometimes by an attitude of empathy.

Although there is not space here to put figures on the respective positions of those involved, it is interesting to note some variations of attitude in France. In most cases, the stated aim is for the database to reach a size where it stabilizes because overall it corresponds to what one gendarme called "the suspectal population," in other words a population associated with "risk management" (Castel, 1981) – in this case, the risk of danger to other individuals. This management encourages a form of "sorting" as a way of easily distinguishing groups ranging from high to low risk of committing offenses (Aas, 2006).

Some interviewees, as it were, in echo of the politicians' statements in the early 2000s quoted in the introduction, suggest that the entire French population should be included in the database, in order to facilitate the identification of perpetrators. In an interview, one police officer, a scientific adviser at the Subdirectorate of Forensic Police, gave the example of a particularly brutal rape-murder case, expressing the kind of empathy for the victim described above, and concluded: "If we'd had all the DNA profiles of every person [in France], we'd have got the culprit straight away" (Police officer 7). In this perspective, the category of suspects should continue to broaden, in a general expansion that would ultimately make all citizens potential criminals. Here the probabilistic reasoning is pushed to its limit. Apart from the political and moral problems it raises, this viewpoint carries the major drawback, which I shall return to, of ignoring the false matches and errors arising from an exhaustive database: the larger the database, the greater the likelihood of matching errors (false positives) between a trace and a suspect.

Other interviewees took a more legalistic position, like this union representative for the PTS: "Is it sufficient, is it excessive, is it insufficient? I don't really have an opinion on that. It's a choice that was made by legislators [...] that's not a question for us to discuss" (Police officer 3). Still others place the emphasis on the regulations introduced, like this union representative with the Judicial Police: "It's real progress. Alongside that, you need to make sure there's a framework, strict controls, to make sure the system isn't abused" (Police officer 4).

In short, while successive legislation from 1998 onward substantially broadened the list of offenses for which genetic samples could be taken, authorized tests on individuals who were merely suspected and, as I shall show below, built these developments into government circulars requiring systematic recording of genetic profiles, police officers, and gendarmes generally subscribe to the probabilistic rationale that leads to the inclusion of a growing number of suspects of various types in the database. Like the position that highlights prevention and repeat offending, described above, this position can be understood in terms of the proximity most of these professionals have with vicious crimes, and their contact with victims in serious difficulty. This probabilistic thinking aligns with institutional configurations, as I show in the next section.

Extended police powers

It should be pointed out that the law distinguishes between "serious or consistent evidence" that makes it *credible* that individuals have committed an offense rendering them liable to *registration* in the FNAEG (described as an "Article 706–54 paragraph 2 suspect" on the FNAEG's requisition form) and "one or more *plausible* reasons" for suspecting that they have committed or attempted to commit an offense that permits DNA comparison *without registration* of their profile in the database (called an "Article 706–54 paragraph 3 suspect" on the FNAEG's requisition form). I shall call the former "paragraph 2 suspects" (sometimes known as suspects "questioned," in the language of police officers and magistrates) and the latter "paragraph 3 suspects" (whom the professionals sometimes call "simple suspects").

Let us consider how categorization distinguishes between the paragraph 2 suspects *registered in* the database and the paragraph 3 suspects *compared to* the database. The latter are often groups of people requested to provide their DNA (which will therefore not be retained in the database) simply because they happened to find themselves near a crime scene. This procedure leads to relatively loose categorization as a suspect, which may involve several hundreds or thousands of individuals only very circumstantially linked to the offense; their classification as suspect is highly transitory, and thus not of the same order as that of the paragraph 2 suspect. Although by definition it involves a large number of individuals, this process, which is often very inefficient because it involves conducting tests almost blind, is relatively little used.[34]

A PTS officer told us that during the first five months of that year (2015), one paragraph 3 suspect was compared for every seventy paragraph 2 suspects entered into the database. In order to understand this ratio, we need to understand first *who* decides on the classification, a question related to the "institutional order" (Jenkins, 2000). Since the 2003 law was passed, an officer of the Judicial Police may enter a record into the FNAEG of her/his own accord, and may also do so on the instruction of the public prosecutor or the examining magistrate. A gendarme who was involved in setting up the FNAEG remembered:

> It just wasn't possible to do it any other way; the magistrate was too snowed under, so Judicial Police initiative [Judicial Police populating the FNAEG] made it possible to test suspects, to compare between a number of suspects as well, so all that developed in the right direction for adding to the database and making it a database that had all the functions necessary to be efficient, and the legislative back-up to be efficient.
>
> *(Gendarme 3)*

Thus today 93% of records entered into the FNAEG for individuals (and 96% of the entries for traces) are registered at the request of an officer of the Judicial Police, and just 7% at the request of a magistrate (4% for traces).[35] In other words, in most cases – except those involving minors or litigious cases – the police officer is the sole judge of what is "serious or consistent evidence," indicating that in the vast majority of cases, responsibility for incorporating records into the database has shifted from the judicial to the police arena. One judge, former president of the Judges' Union (Syndicat de la Magistrature) and critical of current uses of the FNAEG, stated in an interview: "The problem with DNA is that it's the police who decide. It's much more often the police than the examining magistrate. [...] The FNAEG is a police database" (Judge 1).

On this note, technical management of the FNAEG falls under the responsibility of the Central Directorate of the Judicial Police, a department of the Ministry of the Interior. More specifically, the database is populated, consulted, and operated by the Directorate's services located in the town of Écully, in the Rhône département. At the time of my study, the specialist staff of the FNAEG's management department comprised fifteen PTS scientists (three analysts, four technicians, and eight specialist officers). Samples are retained by decision of the public prosecutor, an officer of the Judicial Police, or the examining magistrate, at the Central Department for Storage of Biological Samples (SCPPB), which falls under the responsibility of the gendarmerie. The FNAEG is governed by two committees: the Interministerial Technical Committee for the FNAEG, chaired by a judge from the Directorate of Criminal Cases and Pardons, and made up of police officers, gendarmes, police- and gendarmerie-affiliated experts, and IT staff responsible for technical operation of the database; and the FNAEG Monitoring Committee, chaired by a senior judge from the public prosecutor's office and comprising another judge, a geneticist, and an IT expert. Our research showed that the judge who chairs the Monitoring Committee has relatively few human and financial resources at his disposal (he continues his professional duties in addition to chairing the Committee, and his role in this monitoring is vague, so that in practice monitoring is limited).

The various factors discussed here (the profiling of individuals not convicted, population by Judicial Police officers, and the peripheral role of the Monitoring Committee) have important consequences in terms of power relations because this effectively means largely entrusting the powers and means of investigation to the police, by setting up a database that incorporates both perpetrators and suspects. More generally, the way individuals are classified on the one hand,

and the relationship between these categories and social organization on the other, sheds light on the social and moral order (Bowker and Star, 1999). It appears that inter-institutional power relations put the justice system and the person required to supply their DNA at a disadvantage in relation to the police. Thus the comment made in a different context, that "the prerogatives of the police are expanding, most notably in terms of identity checks" (Fassin et al., 2015 [2013], p. 100), extends to this situation too.

Institutional injunctions and performance targets

In addition to these inter-institutional patterns, intra-institutional rationales are also at play. Although a gendarme from the IRCGN pointed out that "a person in custody is not necessarily a suspect" (Gendarme 4), a PTS officer explained:

> In general, if you had ten people in custody, you'd have to take full records for all ten: so photo, fingerprints and DNA [...]. Once a person is in custody because there is reason [...] to think, those reasons are the same as for taking the DNA sample.
>
> *(Police officer 3)*

In the same vein, a memorandum from the Greater Paris Security Directorate specifies:

> Both physical and genetic fingerprints must be taken [...] for *all persons in custody and questioned under caution* [...]. This procedure must therefore be *systematic* [*in bold and underlined in the original*] in order to ensure the efficacy of the large national databases, the FAED (Fichier Automatisé des Empreintes Digitales, Automated Fingerprint Database) and the FNAEG.

A 2004 ministerial circular similarly emphasized:

> Recording of the genetic profiles of persons who fall within the field of application of the database and of traces must be systematic. [...] Persons placed in custody or liable to be subject to criminal proceedings must be tested and their records entered into the FNAEG.[36]

In fact, many individuals are entered into the FNAEG because they are placed in custody, despite the fact that this may be on grounds of "plausible reason," much broader than the condition of serious or consistent evidence.[37] Thus in practice there is an unbroken process of custody-serious or consistent evidence-entry into the FNAEG, despite the fact that in terms of establishing facts there is not always sufficient material to qualify as serious or consistent evidence. Once again, porosities emerge between overlapping categories; in this case, those held in custody and profiled suspects.

Moreover, in a "results-based culture" (Desrosières, 2008), regimes of categorization of suspects also depend on the evaluation policies of those carrying out the classification. For several years now, the various draft finance laws have included a performance indicator for the police based on a rate of gathering of biological records (the ratio between the number of individuals whose biological samples have been recorded and the number questioned), with the aim of making the FNAEG an exhaustive DNA database. This target rate has progressively risen and was set at 92.2% for the national police in 2020: 64% in 2012, 74.7% in 2014, 84.4% in 2016, 86.5% in 2018, and so on (it is a little lower for the gendarmerie but still rising overall).[38] We should add that officers in the Judicial Police are evaluated, including in relation to fixed targets, and that this has an impact on their career progress. These targets include records entered (taking physical and genetic profiles) for persons questioned under caution, as indicated by the form for police officers' mandatory career appraisal interview, which includes a section headed "Actions to be taken and where appropriate indicators recorded, deadlines for completion, recommendations: physical fingerprinting, genetic records." In this way, as Alain Desrosières argues (2008), the "performance indicators" that structure social life may steer professionals' activity. Their superiors are themselves subject to targets, on the basis of which they will or will not receive a bonus based on a performance indicator, which often includes quality of records taken. At district headquarters level, statistics are gathered on the number of records entered compared to the number of individuals questioned. Thus actors on the ground are themselves under pressure stemming from national directives. The objective of developing the Forensic Police in order to resolve cases is achieved through population of the FNAEG, in the form of figures, by police services, a practice some of those involved call a "politics of numbers."

This politics involves creating statistical tools to measure the supposed efficiency of services or even, as when it was introduced when Nicolas Sarkozy was Interior Minister, setting numerical targets in advance. Since that time, this policy has been repeatedly challenged and then reinstated, without ever disappearing. In other words, the "conventions" (Desrosières, 2008) on which quantification of entries into the FNAEG is based involve a process of datafication. This is manifested in the fact that, in purely statistical terms, it is more in an officer's interest to question, for example, three marijuana users than one dealer. It is also clear that here genetic data are transformed into another kind of data, in terms of encoded performance. While as I have shown statistics do not always amount to a "tool of evidence" in this arena, here they act as a "tool of government" (Desrosières, 2008), in which relations of power are at play: the inter-institutional powers *held* by Judicial Police officers who decide when to enter data into the FNAEG, and the intra-institutional powers *imposed on* these same officers and their superiors on the basis of numerical targets. In sum, these various rationales converge to generate rapid population of the database, as I show in the following section.

Expanding categories

As noted above, the categories of suspect ("questioned under caution") and perpetrator ("convicted") and of traces are distinguished by the period of retention of the data but also by their rate of expansion. Thus for individuals questioned, the number of DNA records has shown a rapid, progressive increase from around 1,400 in 2002 to around 3.3 million in 2018 (150,000 in 2006, 1.2 million in 2010, 2.3 million in 2014). The figure for convicted offenders rose from 2,800 profiles recorded in 2004 to 560,000 in 2018 (104,000 in 2006, 330,000 in 2010, 470,000 in 2014); that for traces moved from 180 in 2002 to 470,000 in 2018 (13,000 in 2006, 93,000 in 2010, 255,000 in 2014).[39] Inclusion in the database is indeed a mass phenomenon, particularly as regards individuals questioned.

The question of the cost of this expansion might be raised here. The Cour des comptes[40] evaluated the funds assigned to the PTS at 357 million euro in 2015. In the same year, court costs related to the PTS were 51 million euro, including 21 million euro for genetic analysis. Overall, the PTS accounts for around 7% of the Interior Ministry's spending on the national police and gendarmerie.[41] Thus practices relating to the FNAEG raise questions less of financial cost than of their effects on the definition and alteration of categories of suspects. Indeed, it is precisely cost-cutting that contributes to the development of these techniques.

Moreover, hitherto classification as a perpetrator or suspect tended to persist, as the dominant rationale behind the expansion of the FNAEG aligns with practices relating to deletion of records. Since the "internal security" law of 2003, suspects' DNA records may be deleted from the FNAEG on instruction of the state prosecutor, acting either routinely as part of her/his regular duties (which is very rare) or at the request of the person concerned when retention of the data no longer appears "necessary given the purpose of the database."[42] Since 2019 there has also been a provision that permits those convicted to lodge a request with the state prosecutor for advance deletion of their genetic profile from these databases, after a specified period.[43] During my field study, prior to the 2021 decree, a senior civil servant from the Ministry of Justice told me that the number of suspect profiles deleted from the FNAEG on these grounds was very low, at 160 per year. In the same order of magnitude, in the year 2014 the FNAEG management service implemented 131 decisions to delete records.[44] From the police's point of view, one reason for this situation relates to the general rationale behind the database, and the type of investigation involved:

> It's a bit complicated to say: we'll ask for John Doe to be deleted because he wasn't convicted, because there's not enough evidence. And then to say seven or eight years later, he committed a crime and we could have caught him with that profile.
>
> *(Police officer 3)*

Individuals are not told – and therefore are usually unaware – that they can request advance removal of their record from the database. Furthermore, in cases where they have to file a request with the public prosecutor, with the assistance of an attorney, the procedure involves a cost. In various situations related to employment, applying for a job in a local authority, or during the recruitment process, for example, there is no requirement for verification of FNAEG status, which involves producing an extract from the police record. This contributes to the fact that the issue is seen as relatively unimportant by those concerned. In short, most individuals profiled forget the FNAEG and may be completely unaware that they belong to one of the categories of individuals profiled, and/or that such categories exist. This confirms two points: first, that the bioidentity discussed in this chapter does indeed relate to "the Other" and not "me"; and second, that the more easily used and the broader a system of categorization is, the less visible it is (Bowker and Star, 1999). Ultimately, the porosity between categories discussed above is accompanied by a hardening of the categories of perpetrator and suspect, owing to the long periods of retention and the small number of records deleted from the FNAEG: once an individual's category has altered in the way described above, the classification tends to last.

Nevertheless, the ECHR ruling against France led to new provisions for deletion of data. The October 2021 decree states that henceforth data relating to suspects who have been acquitted are to be deleted by the FNAEG administration "as soon as it receives communication of the decision"; the decision must be communicated by the competent judicial authority "within the shortest possible time" from the date of the verdict.[45] The difference from the previous situation is therefore that data is to be deleted as of right if the individual is acquitted. As it happens, the CNIL, in the opinion issued shortly before the decree was published, expressed a reservation, noting that deletion of data should be "automatic" and should not depend on a request from the individual concerned. Time will tell how these deletions are carried out, how many records are deleted, and whether deletion is more or less systematic or more unpredictable. To return to the point under discussion above, this will have consequences in terms of the power relations between the police and the justice system. If individuals acquitted have to file a request to have their records removed from the database, as those charged do – in other words, if the record remains in all cases, regardless of the judicial outcome of the offense – the impact of a judicial decision not to convict them is minimized.

International insights

Having described these various professional rationales, it is interesting to note that in some respects they overlap with the situation in other countries.

The United Kingdom's experience

The United Kingdom was the first country to create a national genetic profiles database in 1995, known as the National DNA Database (NDNAD). This followed on from the first implementation of the technique by geneticist Alec Jeffreys in 1984. Almost all offenses may be entered into it, including begging, drunk driving, and taking part in an illegal demonstration, although in practice cost concerns limit the offenses included (Wallace, 2006; Krimsky and Simoncelli, 2011). Until the early 2010s, England, Wales, and Northern Ireland were the only jurisdictions within the Council of Europe that permitted indefinite retention of samples and DNA profiles of any person, whether suspected or judged guilty, whatever their age and the seriousness of the offense committed. In July 2006, the NDNAD contained 1.2 million profiles of individuals who had not been convicted, out of a total of 3.5 million (Lynch and McNally, 2009). This represents a proportion of 34%, still far below France's 75%. Following an appeal by two suspects whose DNA and profiles were to be retained indefinitely (a case I discuss below), the ECHR ruled against the United Kingdom in 2008 for disproportionate infringement of the right to respect of private and family life.[46] In response, in 2012 the United Kingdom passed the Protection of Freedoms Act that permits indefinite retention of the profiles of persons convicted, including of minor offenses (with adjustment for minors), but requires that those of suspects not charged or acquitted be removed from the database after a given period, which may be as long as five years (except in the case of minor offenses, when they must not be retained).[47] All DNA samples from identified individuals must be destroyed after six months. This judgment led the United Kingdom to destroy 7.7 million DNA samples and remove 1.7 million profiles of suspects and children from its database. Furthermore, in 2020 the ECHR issued another unfavorable ruling on the profiling of a person convicted of drunk driving, on a similar basis to its 2008 judgment.[48] Yet these judgments failed to restrain the total number of profiles retained because in September 2022 it had risen to 7 million, amounting to 10% of the UK population, or more precisely 8.5% if we exclude profiles of the same individuals registered under different names.[49]

In contrast to France and the United States at federal level, the British database includes the name, date of birth, gender, and ethnic origin of individuals. Statistics on gender, age, and "ethnic appearance" derived from this database are available. Official statistics show that in 2022, 7.5% of the recorded profiles are from minors aged between 10 and 15, and that 7.5% are from individuals the police categorize as black.[50] As regards this last point, in 2006 a controversy broke out following the publication of statistics that stated that nearly 40% of "black" men, 13% of "Asian" men and 9% of "white" men had their profile recorded in the database, indicating a marked over-representation of black men.[51] Further evidence of this claim came in the 2009 report of the British government's Human Genetics Commission, which stated that the profiles of over three quarters of young "black" men aged between 18 and 35 were recorded in the database, a fact that led civil liberties campaigners and representatives of minorities to raise questions about discrimination.[52] It was emphasized that minorities were more frequently stopped by the police, which put them in a situation of "genetic surveillance."[53] On the opposite side, a British judge reacted to these statistics by calling for profiling to be extended to the entire population, including visitors to the country, so as to avoid "injustice."[54]

Regardless of these statistics, individuals and countries who promote a vision of extensive genetic databases could learn much from the British experience. The ECHR's judgment against the United Kingdom and the destruction of DNA samples and removal of profiles described above do not appear to have altered the match rate for murders, rapes, or other offenses. As the *National DNA Database Strategy Report* for 2013–2014 notes, during the second quarter of 2014 the number of matches was 37 for murders, 127 for rapes and 6,111 for other offenses; during the second quarter of 2013, before the profiles were removed, it was 37 for murders, 103 for rapes, and 6,141 for other offenses. These figures led the authors of one academic article to conclude:

> The "match rate" of the database reached its highest level from 2013–2014 to 2017–2018 (62%-68%). This has been interpreted as an indication of improving performance although the number of loaded subject and crime scene profiles have decreased.
>
> *(Amankwaa and McCartney, 2019, p. 49)*

These points are important because they undermine the common-sense belief that the more extensive a database is, the more effective it is.

The United States' experience

In the United States, the Combined DNA Index System (CODIS) is a national genetic database set up in 1998 and managed by the Federal Bureau of Investigation. CODIS comprises three levels of information: local systems that provide the DNA profiles; state systems that allow individual state laboratories to share information; and the federal (national) system that enables states to compare genetic information. The conditions for participation in the national database (National DNA Index, NDIS) and the DNA data that may be stored in it are specified by federal law: convicted offenders, arrestees, prisoners, crime scene traces, unidentified human remains, missing persons and their families, etc. In November 2020, the NDIS contained over 14 million profiles of individuals convicted, 4.2 million profiles of arrestees, and a million unknown traces.[55] There is provision for deletion of arrestees' data, but this is not automatic and occurs only on the request of the arrestee and provided that the Attorney General receives a certified copy of a final court ruling that the charge was rejected or resulted in an acquittal.

Each of the US states has different laws on the retention of DNA samples, population, and analysis of the information contained in its own database.[56]

Individual states' laws on retention of DNA samples vary widely, resulting in questions being raised about the risk of infringement of privacy, given the information that may be retrieved from the samples. According to Sheldon Krimsky and Tania Simoncelli (2011, p. 238), only eight states forbid the use of genetic databases to obtain information on physical characteristics, predisposition to disease, or genetic conditions. As regards population of the databases, all states collect the DNA of those convicted of crime, and from unidentified traces. Broadening criteria for inclusion, some states also include a series of specific offenses in their field of application, as well as profiles of minors, and a small majority collect samples from arrestees. In November 2020, Alaska (60%), Colorado (57%), North Dakota (67%), South Dakota (61%), Kansas (53%), and Louisiana (71%) held a high proportion of arrestee profiles; the average in the United States was around 20%.

However, even in states that restrict collection of DNA to individuals convicted, local databases may contain DNA samples from suspects because local databases are not subject to state regulations. In 2008 the former mayor of New York, Michael Bloomberg, and his colleagues argued that the more DNA the authorities have, the faster computers will be able to match the right people to crimes, and spare the wrong ones from punishment.[57] Although New York state law stipulates that an individual must be convicted before her/his DNA may be included in its database, at this time Bloomberg was proposing that any person arrested, whatever the offense, should submit a DNA sample to the city's database before the case went to court. However, in early 2020, the city announced that it was reviewing its practices, and the police stated that they would ask for any sample over two years old that was not linked to an ongoing investigation or conviction to be removed from the database, as "we don't want to saturate the database with profiles that aren't yielding any results."[58] Time will tell whether these promised erasures will actually be put into effect.

Thus the view that the largest possible database is the best, observed in France, is shared by police representatives in other countries (Cole and Prainsack, 2015). These international insights illustrate the expansion of genetic databases in other countries but also what we can learn from the restriction of them imposed by the ECHR, which does not affect their efficiency in the case of the United Kingdom.

* * *

To sum up, then, legislation has broadened the scope for DNA to be taken by the police, compared, and stored in the database. My aim in this chapter has been to take a close-up view of the encounter between government policy and the actors involved in constructing categories (Harrits and Moller, 2011), studying how the legislation is put into practice and into discourse by social actors (police officers and gendarmes) in France, and adding counterpoints from other countries. While my aim is not to draw international comparisons, it is evident that certain ways of thinking around "criminal careers" and the extension of profiling recur in various countries. However, one noteworthy difference is that in France DNA samples from identified individuals (in other words those taken, for example following a period in custody, rather than being extracted from traces) are not retained, and this protects against subsequent investigation of the individuals' genetic characteristics. In other countries and regions – some US states, the Netherlands, and others – this DNA is retained, raising questions about the risks of its possible future use.

This study offers an illustration of what happens when actors in the field appropriate categories specified by law. Contrary to the genetic and statistical fixity that might be expected, the example of the FNAEG shows that the categories derived from these scientific approaches and legislative provisions may be dynamic, and to some extent mutually porous. While DNA can exonerate individuals, in the vast majority of cases the retention of profiles in the FNAEG results in *an extension of suspects' bioidentities*. More generally, here bioidentity is the product of a mix of genetic tracers, policies, laws, and professional practices that it in its turn helps to shape. It sits at the point of intersection between sameness and selfhood, within a legal and practical identity where the Other is constituted both as a unique individual (by DNA comparison that demonstrates her/his uniqueness, in the register of sameness) and as a member of a group (of perpetrators and suspects, in the register of selfhood). In this way, we can distinguish two aspects of bioidentity that intersect. Our data reveal the specifically political stakes of the bioidentity attributed to the Other within a knowledge/power. In this way, we can move away from the somewhat apolitical ideas that emerged from early studies of bioidentity in the anthropology of health, where it was linked to individuals voluntarily aligning themselves with a group of patients connected by their genetic mutation. Instead, we can turn our gaze on a mode of categorization, within a sovereign state power, of individuals as suspects or convicted perpetrators, linked by their DNA to their biological and social existence.

The transformation of the traditional categories of perpetrator and suspect, and the development of bioidentities, is articulated with a series of rationales and institutional configurations: *iterative/preventative*, in other words identification after the fact and putative prevention of crime; *probabilistic*, aiming to provide the maximum possibility of success in police investigations (these two are rationales of action); *inter-institutional*, prioritizing the police over the justice system; *intra-institutional*, linked to professional performance (these two are institutional configurations). These various elements interlock and converge toward *an extension and a durability of suspicion* (Vailly and Krikorian, 2018). Thus two dynamics are articulated here: an expansive and pragmatic approach to the use of a technological tool by the actors on the ground is supported by a political will to develop it, demonstrated by the laws introduced since the 1990s in response to social and political perceptions of insecurity and the terrorist threat. This establishes a close relationship between population of the categories of perpetrator and suspect, and resolving cases. This relationship has consequences. Among the police a mechanism of wider inclusion in the database, inspired by a probabilistic rationale for clearing cases, becomes established, assuming that the more information is available, the better we all are collectively. Because of this, there is not (or no longer) acceptance of the risk of including a smaller proportion of individuals in the database, at the cost of the imagined danger of some suspects passing through the net. In other words, these practices are linked to a new "construction of an intolerable" (Fassin and Bourdelais, 2005), in this case intolerance of the risk of missing a case. This helps to explain why, compared to other countries with the same historical context of terrorist risk (Lazer and Meyer, 2004; Hindmarsh and Prainsack, 2010), use of genetic analysis is at a relatively high level in France. Finally, the changes in traditional categories of perpetrator and suspect, and the development of bioidentities, described here, point to the need for research into the point of view of those who oppose the use of genetic databases.

Notes

1 Ceaux, P. (2006, August 23). Guy Georges: Le 'tueur de l'est parisien'. *Le Monde*. In France the judiciary is involved in criminal investigations through the examining magistrate, who oversees the conduct of the investigation [translator].
2 Article 706–55 of the Code of Penal Procedure.
3 French National Assembly, Ordinary session 2002–2003, 3rd session of Thursday January 16 2003; see https://www.assemblee-nationale.fr/12/cra/2002-2003/120.asp (accessed January 21 2021).
4 See the comments reported by Dingreville, A., & Rizet, D. (2008, February 22). Alliot-Marie met la police technique et scientifique au 1er rang de ses priorités. *Le Figaro magazine* and Manach, J.-M. (2007, July 3). La justice simplifie de fichage génétique. *Le Monde*.
5 The law specifies "serious or consistent evidence" that makes it "credible" that the individuals have committed an offense that renders them subject to being included in the FNAEG (the French term for this official questioning is "mis en cause"); article 706–54, paragraph 2 of the Code of Penal Procedure.
6 See questions to the government, responses published in the *Journal Officiel* on April 6 2010, February 12 2013, August 5 2014, and December 8 2015.
7 The law of March 18 2003 on internal security made refusal to provide a DNA sample subject to a maximum penalty of a 15,000 euro fine and twelve months' imprisonment for suspects, and double that for those convicted of offenses.
8 Decision no. 2010–25 QPC of September 16 2010.
9 Aycaguer v. France, June 22 2017, 8806/12, ECHR, Court (Fifth Section), No. 8806/12.
10 "A draft modification of the regulatory arrangements for the FNAEG [...] is currently being drawn up, in order to take account of the Conseil constitutionnel's Decision no. 2010–25 QPC of September 16 2010, which requires that periods of retention of genetic profiles in the database be adjusted depending on the seriousness of the offense or the minor age of the individual." Assemblée nationale, written question no. 121476, response published February 28 2012.
11 Decree no. 2021–1402 of October 29 2021.
12 Commission Nationale de l'Informatique et des Libertés, Consideration no. 2021–009 of January 7 2021.
13 DNA from traces is treated in different ways, depending on the laboratory: destruction of the extract once the genetic profile has been established, storage and dispatch

to the Central Department for the Storage of Biological Samples (Service central de préservation des prélèvements biologiques, SCPPB), or storage at the laboratory.

14 See APEV's website at http://www.apev.org (accessed December 22 2021).

15 With the exception of the segment corresponding to the marker for sex. Article 706–54 of the Code of Penal Procedure.

16 Articles R53–18 and R53–19–1 of the Code of Penal Procedure.

17 The Judicial Police (Police Judiciaire) is the serious crime investigation branch of the French national police force [translator].

18 See Van Renterghem, M. (2006, September 25). La tentation du fichage génétique de masse. *Le Monde*.

19 Dewailly, A. (2008, April 8). Vingt et un ans après les faits, un pompier accusé par son ADN. *Le Monde*.

20 Comments reported by Dingreville, A., & Rizet, D. (2008, February 22). Alliot-Marie met la police technique et scientifique au 1er rang de ses priorités. *Le Figaro magazine*.

21 Dwyer, J. (2008, January 19). License, registration and DNA, please. *The New York Times*.

22 The states listed by the ECHR are: Albania, Austria, Belgium, Bosnia-Herzegovina, Croatia, Denmark, Estonia, Finland, France, Hungary, Latvia, Lithuania, the Republic of Moldova, the Netherlands, Norway, Poland, Portugal, Spain, Sweden, and Switzerland.

23 Case of Gaughran v. the United Kingdom, February 13 2020, pp. 14–15.

24 See Chapters 3 and 4.

25 In 2013, 107,966 matches had been made since the FNAEG was set up. Of these, 95,803 were between a DNA trace found at a crime scene and that of an individual. These are broken down as follows: 73,139 between a DNA trace taken at a crime scene and that of a suspect included in the database; 21,230 between a trace and a convicted offender; 1,247 between a trace and a suspect not included in the database (see below); 187 between a deceased individual and a person identified. Source: Fichier national automatisé des empreintes génétiques, "Rapport d'activité 2013," Police nationale, Direction centrale de la police judiciaire, police technique et scientifique.

26 From the legal point of view, this remark is inappropriate: when a case is dismissed, this decision has not been made, and the dismissal of the case does not have the authority of a case judged. I am grateful to Élisabeth Fortis for this insight.

27 See the Circular of November 29 2013 on combating burglary and other thefts, and the Funding Proposal 2015 and 2018, 176; Police nationale, 152; Gendarmerie nationale; and Maëlys Bernard, Interstats Méthode No. 18, "Élucidation des faits de délinquance par la police et gendarmerie nationales: une nouvelle méthode de calcul," December 2021.

28 Fichier national automatisé des empreintes génétiques, Rapport d'activité 2013, Police nationale, Direction centrale de la police judiciaire, police technique et scientifique. Data as at December 31 2013, calculated from April 2007.

29 Wiles, P. (2017). *Annual Report 2016: Commissioner for the Retention and Use of Biometric Material*. Office of the Biometrics Commissioner, p. 10.

30 Article 706–54, paragraph 5 of the Code of Penal Procedure, and Article A38 of the Code as modified by the decree of August 10 2015.

31 Soyez, F. (2012, July 13). Le fichier des empreintes ADN peut-être en sursis. *Le Figaro*.

32 Desplos, J.-M. (2014, September 8). L'ADN révolutionne le portrait-robot. *Sud-Ouest*. Similarly, a Ministry of Justice spokesperson told the press in 2007: "The more material there is in the database, the more effective it is," Manach, J.-M. (2007, July 3). La justice simplifie de fichage génétique. *Le Monde*.

33 Remarks reported by Dingreville, A., & Rizet, D. (2008, February 22). Alliot-Marie met la police technique et scientifique au 1er rang de ses priorités. *Le Figaro magazine*.

34 Cases in which this practice was used include the rape and murder of a young woman in Pleines Fougères, which resulted in police taking over 400 DNA samples in

1997, and a rape in a high school in La Rochelle, in which in 2014 over 500 DNA samples were taken from adult men and boys at the school.

35 Figures supplied by the PTS.

36 Ministry of Justice Circular of July 27 2004, CRIM-PJ no. 97–28.H5.

37 A person may be placed in custody if there is one or more plausible reasons for suspecting that she/he has committed or attempted to commit a felony or a misdemeanor punishable by imprisonment (rather than by a simple fine). See https://www.service-public.fr/particuliers/vosdroits/F14837 (accessed November 24 2017) and Ministry of Justice Circular of July 9 2008, CRIM-PJ no. 08–28.H5.

38 Source: Draft finance laws for 2015, 2016, 2018, and 2020. "Programme 176: Police nationale; Objectifs et indicateurs de performance 2015 (gendarmerie nationale)"; "Projet annuel de performance, annexe au projet de loi de finance pour 2017."

39 During this period, the published figures did not take into account "replicates" resulting from the same individuals being registered under different names. Data as at December 31 each year, except in May 2016 and March 2018. Source: Questions to the government, responses, published in the *Journal officiel* on April 6 2010, February 12 2013, August 5 2014 and December 8 2015, and personal communication from the PTS.

40 Court of Auditors, France's supreme audit institution [translator].

41 Cour des comptes, La police scientifique et technique. Décembre 2006.

42 Article 706–54–1 of the Code of Penal Procedure.

43 The October 2021 decree set these periods at 3 years where the period of retention is 15 years, 7 years when it is 25 years, and 10 years when it is 40 years.

44 *Journal officiel*, January 5 2016, available at https://questions.assemblee-nationale.fr/q14/14-63410QE.htm (accessed January 21 2021).

45 Article 53–14–1 of the Code of Penal Procedure.

46 S. and Marper v. United Kingdom. Judgment of December 4 2008.

47 Protection of Freedoms Act 2012: DNA and Fingerprint Provisions; Protection of Freedoms Act 2012: How DNA and fingerprint evidence is protected in law. UK Government Home Office, April 4 2014; see https://www.gov.uk/government/publications/protection-of-freedoms-act-2012-dna-and-fingerprint-provisions/protection-of-freedoms-act-2012-how-dna-and-fingerprint-evidence-is-protected-in-law.

48 Bowcott, O. (2020, February 13). Police keeping drink-driver's DNA breached his rights, judges rule. *The Guardian*.

49 Home Office: NPCC. National DNA database strategy board. See https://www.gov.uk/government/statistics/national-dna-database-statistics (accessed November 18 2022).

50 Home Office: NPCC. National DNA database strategy board. See https://www.gov.uk/government/statistics/national-dna-database-statistics (accessed November 18 2022).

51 See http://news.bbc.co.uk/2/hi/uk_news/6979138.stm (accessed March 22 2022).

52 Human Genetics Commission. (2009). Nothing to hide, nothing to fear? Balancing individual rights and the public interest in the governance and use of the national DNA database, Report 2009, p. 4.

53 Robertson, J. (2006, January 5). DNA of 37% of black men held by police. *The Guardian*.

54 Barnett, A. (2006, July 16). Police DNA database 'is spiralling out of control'. *The Guardian*.

55 See https://www.fbi.gov/services/laboratory/biometric-analysis/codis/ndis-statistics (accessed January 7 2021).

56 If the law on access to samples and DNA profiles in a given state differs from federal law, the latter overrides state law for the purposes of participation in the NDIS. DNA Identification Act (42 U.S.C. §14132), see https://codes.findlaw.com/us/title-42-the-public-health-and-welfare/42-usc-sect-14132.html (accessed February 18 2021).

57 Dwyer, J. (2008, January 19). License, registration and DNA, please. *The New York Times*.

58 Sandoval, E. (2020, February 20). N.Y.P.D. to remove DNA profiles of non-criminals from database. *The New York Times*.

References

Aas, K. F. (2006). "The body does not lie": Identity, risk and trust in technoculture. *Crime, Media, Culture: An International Journal*, 2(2), 143–158. doi:10.1177/1741659006065401.

Amankwaa, O. A., & McCartney, C. (2019). The effectiveness of the UK National DNA Database. *Forensic Science International: Synergy*, 1, 45–55. doi:10.1016/j.fsisyn.2019.03.004.

Amankwaa, O. A., & McCartney, C. (2021). The effectiveness of the current use of forensic DNA in criminal investigations in England and Wales. *Wires Forensic Sciences*, 3, e1414. doi:10.1002/wfs2.1414.

Aronson, J. D. (2007). *Genetic witness: Science, law, and controversy in the making of DNA profiling*. Rutgers University Press.

Becker, H. (2018 [1963]). *Outsiders: Studies in the sociology of deviance*. Free Press.

Bourgain, C., & Darlu, P. (2013). *ADN superstar ou superflic? Les citoyens face à une molécule envahissante*. Seuil.

Bowker, G. C., & Star, S. L. (1999). *Sorting things out: Classification and its consequences*. The MIT Press.

Castel, R. (1981). *La gestion des risques: De l'anti-psychiatrie à l'après-psychanalyse*. Éditions de Minuit.

Cole, S. A., & Lynch, M. (2006). The social and legal construction of suspects. *Annual Review of Law and Social Science*, 2, 39–60. doi:10.1146/annurev.lawsocsci.2.081805.110001.

Cole, S. A., & Prainsack, B. (2015). Genetics and forensics. In J. Wright (Ed.), *The International encyclopedia of the social and behavioral sciences* (pp. 955–961), 2nd edn. Elsevier. doi:10.1016/B978-0-08-097086-8.82050-4.

Desrosières, A. (2008). *Pour une sociologie historique de la quantification: L'argument statistique I*. Presses des Mines.

Dew, K., Scott, A., & Kirkman, A. (2016). *Social, political and cultural dimensions of health*. Springer.

Dimond, R., Bartlett, A., & Lewis, J. (2015). What binds biosociality? The collective effervescence of the parent-led conference. *Social Science & Medicine*, 126, 1–8. doi:10.1016/j.socscimed.2014.12.005.

Fassin, D., Bouagga, Y., Coutant, I., Eideliman, J.-S. *et al.* (2015 [2013]). *At the heart of the state: The moral world of institutions*, trans. Patrick Brown. Pluto Press.

Fassin, D., & Bourdelais, P. (Eds.). (2005). *Les constructions de l'intolérable: Études d'anthropologie et d'histoire sur les frontières de l'espace moral*. La Découverte.

Favre, P. (2009). Quand la police fabrique l'ordre social: Un *en deçà* des politiques de la police? *Revue française de science politique*, 59(6), 1231–1248. doi:10.3917/rfsp.596.1231.

Foucault, M. (1983). The subject and power. In H. Drefyus, & P. Rabinow (Eds.), *Beyond structuralism and hermeneutics* (pp. 208–225). University of Chicago Press.

Grimes, D. A., & Schulz, K. F. (2002). Uses and abuses of screening tests. *Lancet*, 359 (9309), 881–884. doi:10.1016/S0140-6736(02)07948-5.

Harrits, G. S., & Moller, M. O. (2011). Categories and categorization: Toward a comprehensive sociological framework. *Distinktion: Journal of Social Theory*, 12(2), 229–247. doi:10.1080/1600910X.2011.579450.

Hindmarsh, R., & Prainsack, B. (Eds.). (2010). *Genetic suspects: Global governance of forensic DNA profiling and databasing*. Cambridge University Press.

Jenkins, R. (2000). Categorization: Identity, social process and epistemology. *Current Sociology, 48*(3), 7–25. doi:10.1177/0011392100048003003.

Jobard, F., Lévy, R., Lamberth, J., & Névanen, S. (2012). Mesurer les discriminations selon l'apparence: Une analyse des contrôles d'identité à Paris. *Population*, 67(3), 423–451. doi:10317/popu.1203.0423.

Keck, F. (2010). Note sur le texte de P. Rabinow, Biosocialité: genèse, enjeux et postérité d'un concept. *Politix*, 90, 39–46. doi:10.3917/pox.090.0021.

Koch, L., & Stemerding, D. (1994). The sociology of entrenchment: A cystic fibrosis test for everyone? *Social Science & Medicine*, 39(9), 1211–1220. doi:10.1016/0277-9536(94)90353-0.

Krikorian, G. (2021). Usages de l'ADN par la police: Les conditions épistémiques de l'absence d'un débat public. In J. Vailly (Ed.), *Sur la trace des suspects: L'incorporation de la preuve et de l'indice à l'ère de la génétique* (pp. 109–135). Éditions de la Maison des sciences de l'homme.

Krimsky, S., & Simoncelli, T. (2011). *Genetic justice: DNA data banks, criminal investigations and civil liberties*. Columbia University Press.

Lazer, D. (Ed.). (2004). *DNA and the criminal justice system: The technology of justice*. MIT Press.

Lazer, D., & Meyer, M. N. (2004). DNA and the criminal justice system: Consensus and debate. In D. Lazer (Ed.), *DNA and the criminal justice system: The technology of justice* (pp. 357–390). MIT Press.

Lynch, M., Cole, S. A., McNally, R., & Jordan, K. (2008). *Truth machine: The contentious history of DNA fingerprinting*. University of Chicago Press.

Lynch, M., & McNally, R. (2009). Forensic DNA databases and biolegality: The coproduction of law, surveillance technology and suspects bodies. In P. Atkinson, P. Glasner, & M. Lock (Eds.), *Handbook of genetics and society: Mapping the new genomic era* (pp. 283–301). Routledge.

Noiriel, G. (Ed.). (2007). *L'identification: Genèse d'un travail d'État*. Belin.

Rabinow, P. (1996). Artificiality and enlightenment: From sociobiology to biosociality. In P. Rabinow (Ed.), *Essays on the anthropology of reason* (pp. 91–112). Princeton University Press.

Ricœur, P. (1992). *Oneself as another*, trans. Kathleen Blamey. University of Chicago Press.

Schramm, K., Skinner, D., & Rottenburg, R. (2012). Ideas in motion: Making sense of identity after DNA. In K. Schramm, D. Skinner, & R. Rottenburg (Eds.), *Identity politics and the new genetics: Re/creating categories of difference and belonging* (pp. 1–29). Berghahn.

Skinner, D. (2011). Mobile identities and fixed categories: Forensic DNA and the politics of racialized data. In K. Schramm, D. Skinner, & R. Rottenburg (Eds.), *Identity politics and the new genetics: Re/creating categories of difference and belonging* (pp. 53–78). Berghahn.

Timmermans, S., & Buchbinder, M. (2010). Patients-in-waiting: Living between sickness and health in the genomics era. *Journal of Health and Social Behavior*, 51(4), 408–423. doi:10.1177/0022146510386794.

Toom, V., Wienroth, M., & M'charek, A. (Eds.). (2023). *Law, practice and politics of forensic DNA profiling: Forensic genetics and their technolegal worlds*. Routledge.

Tutton, R., & Levitt, M. (2010). Health and wealth, law and order: Banking DNA against disease and crime. In R. Hindmarsh & B. Prainsack (Eds.), *Genetic suspects: Global governance of forensic DNA profiling and databasing* (pp. 85–104). Cambridge University Press.

Vailly, J., Kehr, J., & Niewöhner, J. (Eds.). (2011). *De la vie biologique à la vie sociale: Approches sociologiques et anthropologiques*. La Découverte.

Vailly, J., & Krikorian, G. (2018). Durabilité et extension du soupçon: Catégorisations et usages policiers du fichier d'empreintes génétiques en France. *Revue française de sociologie*, 59(4), 707–733. doi:10.3917/rfs.594.0707.

Wallace, H. (2006). The UK national DNA database: Balancing crime detection, human rights and privacy. *Embo Reports*, 7, S26–S30. doi:10.1038/sj.embor.7400727.

Williams, R., & Johnson, P. (2004). "Wonderment and dread": Representations of DNA in ethical disputes about forensic databases. *New Genetics & Society*, 23(2), 205–223. doi:10.1080/1463677042000237035.

Williams, R., & Johnson, P. (2005). Inclusiveness, effectiveness and intrusiveness: Issues in the developing uses of DNA profiling in support of criminal investigations. *The Journal of Law, Medical & Ethics*, 33(3), 545–558. doi:10.1111/j.1748-720X.2005.tb00517.x.

2

RESISTANCE TO THE GENETIC DATABASE

Two activists opposed to the excessive use of advertising billboards "tag" some billboards in a town in northern France. They are caught in the act, and their actions are classified as "vandalism or defacement of property through the use of words, signs or drawings", a recordable offense in terms of the genetic database. They make no claim to innocence – as activists, indeed, they claim their actions – though they prefer to describe them as "daubing" rather than vandalism, but they refuse to provide their DNA to the police. Summoned before the deputy public prosecutor and then before the minor crimes court for the two offences (vandalism and refusal to provide a DNA sample), they launch a media campaign around the case, backed by a support committee made up of artists, political activists from the critical and environmentalist left, and trade unionists. At their trial, dozens of people arrive to support them, and the general secretary of the Syndicat de la Magistrature (Judges' Union), one of the deputies of the town's Green Party mayor, and a schoolteacher are called as witnesses. In response to a question from the judge, one of those charged says: "I don't think I should be included in a database originally created for sex offenders" (Activist 1). The public prosecutor responds:

> When a person commits an offense defined in law, they are obliged to submit [to DNA sampling], otherwise it's too easy: for now I admit what I did, but later it'll be: 'No trace, no case,' and I can say, as there are no traces, 'it wasn't me'. Even if the motivation is different, we can't make a distinction: that is the law. I ask you to find the defendants guilty.
>
> *(Judge 2)*

He asks for a one-month suspended prison sentence for the vandalism, and two months suspended for the refusal to provide DNA. The two daubers, as they

DOI: 10.4324/9781003456056-4

describe themselves, are eventually acquitted of vandalism but sentenced to a suspended 500-euro fine for the refusal to provide DNA. More generally, some of those opposed to DNA sampling are repeatedly convicted of refusal to provide a sample because the demand is reiterated: just because a person is convicted once does not mean that the offense disappears when they refuse a second time. In this vein, the public prosecutor in the case of an anti-GMO (genetically modified organism) activist, a "GMO reaper" who repeatedly refused to provide his DNA, spoke of a "continuous offence" in a 2006 press statement: "As long as he continues to refuse to provide DNA, I shall continue to charge him and he will be summoned again. He could go to jail for repeat offending."[1]

These preliminary examples take us straight to heart of the reasoning behind refusals to provide a DNA sample, and the effects highlighted by this reasoning. These practices of profiling, and these refusals to provide a DNA sample, produce effects where the definition of actions ("vandalism", etc.) plays an important role. Through the intermediary of language, not only descriptions but also legal definitions and classifications ("convicted of refusal to provide DNA", "questioned under caution", etc.) are formed. And these classifications interact with the individuals classified, thereby contributing to "making up people" (Hacking, 2000), who may express resistance to such classifications. Following on from the previous chapter, the questions raised here may thus be formulated as follows: from the point of view of those opposed to genetic profiling, how does the shift of identities (either attributed to individuals or claimed by them) articulate with the effects contested by these opponents on the legal and scientific levels? What bottom-up role do these actors play in the "government" of the FNAEG, as previously defined?[2] Before responding to these questions, it will be helpful to briefly consider international studies of how such databases are received in various countries.

International reception of genetic databases

Studies of the acceptance of genetic databases show that in the United Kingdom the majority of those interviewed among the public see the use of DNA in forensics and criminal investigations "as the least controversial and most beneficial of genetic applications" (Wilson-Kovacs et al., 2012, p. 288), that in New Zealand and Serbia the majority of the population agrees with practices aimed at identifying criminals (Veth and Midgley, 2010; Curtis, 2014; Teodorovic et al., 2017), and that in Portugal there is "acknowledgement of the investigative potential of forensic DNA technologies and a relegation of civil liberties and human rights to the background, owing to the perceived benefits of protecting both society and the individual from crime" (Machado and Silva, 2014, p. 132). Overall, it seems that across various countries the public perception of genetic databases is that they are beneficial for society and that they provide reliable results that help to identify offenders; this perception sometimes goes hand in hand with limited understanding of the processes involved (Curtis, 2014). There is a marked absence of debate in a number of countries (the United States, United Kingdom, and France, as I shall discuss). Machado and Granja (2022) describe the difficulty NGOs critical of the extension of "genetic surveillance" have in mobilizing the public around these issues in Europe. Despite this, there have been opposition campaigns focused on the breach of human rights and the development of the surveillance society (Etzioni, 2004); questions have been raised around issues of civil liberties and the misuse of genetics (Machado and Silva, 2014; Teodorovic et al., 2017), particularly in the media (Hindmarsh, 2010), and concerns expressed in the field of legal ethics (Guillen et al., 2000; Gamero et al., 2004). It is important to note that this is not always blanket opposition: positions may shift depending on the seriousness of the offense or the status (convicted or suspected) of the individuals profiled (Curtis, 2014). As I have noted, the United Kingdom is leading the way in development of genetic databases. According to GeneWatch, a British not-for-profit organization that monitors the evolution of genetic technology and its impact on human rights, DNA may be an important tool in criminal investigations, but the issue of the duration of retention of profiles for individuals acquitted, or convicted of minor offenses, has not yet been resolved. GeneWatch further argues that indefinite retention of the profiles of children who have committed more than one minor offense, and adults who have committed a single minor offense, is still excessive.[3] In short, although the public perception of these practices appears positive in the population overall, more critical questioning emerges when opinions are assessed more closely in relation to specific situations, particularly among activists and advocacy organizations (Curtis, 2014; Williams and Wienroth, 2014a; 2017).

In the United States, Dorothy Nelkin and Lori Andrews (1999) note the lack of public opposition during the 1990s to the tissue banks set up for the purposes of identifying individuals. However, they discuss the case of a number of military personnel who refused to provide DNA for the purposes of identifying their bodies should they die in the field. For example, in 2005, two Marines were ordered by their senior officers to provide blood samples and cheek cells to be included in a huge tissue bank launched in 1992, in order to limit the number of "unknown soldiers" killed in combat whose remains are unidentified. The two men refused and were court martialed. They argued that they wished to "have control of [their] DNA" and feared that it would be used for purposes other than identification, or without their consent. Ultimately, the military judge dropped the charges on the grounds that there were no regulations concerning the consequences of refusing to comply with the program. However, the two men lost their civil suit, when the court judged that the request for a sample was valid. In 1996 another, African American, soldier also refused to give tissue samples but for slightly different reasons relating to racism. He wrote: "Until the issue of racism is resolved, Afro-Americans should retain possession of their genetic material." At court martial he was sentenced to 14 days' hard labor and a two-grade reduction in rank. The same year, a Native American marine refused to provide his DNA for reasons of religious conviction. He was convicted, downgraded, and lost 40% of his salary but applied for a waiver on grounds of religious freedom, which he was eventually granted. Nelkin and Andrews make the interesting point that these refusals indicate a position that challenges the general assumption of the military's authority over soldiers' bodies. Here, in effect, DNA implies a risk for the appellants that goes beyond the usual military intrusion into bodies because it allows for its potential use in the fields of medicine or the law (Nelkin and Andrews, 1999). Nevertheless, as I have noted, these examples of opposition to genetic databases remain relatively rare in the United States.

It is not always possible, from these various studies, to gain a detailed picture of the discourse and concerns of those opposed to genetic profiling. Here I am interested more in political forms involving citizen action than in the institutional and judicial framework. My primary mode of investigation takes forms of resistance to the various kinds of power as a starting point and "[uses] this resistance as a chemical catalyst" (Foucault, 1982, p. 780) to reveal the contested social effects of profiling practices. Moreover, Foucault (1991a, p. 75) argues, "to analyze 'regimes of practices' means to analyze programmes of conduct which have both prescriptive effects regarding what is to be done (effects of 'jurisdiction'), and codifying effects regarding what is to be known (effects of 'veridiction')." In the first part of this chapter, following a few general remarks outlining the background to opposition to police databases in France, I present the "effects of jurisdiction" of genetic profiling: in other words, the effects of genetic profiling applied to populations, in terms of the production and implementation of law ("what is to be done"). I show that those who oppose the broad coverage of the database do so on the grounds of civil liberties, against a more general background of power relations supportive to the database. They do not contest the targeted use of DNA in the register of "sameness" (Ricœur, 1992). It is rather as if they contest the shift from this use to one extended to entire populations, which transforms the bioidentity of those profiled, who are then categorized as long-term suspects or criminals, in the register of "selfhood" (Ricœur, 1992). I then present the "effects of veridiction" – that is, the effects in terms of what social actors consider to be true or false ("what is to be known") regarding medical data or data relating to origin, which these activists claim are contained in genetic profiles. This helps to make clear how the scientific arguments put forward by opponents reinforce their point of view. Once again, the identity of individuals profiled appears to extend beyond the frame of comparison of genetic profiles (in the register of sameness) into the register of characterization of individuals (according to their predisposition to a disease or their origin, in the register of selfhood), but this time on the basis of scientific arguments.

Large-scale profiling

Studying the FNAEG invites consideration of the wider context of police and court databases in France, which, as I shall show, has an influence on discussions. I have noted that the number of both biometric and non-biometric databases used for information, identification, and administration is consistently rising in France, as is the number of so-called "security" laws. As described above, in October 2018 a National Assembly information commission published a report noting 106 databases available to the security forces (police and gendarmerie) – 70 more than in 2007. The report argued that the databases were "excessive in number and form an overly complex whole" and called for rationalization, digitization, and interconnection rather than placing restrictions on profiling.[4] Here, rather than giving a general overview of police and court databases, I focus on three such databases that are particularly heavily used and that are worth briefly outlining in order to understand the rationales underlying them.

The most extensive, and currently most widely used, database in France is the Traitement d'Antécédents Judiciaires (Criminal Records Database, TAJ), set up in 2011 to replace the national police's STIC and the gendarmerie's JUDEX, which were then abolished. The TAJ is a police investigation database (available to both police and gendarmerie) used in criminal investigations (seeking perpetrators of offenses), administrative inquiries (recruitment to sensitive posts), and some information searches. Its purpose is to support investigation and to facilitate the recording of offenses, the search for perpetrators, and the gathering of evidence. It contains data on individuals "questioned under caution" in criminal investigations, and thus not only those convicted but also those subsequently acquitted, as well as data on victims. By the end of 2018, it contained 18.9 million profiles of individuals. A suite of data, including photos, is retained for each individual questioned. This prompted the advocacy organization La Quadrature du Net, which campaigns for internet freedom, to lodge an appeal with the Conseil d'État,[5] on the grounds that the Code of Penal Procedure allows the police and gendarmerie to use facial recognition on these photographs. However, the Conseil d'État rejected this appeal in 2022. In addition, the National Assembly information commission's report, cited above, noted a number of inaccuracies in the TAJ, and that police administrators and gendarmerie officers sometimes updated it in a hurry. Victims might thus be recorded erroneously as perpetrators.[6] This was already the case with the STIC, since, according to the CNIL, 40% of the STIC records examined contained errors and gave rise to corrections of "decisive" information – in other words information that led to the inclusion of the individual questioned in the database.[7] These errors are not without consequence: the CNIL pointed out that in 2013 people had been refused access to certain jobs, a residence permit, or French nationality on the basis of incorrect criminal records data. Moreover, this is one of the databases highlighted for police officers' use of data for personal reasons unconnected with the database's official purpose or any operational need: the report of the Inspection Générale de la Police Nationale (General Inspectorate of the National Police, IGPN) listed 21 investigations of failure to comply with the rules for use of databases involving misappropriation of personal data. This figure probably represents only a fraction of the actual number of illicit consultations.[8]

Another widely used database is the Fichier Automatisé d'Empreintes Digitales (Automated Fingerprint Database, FAED). It is used to search for and identify perpetrators of crimes and individuals who receive a prison sentence. It is also used in the search for missing persons and the identification of individuals who have died or been seriously injured. In 2018 it contained records of 6.2 million individuals, again including those "questioned under caution" but not convicted, and around 220,000 traces.[9] In 2013 the European Court of Human Rights ruled against France on the subject of the FAED, citing disproportionate interference with a suspect's right to respect for private life. The terms of the ruling were roughly the same as those of the court's rulings against France and the United Kingdom on genetic profiling.[10] In September 2021, the CNIL also called the Ministry of the Interior to account over the FAED, in connection with the deletion of data.[11] The CNIL pointed out that many records relating to individuals who had been definitively acquitted or discharged, which should have been deleted from the database under the decree on the FAED, had not been erased. Individuals, then, continue to have their data compared to traces left at crime scenes, and are thus kept under a form of suspicion despite having been exonerated.

The Titres Électroniques Sécurisés system (Secure Electronic Documents, TES) is different in scope, being designed to bring together the digitized photographs and fingerprints, the eye color, and postal and email addresses of all those who hold or have held an identity card or passport – in other words, almost all French citizens.[12] It therefore sits apart from the world of criminal cases, facilitating automatic comparison of fingerprints with those registered under the same identity, in order to prevent identity theft. It is unique in its vast coverage and the nature of the digitized information it contains. Its introduction sparked protests, leading the government of the day, which insisted that there was no alternative to digitization of the identity photo, to grant the possibility for anyone to ask for their digitized fingerprint to be deleted 90 days after a request for identity documents (at that time the paper copy of fingerprints was retained for 15 years). The extent to which this possibility is communicated, understood, and received by French citizens suggests an interesting avenue for research. For obvious reasons concerning civil liberties, the CNIL warned of the need to restrict access to the database so that it could only be consulted on the basis of the identity of the holder of the document, not on the basis of her/his face or fingerprints. The ministry confirmed that this was the case, since the TES database could only compare an identity with a fingerprint and could not be used to discover identity from a fingerprint. This leaves unanswered the question of its possible future evolution, since it would be easy for a government to alter the nature of the database and make it possible to use the data to trace back to an identity. In other words, with fingerprints and the photo, both digitized, as well as an address, the police would possess an extremely powerful tool with particularly problematic consequences for civil liberties.

Given this overall picture, it is clear that the FNAEG is typical of general developments in profiling, in terms of the expanding volume of data held, the integration or correlation with biometric data, and the inclusion of large numbers of suspects. One of the common elements of the FNAEG, the TAJ, and the FAED is that they contain records of minors and of individuals merely suspected by the police, many of whom have not been convicted. At the same time, the FNAEG has specific features that relate to the nature of the genetic data held, such as non-retention of DNA samples from persons identified in France. Having sketched this overview, I now return to the subject of opposition to current uses of the FNAEG.

Effects of jurisdiction

"Criminal" and "citizen": how profiling influences definitions

As noted above, the laws on "everyday security" and "interior security" penalized refusal to provide a DNA sample. However, the situation is more complex because there is a level of ambiguity in the law. Refusal to provide DNA when conditions permit it to be required is an offense, yet under the bioethical principles of the Civil Code, which guarantees the inviolability of the human body, a cheek or blood sample cannot be taken by force (except where the individual is sentenced to ten or more years in prison).[13] A memorandum from the Ministry of Justice highlighted the situation with regard to sampling:

> While a sample may not be taken by force, the need for consent does not constitute a formality requiring that the individual's agreement be recorded in a statement or a written authorization signed by that individual.[14]

In short, DNA may not be taken without consent (except where the individual has been sentenced to ten or more years in prison), but refusal to provide it is an offense. Moreover, other Ministry of Justice memoranda which remain in force insist: "Refusal to provide DNA samples by persons held in custody or convicted should always be prosecuted."[15] Thanks to this systematic prosecution, it is possible to estimate the number of refusals to provide DNA, since the number of convictions for such refusal has varied, from 382 in 2005 to 542 in 2013, peaking at 604 in 2008. More recently, over the period 2018–2022, the number has averaged 681 each year.[16] It is worth noting that while the conviction rate for people charged with refusing to provide DNA is high, the penalties are generally light, consisting of fines or suspended prison sentences, or sometimes adjusted sentences, as the courts treat those who refuse to provide DNA differently depending on whether they are convicted of a sex offense or a minor crime. While judges apply the law strictly, the somewhat symbolic nature of some penalties (100-euro fines) suggests that they are not always comfortable with these minor infractions, particularly if the individual has been acquitted of the main offense but prosecuted for the refusal to provide DNA, as in the example at the head of this chapter.

One of the groups spearheading resistance to the FNAEG were the anti-GMO activists: following an internal debate on whether or not they should provide their DNA, the majority of them chose to refuse. However, in 2008 a specific offense of destruction of genetically modified crops, not recordable for the purposes of the FNAEG, was created so that these activists were no longer affected (it is worth noting that convictions for refusal to provide DNA reached a peak in that year). This is sometimes seen as a way for the government to circumvent opposition, as one police officer I interviewed suggests: "Now they're not in the database anymore, things have calmed down, there's no longer a problem ..." (Police officer 8). This political desire not to arouse inconvenient opposition also emerges in the memorandum cited above, which emphasizes the need for systematic sampling and prosecution of those who refuse but urges that it be done in such a way as not to encourage criticism of the FNAEG. Thus road traffic offenses, which are liable to involve a large proportion of the French population, are not subject to the requirement to provide DNA, as they would be likely to "fan criticism of the database and lead to widespread refusal to provide a sample."[17]

Apart from the anti-GMO campaigners, public contestation of the FNAEG comes predominantly from political and trade union activists who form a broadly interconnected network among union, environmentalist, and anarchist groups. These networks are sometimes supported by professionals – including lawyers and judges – who are members of the Syndicat de la Magistrature (Judges' Union), the second largest judges' union in France, the Syndicat des Avocats de France (French Lawyers' Union), and the Ligue des Droits de l'Homme (Human Rights League), three organizations that are politically on the left and at the forefront of defense of civil liberties. Those who oppose profiling work extend the reach of their actions beyond these groupings, generating media campaigns as in the case of the "daubers" cited above. They seek to use the trial as a platform for promoting their cause and generating public debate, following a time-honored tradition.[18] Thus the trial becomes a platform on which to construct a social problem in the arena of both courts and media (Bonneuil et al., 2008).

Opponents seek to broaden their campaign because challenging mass genetic profiling is not an idea that is widely shared in France. As one lawyer defending political activists put it: "It's clear that French society sees the FNAEG as an excellent method of surveillance [...]. It's always been really difficult to criticize this system" (Lawyer 1). A spokesperson for the Ligue des Droits de l'Homme went further in the press: "The subject doesn't get people fired up."[19] My interviewees suggested a range of reasons why individuals might agree to provide their DNA: being unaware that they could refuse, fear of a harsher sentence or having their custody extended in sometimes oppressive conditions, legal costs arising from a trial for refusal to provide a sample, the restrictive procedures for consulting the FNAEG, and the fact that the FNAEG has become normalized alongside other profiling practices. One other reason is the relatively "painless" nature of the database, which cannot be consulted by employers or administrative authorities.

According to Armand Mattelart and André Vitalis (2014, p. 194), "it is precisely this invisibility that contributes much of the power and efficacy" of profiling.

The broad range of those opposed to profiling, however, are very alarmed by the significant growth of databases for police and judicial use, and in particular of the FNAEG, which they see as liable to infringe on individual liberties. It is important to point out that protests against the FNAEG concern not the use of genetics in criminal law in general (i.e., DNA comparisons between a trace and a suspect identified by traditional investigative methods, or even the use of a database in the case of serious crimes such as murder or rape) but rather certain extended uses of the database in terms of the individuals concerned, types of offense, length of retention of data, etc. In other words, in terms of the broader population, for they seek to dissociate *large-scale genetic profiling* from *the use of genetics* to compare DNA from a trace with that of a suspect identified in a case (or the DNA of an unidentified body with that of a person thought to be related to her/him). A lawyer for activists illustrates this point of view:

> Between asking a certain specific individual to provide her/his DNA to confirm that it does not match the DNA found at a crime scene, and profiling millions of people, there's a huge difference. [...] I mean, ultimately, that's tantamount to suspecting those millions of French people of being potential criminals.
>
> *(Lawyer 2)*

An anti-FNAEG activist argues: "It's no longer a record system searched on the basis of information found in the context of specific cases, it's a database of potentially dangerous individuals" (Activist 2). A joint press release from the Ligue des Droits de l'Homme, the Syndicat de la Magistrature, and the Syndicat des Avocats de France expresses similar views: "Being registered in the database is becoming a penalty in itself, and creates a presumption of guilt based on a database of permanent suspects."[20] Here it is the effects of jurisdiction of genetic profiling that are called into question (should millions of individuals be profiled? who is a suspect? who is a criminal?). And although the legal definition used in prosecutions makes no distinction between breaches of common law and offenses arising from trade union, political, or campaigning activity, these opponents do not consider themselves offenders, still less criminals, as one of them argues:

> [Profiling] should be reserved for criminals who are actually potentially dangerous. But trade unionists and campaigning activists acting within their trade union mandates are not criminals. [...] There's absolutely no question here of individual corrupt, criminal acts intended to harm others.
>
> *(Activist 3)*

Thus in their minds there is a moral aspect to their refusal to be assimilated with criminals, and indeed a perceived attack on their honor. In this vein, a CGT[21] member at the former Continental tires factory told the press at the end of his appeal court trial, during which he was sentenced to a fine of 1,200 euro for refusing to provide a DNA sample: "The worst thing is not the fine, it's being convicted, being treated like a criminal." This widely publicized trial occurred in the context of a months-long industrial dispute over the cutting of more than one thousand jobs, during which the defendant had enabled workers to obtain severance pay.[22] He had been asked to provide his DNA because he had participated in the vandalization of a subprefecture;[23] the defendant had been discharged initially on grounds of the "disproportion between the intention of the law [...] and the means for achieving it," but the public prosecutor had appealed.

For these activists, the distinction between them and criminals is not just legal but symbolic: they seek to establish a boundary between themselves and other social groups by defining their own identity and status in opposition to these others. When they argue that *I* am not a sex offender, so I should not be in the same database as *rapists*, the demand for individual and collective rights (the right of a given person or group of persons not to be included in the database) is correlated with the production of a collective alterity that can be incorporated in the database because they are "real" criminals. There is a parallel with this position of alterity in the history of the labor movement: according to Foucault (1991b), during the 19th century, labor movements and their leaders were forced – in order to escape police repression and accusations that they were bands of murderers, thieves, and alcoholics – to mark their difference from the criminal population. Foucault argues that this led them to support separation between common-law prisoners and political prisoners in more recent times. It is worth adding that this position comes up against the fact that often, in democracies, breaches of the law are not considered political phenomena.

But this position is not unanimous among opponents of profiling. For example, one judge, a senior officer of the Syndicat de la Magistrature who advocates for activists, explains:

> It would be worrying and counterproductive to draw a distinction between the nice guys, those who are profiled in the context of a political campaign, and who should be excluded from the process, and those who are less defendable like juvenile offenders ... [...] It would be prejudicial to stay holed up in the righteous enclave of political and trade union activists.
>
> *(Judge 3)*

According to this second point of view, limiting the campaign to arguing that trade unionists should not be included in the database fails to fully comprehend the problem, which is the extension of the FNAEG and the length of retention of data.

Moreover, not only do these opponents not consider themselves criminals, but they present themselves as champions of causes of general concern: "We're [working] to defend the collective, in the general interest of workers," said one of them in an interview (Activist 4). In a similar vein, in a trial for refusal to provide a DNA sample, the lawyer for an "anti-billboard" activist argued: "These people are whistleblowers, citizens who are sending a message, acting openly, they are citizens who are alerting us" (Lawyer 3). Some activists we interviewed even saw themselves as creators of law: they commit an act punishable under the law in order to change it (to exempt traditional trade union activity from criminal law, limit the use of advertising billboards, etc.), as one anti-GMO activist explained:

> I refused to be labelled as a criminal because I was acting as a citizen, and I was doing it [digging up GM crops] in order to change the law, so that there's recognition under the law. I think that by working through the justice system, citizens can get the judge to take decisions that afterwards, through case law, will help to drive changes in the law.
>
> *(Activist 5)*

During his trial for refusal to supply a DNA sample, another declared:

> I recognize that society has to protect itself against those who have committed crimes, rape, or torture, and that their DNA should be taken when they are convicted, but for that very reason I refuse to be included in the same database as them.
>
> *(Activist 6)*

Let us consider the implications of these remarks in greater depth. In the first place, these statements ("It's always been really difficult to criticize this system"), and the relatively small number of refusals to provide DNA compared to the number of individuals profiled, confirm my initial hypothesis. Profiling is evidence of a form of power *tolerated* by the majority of the population, either because people are indifferent to it or because they approve of it: overall the French population is not massively opposed to the kind of power represented by large-scale, rather than individual, genetic profiling. Profiling persists by virtue of being not imposed but overall tolerated or accepted, even if at certain times more active opposition arises. In general, as I have noted, there is a majority acceptance of genetic databases in various countries, notwithstanding some degree of opposition. As noted in the introduction, this attitude forms part of a context of popular indifference or acceptance – even sometimes of demand – for surveillance cameras in public spaces, monitoring of digital spaces, etc.

Secondly, opposition to the use of databases, particularly genetic databases, is linked to their scope, extended to entire populations. It is not directed at isolated comparisons between an individual suspected in the context of a traditional investigation and a trace left at a crime scene. For opponents of this aspect of profiling, the effects of jurisdiction produced by court and police categorizations (convicted of a crime, suspect etc.) are a central issue, as they refuse to be assimilated with a suspect or criminal population. Again, following Ricœur (1992), they do not contest the targeted use of DNA in the context of comparison of genetic data that enables matching of two identical genetic profiles, in the register of sameness. Rather, it seems that they contest the move between this use and a use extended to entire populations that changes the bioidentity of individuals profiled, who are assimilated with long-term suspects or criminals, in the register of selfhood ("that's tantamount to suspecting those millions of French people of being potential criminals"). Here it is the shift in the selfhood of individuals (who may move from the status of innocent to suspect or guilty, as interviewees contend), rather than their sameness (which derives from the isolated comparison of genetic markers) that is contested. And the FNAEG, which is supposed to be concerned with identification (in the register of sameness), maintains a confusion between sameness and the identity of the individual (in the register of selfhood).

Thirdly, far from seeing themselves as "criminals," these political opponents consider themselves "legal entrepreneurs," to paraphrase Becker (2018 [1963]) in his discussion of the "moral entrepreneurs" who work to change moral norms and laws. Moreover, they are not isolated individuals but form an interconnected network and see themselves as a citizen collective. Their position offers the opportunity for deeper analysis of the concept of "biological citizenship" (Petryna, 2002), as discussed in the sociology of health and the living being. Borrowing the term coined by Adriana Petryna in relation to those exposed to radiation from Chernobyl, Nikolas Rose (2007) portrays a biological citizenship that takes account of projects undertaken by citizens and linked to their biological existence as human beings. The element of choice and responsibility pertaining to individual actors in this concept makes it particularly apposite to the medical context (prenatal testing, etc.). Expanding the concept by taking it beyond the medical and health sphere, some authors adapt it substantially, applying it to the case of suspects whose data are incorporated into genetic databases by the state:

> If we think of [these genetic databases] as a form of genetic citizenship or biological citizenship, then [they] clearly have very different features than [those used in a medical context]. [...] This is not about self-definition but definition by the state.
>
> *(Tutton and Levitt, 2010, pp. 97–98; see also Heinemann and Lemke, 2014)*

In the present case, the situation is different again because the definition of citizenship produced here is not only that produced by the state (by virtue of genetic identification) but also that produced by the actors themselves (by virtue of collective action). Although, as I shall show, the specifically biological aspect of the debate may also come into consideration, the citizenship produced, at least in the first instance, emerges in opposition to biological citizenship because these opponents refuse the "biological" or the "bio" in bioidentity. To take up the distinction proposed by Agamben (1995), their position is rooted not only in the point of view of the *zoe*, or "bare life", the simple fact of being alive, but rather, and much more, in that of *bios*, as actors in "political life" organizing collectively. Or simply as citizens, if we take the term "citizens" to refer to the concept of individuals fully engaged in social action and/or whose rights are recognized. The exercise of political citizenship becomes a criterion of identity of individuals who understand themselves as members of the *polis*. In contrast to the situation observed in Portugal, where those considered by organizers of genetic profiling to be "good citizens" are those who voluntarily provide their DNA (Machado and Silva, 2009; 2016), here the opponents who refuse to provide their DNA proclaim their identity as citizens ("I was acting as a citizen"). As if in echo to the extension of profiling, these activists define a collectively organized political citizenship that seeks to influence the limits of state power over individuals (Vailly and Bouagga, 2019).

The argument for proportionality and private life

Public contestation by opponents of profiling is underpinned by arguments made in court battles, as suggested by the way they use trials to defend their cause. In their view, condemning profiling as a manifestation of an increasingly "punitive" state raises political and moral questions that have a legal aspect: the principle of proportionality. Anti-GMO activists drew on this argument, which is now promoted in legal challenges to the FNAEG, early on in their trials for refusal to provide a sample. To be more specific, the disproportion cited in trials or described in interviews may relate to the disproportionate infringement of rights compared to the minor nature of the offense, even when, as in the example at the beginning of this chapter, the way the actions are described portrays them as relatively serious ("vandalism" for graffiti, etc.). The disproportion cited may also relate to the methods of arrest, the processing of data in terms of how long they are retained and whether they are deleted, or the link to private life. When they use the argument of interference in the right to private life, lawyers and defendants draw on Article 8 of the European Convention of Human Rights, according to which "everyone has the right to respect for his private and family life, his home and his correspondence."[24] They base this argument on European case law, S. and Marper v. United Kingdom, an ECHR case which led to the ruling against the United Kingdom, discussed in Chapter 1.[25] I now describe the case in detail. In 2001, an 11-year-old youth was arrested for attempted robbery with violence, and a man was arrested for harassment of his partner.[26] A DNA sample was taken from each, to be incorporated in the UK database for an indefinite period. The youth was acquitted and the man discharged, as he had reconciled with his partner and she had withdrawn her complaint. As they had not been convicted, they asked for their DNA samples to be destroyed, but the police refused. Between 2002 and 2004, they appealed to the Administrative Court, the Court of Appeal, and the House of Lords in turn, arguing that retention of the samples meant they were still under suspicion despite the fact that they had been acquitted, and that retention of the samples and genetic profiles constituted a breach of their right to respect of private life. All three courts ruled against them, with counsel for the Home Secretary arguing that retention of these samples had nothing to do with the offenses of which they had been acquitted but was intended to assist investigation of potential future offenses. The appellants therefore appealed to the European Court of Human Rights, which ultimately ruled in their favor. According to the ECHR's unanimous decision, general and undifferentiated lifelong retention of DNA profiles and samples of suspects represents a disproportionate breach of the right to respect of private and family life, protected under Article 8 of the European Convention. It therefore contravenes the requirement for proportionality between the alleged actions and the need for genetic sampling. The Court also noted that there were only limited possibilities for an acquitted individual to have her/his data removed from the nationwide database or the materials destroyed. It was particularly concerned that individuals who had not been found guilty of any offense and had the right to presumption of innocence were treated in the same way as those convicted, given the right of any person found innocent that "no suspicion regarding an accused's innocence may be voiced after his acquittal." Clearly, then, the category of suspects was central to debates and decisions around this European case law.

More recently the ECHR ruled against the United Kingdom in the case of a man arrested in Northern Ireland for drunk driving in 2008. He was taken to the police station and a DNA sample was taken to be incorporated into the UK database. In court, the defendant was sentenced to a £50 fine and a one-year driving ban. Two months later, he asked for his DNA to be destroyed, arguing that it was being retained unlawfully. The sample was destroyed in 2015, but his DNA profile was retained for an indefinite period. In the High Court of Justice of Northern Ireland, he argued that this retention interfered with the respect of his right to private life and was unlawful, but his case was dismissed. He then applied to the ECHR, which judged that the applicant's biometric data were retained "without reference to the seriousness of the offence or the need for indefinite retention." It further noted that there was no provision for the applicant to apply to have the data concerning him deleted if conserving it no longer appeared necessary. As in the Marper ruling, the court concluded that there was disproportion in the interference with private life and ruled against the United Kingdom. I shall return to the "arm of the law" (Israël, 2020) and the role of European law in these disputes below.

Coming back to France, in June 2017 the ECHR unanimously ruled against France with regard to the FNAEG for the first time. The appellant was a farmer who had participated in a demonstration organized by a farmers' union in 2008 and had been taken into custody. He was brought before the criminal court for immediate summary trial[27] and "charged with intentional violence not entailing total unfitness for work, against gendarmes whose identity has not been established [...], using or threatening to use a weapon, in this instance an umbrella."[28]

Sentenced to a two-month suspended prison sentence for what was described as "armed violence" and a 500-euro fine for refusal to provide a DNA sample, he appealed to the ECHR after the Court of Appeal upheld his conviction and his appeal to the Court of Cassation was dismissed. Once again, in the view of the ECHR, "the applicant's conviction for having refused to undergo DNA profiling for inclusion in the FNAEG amounted to a disproportionate infringement of his right to respect for private life, and therefore cannot be deemed necessary in a democratic society"; the court noted that the law provided for no differentiation according to the nature and/or seriousness of the offense committed.[29] It judged that in the absence of any adjustment of the maximum 40-year duration of retention according to the seriousness of offenses, the 40-year period "is, in practice, treated as indefinite storage, or at least as a norm rather than a maximum."

Since this ECHR ruling, a number of activists have been discharged in trials for refusing to provide a DNA sample: it appears that judges are assessing the proportionality of profiling to the seriousness of the offense on a case-by-case basis.[30] In similar vein, in September 2021 the Court of Cassation upheld the acquittal of five people charged with refusing to provide a DNA sample following their conviction for "aggravated theft" ("gang theft by deception") after they removed the portrait of the President from the town hall and replaced it with a banner reading "social climate justice, Macron out" as part of a "non-violent COP21 action."[31] The Court judged that since the offense was not of a type to cause harm, there was disproportion between the triviality of the offense and the interference with the respect to private life entailed by incorporation in the FNAEG. This shows that the seriousness of an offense, such as aggravated theft, cannot be judged in isolation from the context in which it is committed. However, other activists had their convictions for refusing sampling upheld, as another example shows. During a Yellow Vest demonstration in 2019, scuffles broke out between demonstrators and police officers, a police station was vandalized, and a number of individuals were arrested. One of them, after a spell in custody, was sentenced at an immediate summary trial to four months' imprisonment for aggravated vandalism and two months for refusal to provide a DNA sample. She appealed this sentence and was discharged for the first offense but convicted of the second. She then appealed to the Court of Cassation, on grounds of the contradiction between the conviction for refusal to provide DNA and the discharge from the former charge. In 2020 the Court ruled that the acquittal in the Court of Appeal did not remove the suspicion weighing over her, and did not bring into question the constitutive evidence of the case at the point of the offense. The Court also stated that there was no disproportionate interference in private life, because there was provision for the individual to request deletion of these data. In short, the Court of Cassation ruling shows that the possibility of seeking deletion reinforces the detainee's obligation to agree to DNA sampling.[32] Both a new awareness of proportionality in prosecutions and certain tensions at work in the Court of Cassation's rulings thus emerge. How these will play out in the new context of the October 2021 decree remains to be seen.

The question of proportionality and private life gains further traction in view of the relational character of DNA. In his trial, one activist argued: "The FNAEG is an invasion of privacy. It's not just me that's being profiled, it's my parents and my son. We have to be aware of this!" (Activist 7). At another trial the partner of an activist, called as a witness, objected: "By taking part of Mr X's [her partner's] DNA, they're also taking our children's DNA [...], so on behalf of my children, this refusal of profiling concerns me" (Activist 8). Another activist prosecuted following a trade union action in an agricultural processing factory in northern France, relieved at being acquitted, said on regional TV: "DNA is something private. It's something we all inherit from our ancestors." This perceived "privacy" of DNA points to a specific feature of the FNAEG not shared by other databases, in that genetic information is dual in nature: it is both individual by definition and shared within kin groups (Vailly, 2024). This characteristic, which is traditionally ascribed a form of "genetic exceptionalism" (Murray, 2019) compared to other modes of identification such as fingerprints, is not surprising given that genetics is defined as "the science of heredity." It emphasizes that notions of the individual and the collective are intrinsic to DNA, and are expressed here in terms of private and family life. The private life in question is not only that of individual activists but also that of their family collectively, as a biological entity. In parallel to the political citizenship discussed above, they defend private life as the separation between the public arena and the family group. In short, here the effects of jurisdiction on bioidentities criticized by opponents extend to the biological family.

Two points are worth noting by way of conclusion to this section. Firstly, the FNAEG produces "effects of jurisdiction" (Foucault, 1991a) in the sense defined above. The first effect is the direct effect the FNAEG produces on the law: the database makes it possible to compare DNA profiles, contributes to the solving of crimes, and provides evidence for trials (*probative effect*). The second effect produced by the FNAEG *goes beyond* the law in that it produces a majority category midway between the innocent and the guilty: individuals who have been questioned under caution, and profiled but not convicted (*suspicion effect*). The third effect of jurisdiction is that individuals may be convicted for refusing to provide DNA even if they are acquitted of the initial offense (*penalization effect*). Such individuals therefore pass from the status of suspect (of an initial offense) to convicted (for refusal of sampling). Here it should be noted that between 2004 and 2013 the majority of those convicted of refusing to provide DNA were people who had been questioned (63%, between 200 and 400 individuals per year); fewer had been convicted of a misdemeanor (31%, between 100 and 200 individuals per year) or a serious crime (6%, between 10 and 60 people per year).[33] The fourth effect lies in the decoupling between recordable offenses (for example graffiti, which is categorized as vandalism, is a recordable offense for the purposes of the FNAEG) and the type of investigation that calls for genetic data (DNA profiles are not analyzed in the *search for perpetrators* of graffiti because the damage is not considered sufficiently serious). This fosters proximity within the database between terrible crimes and less serious actions that are subject to the requirement of a DNA sample (*effect of proximity between criminal offenses and political or trade union actions*). This effect is amplified by the fact that the law makes no distinction between common-law offenses and political or trade union offenses. It is the latter three effects that opponents of DNA profiling indirectly contest.

Secondly, compared to other studies of this subject, the French case discussed here offers a deeper insight into opposition to profiling (seeing oneself as a citizen, contesting intrusion into family life, etc.). It also highlights two points. First the power relation in favor of the police, discussed in Chapter 1, is tolerated by the majority of the population, who overall do not express opposition to profiling. Second, what emerges is a porosity not only between perpetrator and suspect, as noted, but also between the individual acquitted of an offense and one convicted of refusal to provide DNA. What opponents contest is the fact that identity in the sense of "selfhood," in the categories of perpetrator and suspect, as well as that of their biological family, is united in the database, becoming in both cases the identity of lasting suspects or "criminals." They also protest the fact that their identity may become that of an individual convicted for refusal of DNA sampling: in all three cases (suspect, convicted of an offense, convicted for refusal), individuals are no longer innocent and, in their view, are placed in the same category as criminals.

Effects of veridiction

The circulation of knowledge

Chapter 1 explored the position of police officers with regard to the nature of non-coding DNA markers. Examining the genealogy of the FNAEG helps to give a sense of the importance of this argument in legitimizing the database. At the outset, in 1999, the CNIL raised the issue of "non-coding" material, issuing a favorable opinion on the FNAEG, provided that genetic profiles were derived only from "segments of DNA that do not allow the organic, physiological or morphological characteristics of the individuals concerned to be determined."[34] In 2001 a report by the Parliamentary Office for Evaluation of Scientific and Technical Decisions (Office parlementaire d'évaluation des choix scientifiques et techniques) noted:

> Since the markers used in expert evidence relate only to the non-coding part of the genome and therefore cannot provide information on any genetic feature outside of the targeted objective (ethnic origin, disease or predispositions to pathologies), taking a genetic fingerprint is no less respectful of fundamental human rights than taking a physical fingerprint.[35]

In 2003 Christian Estrosi, the rapporteur for the law on interior security, told the parliamentary deputies gathered to vote on the law:

> If you try to obtain the smallest piece of information about the individual – state of health, metabolism, hair or eye color, skin color, etc. – from a genetic profile registered in the FNAEG, you won't be able to, because these profiles are non-coding. It is absolutely impossible.[36]

Moreover, it was on the basis of this argument that the Conseil constitutionnel ruled in 2010 that the FNAEG was constitutional.[37] Thus the non-coding nature of the markers used in genetic profiles constituted a key element in the approval of the FNAEG. But this is contested by opponents – or the organizations that support them (Syndicat de la Magistrature, Syndicat des Avocats de France, Ligue des Droits de l'Homme) – who argue that genetic profiles could supply information other than that used for identification. It is the nature of the markers themselves that is in question.

The issue of the information that is or is not provided by the FNAEG's markers was raised by an activist opposed to extensive use of advertising billboards. He was required to provide a DNA sample but had his doubts about the "non-coding" nature of the markers and sought information on the subject on the internet. His attention was drawn to a press release about a scientific article unrelated to the FNAEG, which demonstrated a link between non-coding segments and a genetic disease (Pierre Robin syndrome). This suggested that in general, non-coding DNA sequences were not necessarily uninformative. Seeking to find out more, he contacted a genetics researcher who delved into the more specific question of the FNAEG's markers. In an interview, she explained the link between the population-wide nature of the database and the information gathered:

> When you have a large database, you need a lot of [genetic] markers because otherwise there's a risk of confusing two individuals. And once you have a lot of markers, you're going to have information.
>
> *(Geneticist 1)*

What sort of information are we dealing with here? This geneticist pointed to an Italian study that showed that one of the markers used in the FNAEG (D2S13–38) may be associated with a predisposition to a rare disease (pseudohyperkalemia), and a Chinese study that showed that a different marker also used in the FNAEG (D2S1S11–38) may be associated with increased risk of coronary heart disease.[38] She also found an article that demonstrated that it would be possible to obtain some information on an individual's geographical origin, with 86% reliability, from the 17 markers used in the FNAEG, which are also those most widely used internationally.[39] This Portuguese study reported:

> Our confirmation of an 86% accuracy of individual population affiliation for the common 17 STR genotype profiles shows that this well known forensic set of STRs has also a considerable amount of information for population assignment, besides being excellent for individual identification.[40]

These Portuguese researchers also developed an open-access software program, PopAffiliator, that can be used to derive these indications of a person's origin from her/his genetic profile, although the information gathered is relatively broad (on a continental scale – Asia, Africa, Europe) as the markers were not chosen to distinguish population groups. Until that point, "ethnic" or "racial" categories were entirely absent from the FNAEG, in contrast to the situation in other countries, notably the United Kingdom.

This French geneticist, who was herself involved in campaigning for researchers to act in their capacity as citizens, gave evidence at the trials of a number of activists who had refused to provide DNA, highlighting the kind of information that could be detected from the markers in profiles. She spoke on the subject with lawyers, and some gradually began to take up the theme. This remark by a lawyer observing a trial for refusal to provide a DNA sample demonstrates the role this argument can play;

> Dr [anonymous], a researcher at the Institut national de la santé et de la recherche médicale (National Institute for Health and Medical Research, Inserm), who has a doctorate in genetics and statistics [...] has some very interesting things to say about the FNAEG: for example that today the DNA segments that it is permitted to sample can reveal [...] a person's geographical origin, their ethnic origin, some of their pathologies. Under Article 704–55 of the Code of Penal Procedure, only non-coding segments of DNA may be taken. So today, the data available to us, the data that can be extracted from a DNA segment, are illegal! Illegal, because those data are not neutral, they talk. [...] Today, the block placed when the law was passed, [saying]: 'We're not going any further in what we can decode,' that block no longer exists! The basic contract has been broken!
>
> *(Lawyer 4)*

The partner of an activist called as a witness in his trial protested:

> We know that DNA is much more coding than they say; it says more than people think, so ... this refusal of profiling concerns me too.
>
> *(Activist 7)*

Thus the idea of "speaking" markers, rooted in scientific arguments relating to the development of scientific knowledge about non-coding DNA, has become established and is common currency in activist circles. For those most au fait with the subject, the case is proven, and published articles provide the evidence.

In these people's view, taking genetic profiles sets up new categories, classing individuals by continental or sub-continental origin. Moreover, genetic techniques produce forms of knowledge drawn from DNA markers that are all the more informative when they are taken from a large database ("when you have a large database, you need a lot of markers [...]. And once you have a lot of markers, you're going to have information"). The management of large populations determines the amount of information available from genetic profiles, which in return makes it possible not only to *identify* individuals but also to *characterize* them. Once again, the individual identity in question appears to go beyond comparison between genetic profiles (in the register of sameness), extending into the characterization of individuals (in relation to their predisposition to a disease or their origin, in the register of selfhood) – but here on the basis of scientific arguments.

In the time since I conducted my field research, new links have been revealed between the expression of genes involved in disease and markers used in the FNAEG. For example, in 2022, a team of researchers at Stanford University showed that three genetic markers used in the United States federal database, CODIS, and also included in the list used for the French database (CSF1PO, D3S1358, and D18S51), may be associated with the expression of genes involved respectively in psychiatric disorders, Perrault syndrome (a rare condition causing deafness in both sexes, and sometimes infertility in women), and MELAS syndrome (a neurological disease), as well as serious skin and platelet disorders.[41] Given the body of research and studies built up by biological research organizations, it appears that today it would be difficult to find 20 or so genetic markers that are both informative in terms of identifying individuals and devoid of any role in the expression of genes involved in disease. The early regulatory frameworks thus now stand on shaky ground.

Between science and law

The argument about the information that may or may not be provided by genetic profiles was deemed sufficiently serious for lawyers acting on behalf of opponents of profiling to take it up in Priority Questions of Constitutionality (Questions Prioritaires de Constitutionnalité, QPC). This is an opportunity open to any citizen, in the context of a trial, to contest a law she/he deems not consistent with the French constitution. Without describing the legal process of the various stages of these QPC here, I shall note the main arguments in the courts that judged whether they were admissible and ruled that genetic profiling practices did indeed conform with the constitution.[42] This response was based mainly on the prohibition on using such information on individuals, should it be available: "Neither the contested provisions nor the data resulting from them and incorporated into the FNAEG authorize the examination of genetic characteristics of persons [...] but only their identification from genetic profiles."[43] But according to the lawyer leading on this case:

> [According to] the line set by the legislation [...], the point is not even *to be able* to do it [examine phenotypical characteristics] if it should happen that someone wanted to change the use of the database. [...] One of the safeguards that was put in place was that these databases contained only non-coding segments; in other words, that they made anything other than identification of the person *impossible*. And that's not the case.
>
> *(Lawyer 2)*

The key point here is not only the *prohibition* on using individuals' phenotypical information but above all the *impossibility* of doing so, in the spirit of the law that specified "non-coding" materials precisely for this reason. This lawyer further argues, in relation to the political context of the rise in far-right ideas and the potential political use of such data:

> These are segments that are going to be kept for 50 years, and do you know what's going to be happening in France in 50 years? I have no idea, I don't know; X [the leader of a far-right party] is going up in the polls, I have no idea. So maybe these databases that contain the details of millions of people might someday be used to find out people's geographical origin, we don't know.
>
> *(Lawyer 2)*

When drawing on these scientific arguments, opponents sometimes link back to France's history, the dark days of World War Two, and the country's registers of Jews, as well as to its potential future, in the context of the rising electoral popularity of the far right. They point out that in the anti-Jewish raids during the war, the police service used punched cards to optimize classification criteria, record-keeping, and efficiency:

> When you create population records, and especially of a political population like us, opponents, dissidents, you know how it starts, but you don't know how it will end. [...] They put people in cattle trucks [reference to World War Two].
>
> *(Activist 9)*

Some of them back up their views with personal experience; for example, of a grandfather who added names of Jews to a file during World War Two and lived with their death on his conscience. These concerns are not expressed only in interviews or during trials but are sometimes taken up in the popular press; for example, in these excerpts from articles in national and regional newspapers:

> This DNA profiling could be extremely dangerous. When Jews were asked to register as such under the Vichy regime, they were confident they had done nothing wrong and had to comply. But they ended up in Nazi concentration camps. A change of government or policy can happen at any time.[44]

> If the far right comes to power tomorrow, there's no knowing how these databases might be used. Until recently people thought that this database couldn't be used to categorize the population in terms of origin, but the [anonymized] geneticist [...] has shown that's not the case.[45]

While in other countries some concerns about misuse of genetic data arise out of lack of trust in institutions (Machado and Silva, 2016; Teodorovic et al., 2017), here they have a particular resonance stemming from their political and historical context. Some of the courts that ruled on whether the Priority Constitutional Questions were admissible responded that the question was a technical one and therefore outside of their purview. Another argument made by one of these courts was that it was for the government to legislate the number and nature of segments to be analyzed in genetic profiles, in response to the development of knowledge, and not for the courts to respond to the question. The technical nature of the argument about the information that could be derived from profiles has other repercussions because it limits the extent to which opponents and their lawyers can make use of it. Neither the FNAEG Monitoring Committee nor the Interministerial Technical Committee for the FNAEG have produced public reports on these questions.

Thus opponents of DNA profiling firstly highlight scientific reasoning, according to which taking genetic profiles no longer ensures the *impossibility* of deriving information – for example, on categories of origin by continent or sub-continent – but is subject merely to a *prohibition*, which could one day be challenged. Secondly, the potential political use of databases constitutes a further key issue in their argument. Here we find confirmation of the suggestion that studying genetic markers in order to study people's origin "[lends] renewed authority to biological conceptions of human difference and [provides] fodder for national debates over belonging, self-definition, and political power" (Wailoo et al., 2012, p. 2). In France employers do not currently misuse DNA to keep individuals out of certain jobs, in contrast to the situation in the United States (Etzioni, 2004). For this reason, opponents in France do not use arguments about job discrimination, preferring to highlight the risk of political use of profiling, following the practice that prevailed during World War Two. The French historical context of collaboration between France and the Nazi regime clearly emerges as a major factor in understanding how the FNAEG is problematized in France. Opponents are seeking to introduce more or less effective citizen monitoring of the relationship between genetic techniques and potential biopolitical uses of identity ("maybe these databases that contain the details of millions of people might someday be used to find out people's geographical origin"). To my knowledge, this is the first time that this issue of the information contained in markers used in forensic science has been raised so directly in public debate. In contrast to other studies that emphasize the separation between scientific and lay knowledge (such as Williams and Wienroth, 2014b), or concerns around the use of information by the state, rather than the intrinsic properties of DNA (Williams and Johnson, 2004), the present study reveals not only an appropriation of knowledge by laypeople but also that citizens are driving these new debates using scientific arguments. Nevertheless, as I have shown, these arguments remain relatively limited, owing to their technical nature.

* * *

Thus genetic analysis applied to entire populations, rather than merely individuals, in the context of criminal investigation, shifts bioidentities through effects of both jurisdiction and veridiction (Foucault, 1991a), which are at the root of opposition to profiling. These effects are manifested firstly in the fact that there is no distinction between common-law and political offenses, secondly in the fact that people are convicted of refusal to provide a DNA sample even if they have been acquitted of the initial offense, and finally in the production of a majority category comprising a group midway between the innocent and the convicted: those who have been questioned under caution and profiled but not convicted. Opposition is to an approach centered not on dangerous *individuals* but on a *population*: opponents distinguish between comparison of the DNA of a person identified in the context of a specific case with a trace from a crime scene, and the profiling of millions of individuals. Drawing on Ricœur, I have shown that one of the main points of contestation in this context concerns the transformation of individuals' bioidentity ("that is tantamount to suspecting those millions of French people of being potential criminals"). In the view of opponents of profiling, this goes beyond the scope of comparison of profiles (in the register of sameness), extending into the register of lasting suspicion (when people become suspects profiled for 15 or 25 years, in the register of selfhood), or the characterization of individuals (depending on their predisposition to a disease or their origin, also in the register of selfhood).

This shift in bioidentities has significant features. While comparison of individual profiles demonstrates the *permanence* of biological identity, the use of large-scale databases generates identities that are not permanent but may shift between the innocent, suspects, and the guilty. In short, while I have adapted the concepts of sameness and selfhood initially reserved for the "self" (Ricœur, 1992) to the "Other" (the person perceived as criminal) and the "self" (the person who perceives her/himself as a citizen), they also help to extend the distinction discussed in Chapter 1 between two interwoven aspects of bioidentity. Moreover, while I have shown that the policy under discussion here is concerned both with punishment and with policing, the low level of opposition to the extended database among the French population points to a configuration of power relations that cannot be reduced to surveillance imposed from on high, and makes it possible to verify the hypothesis I put forward on this subject in the introduction.

Finally, these practices have "effects of veridiction" (Foucault, 1991a, p. 75). Some of those who oppose genetic profiling draw on scientific arguments that information about rare diseases or origin could be derived from the FNAEG, despite the fact that this was not its original purpose. According to the geneticist who supports their campaign, it is the very size of the database that makes such information available (the larger the population studied, the more markers are needed to identify individuals; the more markers are analyzed, the more information emerges). In other words, like population-wide profiling, these techniques establish statistical probabilities that prompt new, scientifically-grounded resistance. In the view of opponents, the guarantees accompanying the database thus become even less trustworthy. The uses to which information drawn from DNA could be put are particularly sensitive in two respects: that of the individual's family, whom by definition share these genetic data, and that of potential biopolitical use of identity by an authoritarian government.

To paraphrase US Attorney General Janet Reno (Jasanoff, 2004, p. 342), these opponents align with the position that "the challenge is to learn how to govern, rather than be governed by, the power of DNA." As they see it, not only is a securitarian era coinciding with rapid technological development, but technology has the capacity to serve a potentially authoritarian drive toward political surveillance in the relatively near future. This last point helps to resituate these debates in the French context, marked as it is by the history of World War Two with its registers of Jews, and by the electoral rise of the far right. Going beyond these findings, the research presented in this chapter invites further analysis of the police and courts' use of genetic data in terms of suspects' geographical origin.

Notes

1 AFP (2006, 29 September). Un jeune faucheur d'OGM condamné pour avoir refusé de donner son ADN. *Le Monde.*
2 Here I discuss public contestation of the FNAEG, rather than individual refusals under common law, which would require a different research method, are few in number, and not highly visible, as they are not widely publicized.
3 See http://www.genewatch.org/sub-539478 (accessed 9 February 2021).
4 Rapport d'information sur les fichiers mis à la disposition des forces de sécurité, présenté par les députés Didier Paris et Pierre Morel-À-l'Huissier, Assemblée Nationale, October 17 2018, p. 20.
5 The Conseil d'État (Council of State) acts as legal adviser to the executive, and as supreme court for administrative justice [translator].
6 Rapport d'information sur les fichiers mis à la disposition des forces de sécurité, présenté par les députés Didier Paris et Pierre Morel-À-l'Huissier, Assemblée Nationale, October 17 2018, p. 31.
7 Anonymous (2013, June 13). La CNIL alerte sur les défaillances des fichiers de police. *Le Monde* with AFP.
8 Rapport annuel de l'Inspection générale de la police nationale 2022, https://www.interieur.gouv.fr/Publications/Rapports-de-l-IGPN (accessed September 25 2023).
9 See CNIL website, https://www.cnil.fr/fr/faed-fichier-automatise-des-empreintes-digitales (accessed February 17 2021).
10 M.K. v. France, Judgment April 18 2013.
11 See CNIL website, https://www.cnil.fr/fr/fichier-automatise-des-empreintes-digitales-rappel-lordre-du-ministere-de-linterieur (accessed December 6 2021).
12 Set up in 2005 to centralize data relating to holders of electronic passports, it was extended in 2016 to those applying for identity cards, and its final/completed version/regulations on its final form was/were published in the *Journal Officiel* in 2018.

13 Articles 16.10 and 16.11 of the Civil Code. Information report no. 2235, registered January 20 2010. Alain Claeys and Jean Leonetti, members of the National Assembly.
14 Bulletin officiel du ministère de la Justice no. 80 (October 1–December 31 2000). Circulaire de la direction des Affaires criminelles et des Grâces. Signalisation des circulaires du 1er octobre au 31 décembre 2000, p. 7.
15 Ministry of Justice memoranda of July 27 2004 and July 9 2008, CRIM-PJ no. 08–28.H5.
16 Source: Ministry of Justice statistics and Agence France Presse (press release April 13 2023).
17 Ministry of Justice memorandum of July 9 2008, CRIM-PJ no 08–28.H5, p. 4.
18 As illustrated by a 19th-century newspaper article that states: "The space of the courts [...] is an arena that resounds with the cries of [political] combatants," *La Fraternité*, November 1841.
19 Fessard, L. (2011, September 10). Empreintes génétiques: "Refuser le prélèvement, c'est aggraver son cas." *Médiapart*.
20 Ligue des Droits de l'Homme, Syndicat des Avocats de France, Syndicat de la Magistrature, Le FNAEG, ne vous en fichez pas! Press release, November 21 2021.
21 Confédération Générale du Travail, one of the largest French trade unions [translator].
22 Anonymous (2012, February 6). Xavier Mathieu condamné en appel. *L'Humanité*.
23 Subprefecture – the building housing the local government administration [translator].
24 This principle was argued by anti-GMO activists accused of "wilful destruction of public property." They refused to provide a DNA sample for inclusion in the FNAEG. Following their conviction and their appeal to the European Court of Human Rights, the French government sought a settlement, offering them 1,500-euro compensation for harm suffered. However, revelation of these negotiations to the press rendered the appeal inadmissible in court. Deceunink v. France, Mandil v. France, Barreau et al. v. France. European Court of Human Rights, Judgments of December 13 2011. https://hudoc.echr.coe.int/eng#%22dmdocnumber%22:[%22899156%22],%22itemid%22:[%22001-108777%22] (accessed February 15 2021).
25 They also drew on the ECHR's 2013 ruling against France on the matter of the Automated Fingerprint Database (FAED), transposing it to the FNAEG, since this ruling had cited the concept of proportionality and privacy in precisely the same terms as the Marper judgment. M.K. v. France, Judgment of July 18 2013. They sometimes also cited the reservation expressed by the Conseil Constitutionnel as to proportionality between the seriousness of the offense and the length of retention of data.
26 S. and Marper v. United Kingdom, Judgment of December 4 2008.
27 A fast-track court procedure where a person charged with a minor offense is tried shortly after being taken into custody, by decision of the public prosecutor [translator].
28 Aycaguer v. France, ECHR, June 22 2017, see https://hudoc.echr.coe.int/fre?i=001-175007 (accessed May 22 2023).
29 ECHR press release 2015 of June 22 2017 https://hudoc.echr.coe.int/fre?i=001-175007 (accessed May 22 2023).
30 Hourdeaux, J. (2018, April 20). Fichage génétique: La France toujours dans l'illégalité. *Médiapart*.
31 Court of Cassation ruling of September 22 2021.
32 Decree no. 1994 of October 28 2020, Court of Cassation – Criminal Chamber, https://www.courdecassation.fr/jurisprudence_2/chambre_criminelle_578/1994_28_45805.html, and Engel, F. (2020, November 16). Répression du refus de se soumettre à des prélèvements biologiques. *Dalloz actualité*.
33 Source: Ministry of Justice statistics.
34 Commission Nationale de l'Informatique et des Libertés 1999, 20th annual report, p. 37, and Gerbaud, A. (2012, July 4). Le fichier aux deux millions d'empreintes génétiques sur la sellette. *Politis*.
35 Christian Cabal, Office parlementaire d'évaluation des choix scientifiques et techniques, "Rapport sur la valeur scientifique de l'utilisation des empreintes génétiques

dans le domaine judiciaire," June 7 2001, see https://www.assemblee-nationale.fr/rap-oecst/empreintes_genetiques/r3121-1.asp.
36 National Assembly, 2002–2003 Ordinary Session, 45th day of sitting, 120th session, 3rd session of Thursday January 16 2003, see https://www.assemblee-nationale.fr/12/cri/2002-2003/20030120.asp, p. 296 (accessed January 21 2021).
37 "The contested provision does not authorize examination of the genetic characteristics of persons who have had samples taken, but only allows for them to be identified from genetic profiles." Decision no. 2010–25 QPC of September 16 2010, p. 5.
38 Carella, M., d'Adamo, A. P., Grootenboer-Mignot, S., Vantyghem, M. C. et al. (2004). A second locus mapping to 2q35–36 for familial pseudohyperkalaemia. *European Journal of Human Genetics, 12*, 1073–1076; Hui, L., Jing, Y., & Weijian, Y. (2011). Novel association analysis between 9 short tandem repeat loci polymorphisms and coronary heart disease based on a cross-validation design. *Atherosclerosis, 218*, 151–155.
39 In August 2018, the number of markers examined was set at 21 under the Decree of August 10 2015-art. 2(V).
40 Pereira, L., Alshamali, F., Andreassen, R., Ballard, R. et al. (2011). PopAffiliator: Online calculator for individual affiliation to a major population group based on 17 autosomal Short Tandem Repeat genotype profile. *International Journal of Legal Medicine, 125*(5), p. 630.
41 Bañuelos, M. M., Zavaleta, Y. J. A., Roldan, A., Reyes, R.-J. et al. (2022). Associations between forensic loci and expression levels of neighboring genes may compromise medical privacy. *PNAS, 119(40)*, e2121024119.
42 See Judgment of the Tribunal de Grande Instance de Senlis (Senlis Regional Court) of March 21 2012, Ruling of the Court of Cassation of June 19 2012, Judgment on Appeal of Senlis Regional Court of November 26 2012, Judgment of the Amiens Court of Appeal of June 13 2014, Ruling of the Court of Cassation of June 10 2015.
43 Ruling of the Court of Cassation of June 10 2015.
44 Fessard, L. (2011, September 19). Ils ont refusé de donner leur ADN. *Médiapart.*
45 Fessard, L. (2011, September 19). Ils ont refusé de donner leur ADN. *Médiapart.*

References

Agamben, G. (1995). *Homo sacer: Sovereign power and bare life.* Stanford University Press.

Becker, H. (2018 [1963]). *Outsiders: Studies in the sociology of deviance.* Free Press.

Bonneuil, C., Joly, P. B., & Marris, C. (2008). Disentrenching experiment: The construction of GM–Crop field trials as a social problem. *Science, Technology & Human Values*, 33(2), 201–229. doi:10.1177/0162243907311263.

Curtis, C. (2014). Public understandings of the forensic use of DNA: Positivity, misunderstandings and cultural concerns. *Bulletin of Science, Technology & Society*, 34 (1–2), 21–32. doi:10.1177/0270467614549415.

Etzioni, A. (2004). DNA tests and databases in criminal justice: Individual rights and the common good. In D. Lazer (Ed.), *DNA and the criminal justice system: The technology of justice* (pp. 197–223). The MIT Press.

Foucault, M. (1982). The subject and power. *Critical Inquiry*, 8(4), 777–795.

Foucault, M. (1991a). Questions of method, trans. Colin Gordon. In G. Burchell, C. Gordon, & P. Miller (Eds.), *Studies in governmentality* (pp. 73–86). University of Chicago Press.

Foucault, M. (1991b). Michel Foucault on Attica: An interview. *Social Justice*, 18(3), 26–34.

Gamero, J. J., Romero, J. M., Peralta, J. L., Corte-Real, F. *et al.* (2004). DNA technology application procedures in forensic practice: Social and ethical conditioning II. *International Congress Series, 1261*, 571–573. doi:10.1016/S0531-5131(03)01780-1.

Guillen, M., Lareu, M. V., Pestoni, P., Salas, A. *et al.* (2000). Ethical-legal problems of DNA databases in criminal investigation. *Journal of Medical Ethics*, 26, 266–271. doi:10.1136/jme.26.4.266.

Hacking, I. (2000). *The social construction of what?* Harvard University Press.

Heinemann, T., & Lemke, T. (2014). Biological citizenship reconsidered. *Science, Technology & Human Values*, 39(4), 488–510. doi:10.1177/0162243913509414.

Hindmarsh, R. (2010). Biosurveillance and biocivic concerns, from 'truth' to 'trust': The Australian forensic DNA terrain. In R. Hindmarsh, & B. Prainsack (Eds.), *Genetic suspects: Global governance of forensic DNA profiling and databasing* (pp. 262–287). Cambridge University Press.

Israël, L. (2020). *L'arme du droit*, 2nd edn. Presses de Sciences Po.

Jasanoff, S. (2004). DNA's identity crisis. In D. Lazer (Ed.), *DNA and the criminal justice system: The technology of justice* (pp. 337–355). MIT Press.

Machado, H., & Granja, R. (2022). *Genetic surveillance and crime control: Social, cultural and political perspectives*. Routledge.

Machado, H., & Silva, S. (2009). Informed consent in forensic DNA databases: Volunteering, constructions of risk and identity categorization, *BioSocieties*, 4, 335–348. doi:10.1017/S1745855209990329.

Machado, H., & Silva, S. (2014). Would you accept having your DNA profile inserted in the national forensic DNA database? Why? Results of a questionnaire applied in Portugal. *Forensic Science International*, 8, 132–136. doi:10.1016/j.fsigen.2013.08.014.

Machado, H., & Silva, S. (2016). Voluntary participation in forensic DNA databases: Altruism, resistance, and stigma. *Science, Technology & Human Values*, 41(2), 322–343. doi:10.1177/0162243915604723.

Mattelart, A., & Vitalis, A. (2014). *Le profilage des populations: Du livret ouvrier au cybercontrôle*. La Découverte.

Murray, T. (2019). Is genetic exceptionalism past its sell-by-date? On genomic diaries, context and content. *American Journal of Bioethics*, 19(1), 13–15. doi:10.1080/15265161.2018.1552038.

Nelkin, D., & Andrews, L. (1999). DNA identification and surveillance creep. *Sociology of Health & Illness*, 21(5), 689–706. doi:10.1111/1467-9566.00179.

Petryna, A. (2002). *Life exposed: Biological citizens after Chernobyl*. Princeton University Press.

Ricœur, P. (1992). *Oneself as another*, trans. Kathleen Blamey. University of Chicago Press.

Rose, N. (2007). *The politics of life itself: Biomedicine, power and subjectivity in the twenty-first century*. Princeton University Press.

Teodorovic, S., Mijovic, D., Radovanovic Nenadic, U., & Savic, M. (2017). Attitudes regarding the national forensic DNA database: Survey data from the general public, prison inmates and prosecutors' offices in the Republic of Serbia. *Forensic Science International*, 28, 44–51. doi:10.1016/j.fsigen.2017.01.007.

Tutton, R., & Levitt, M. (2010). Health and wealth, law and order: Banking DNA against disease and crime. In R. Hindmarsh, & B. Prainsack (Eds.), *Genetic suspects: Global governance of forensic DNA profiling and databasing* (pp. 85–104). Cambridge University Press.

Vailly, J. (2024). Genetics. In W. C. Cockerham, J. Gabe, S. Quah, & J. M. Ryan (Eds.), *The Wiley-Blackwell encyclopedia of health, illness, behavior, and society*, 2nd edn. Wiley-Blackwell (in press).

Vailly, J., & Bouagga, Y. (2019). Opposition to the forensic use of DNA in France: The jurisdiction and veridiction effects. *BioSocieties*, 15(3), 394–419. doi:10.1057/s41292-019-00150-y.

Veth, J. S., & Midgley, G. (2010). Finding the balance: Forensic DNA profiling in New Zealand. In R. Hindmarsh, & B. Prainsack (Eds.), *Genetic suspects: Global governance of forensic DNA profiling and databasing* (pp. 288–308). Cambridge University Press.

Wailoo, K., Nelson, A., & Lee, C. (Eds.). (2012). *Genetics and the unsettled past: The collision of DNA, race, and history*. Rutgers University Press.

Williams, R., & Johnson, P. (2004). "Wonderment and dread": Representations of DNA in ethical disputes about forensic databases. *New Genetics & Society*, 23(2), 205–223. doi:10.1080/1463677042000237035.

Williams, R., & Wienroth, M. (2014a). *Public perspectives on established and emerging forensic genetics technologies in Europe*. EUROFOGEN-NoE.

Williams, R., & Wienroth, M. (2014b). Identity, mass fatality and forensic genetics. *New Genetics and Society*, 33(3), 257–276. doi:10.1080/14636778.2014.946005.

Williams, R., & Wienroth, M. (2017). Social and ethical aspects of forensic genetics: A critical review. *Forensic Science Review*, 29, 145.

Wilson-Kovacs, D., Wyatt, D., & Hauskeller, C. (2012). "A Faustian bargain?" Public voices on forensic DNA technologies and the national DNA database. *New Genetics and Society*, 31(3), 285–298. doi:10.1080/14636778.2012.687085.

PART 2

Predicting the appearance of suspects

3

THE PROBLEM OF SUSPECTS' ORIGIN

While the aim of genetic profiles, which are routinely used today, is identification via comparison of profiles (after the manner of physical fingerprints), this chapter considers a newer technique that is beginning to be used in criminal investigations. This technique uses DNA to predict the appearance and/or – the focus of this chapter – the "origin" of a suspect, as a supplement to or substitute for eyewitness testimony. (For ease of legibility, I omit the inverted commas around the term "origin" in the remainder of this chapter.) Indeed, the term "genetic witness," coined by historian Jay Aronson (2007) to refer to traditional genetic profiles, seems particularly apposite to this technique. Some social actors even describe this approach as a "genetic photofit," though this seems inappropriate given the relatively limited number of features available for analysis (as I shall show in the next chapter), at least at the present time. Thus the broad geographical origin of individuals (at the level of continent or sub-continent), determined on the basis of DNA traces, has been used in several hundred police investigations notably in the United States, the United Kingdom, the Netherlands, and Spain (Sankar, 2010). Following the terrorist attacks in Madrid in 2004, at a time of heightened political tension, investigators were uncertain whether responsibility lay with ETA, the Basque separatist organization, or Al-Qaïda. Subsequently, a parliamentary information commission established that the government at the time, over-hastily and with an eye to forthcoming elections, had attributed the massacre to ETA,[1] despite the fact that a range of evidence, together with genetic analysis, showed that the suspects were of Arab rather than Basque origin.[2] Nonetheless, examples where these kinds of tests have proved useful in police inquiries are still few and far between, and have been described in a handful of cases in the United States (Fox, 2010) and the Netherlands (M'charek et al., 2020).

One well-known example is that of a series of five rape-murders that took place in Louisiana, in the United States, in 2002–2003 (Fox, 2010). The police

DOI: 10.4324/9781003456056-6

had been following a false lead, based on several witness testimonies, looking for a "white" suspect, but the investigation had stalled as all the "white" suspects questioned were ruled out. The police even took DNA samples from 1,200 white men, without result. After lengthy fruitless searches, in 2003 detectives called on a geneticist, who asserted that, on the basis of the DNA left at the crime scenes, he would be able to detect the percentage of genetic material from four possible groups (sub-Saharan African, American, South-East Asian, and European). After blind control tests on twenty individuals proved convincing, the geneticist, by studying 176 genetic markers selected for the information they could provide about origin, established that after all the suspect was "black" – more precisely, of 85% African and 15% Native American origin. This result led to a major refocusing of the investigation and contributed to the arrest of the culprit a few months later. The irony of the story is that the man had been suspected before this genetic analysis was carried out but had been ruled out of the investigations when the detectives discovered that he was black.[3]

Epistemologically, this approach shows that forensic science has entered into the very lively biomedical debates about genetic identification of individuals' "geographical," "ethnic," or "racial" origin that have arisen since the sequencing of the human genome at the turn of the new millennium.[4] From a political point of view, there is a need to analyze the social stakes involved in the discourses and practices that this approach articulates, by virtue of its weaving together of DNA, individual origin, appearance, and criminality. But although these new genetic tests are the subject of growing interest in the social sciences (M'charek, 2008; 2013; Vailly, 2017 [2016]; Wienroth, 2018; Skinner, 2020 [2019]), the number of field studies remains limited. My contribution to this research will be to show how these innovations were (de)problematized in the public arena in France – a country where overall the human and social sciences have shown little interest in genetics-driven shifts in attitudes to origin – taking seriously the question of historical, social, and political context. How and why are the new origins identified by forensic genetic tests sources of problematization or, conversely, of deproblematization? What technical and scientific practices, what political analyses, and what moral questioning do social actors articulate when considering them? How does France's history and republican identity influence the problematization of genetic origin? The key role of the social sciences is to dissect the mechanisms of these processes, in a context where French society is increasingly a place of discourse and debate around origin (Fassin and Fassin, 2006).

Socio-historical context

Before presenting my results, I should like to lay out a few points pertinent to my analysis. Foucault uses the term "problematization" in a variety of ways (Gros, 2014). In a relatively restricted sense, he uses it to designate practices that "pose a problem" or "provoke difficulties":

> for a domain of action, a behavior, to enter the field of thought, it is necessary for a certain number of factors to have made it uncertain, to have made it lose its familiarity, or to have provoked a certain number of difficulties around it.
>
> *(Foucault, 1984, p. 388)*

This approach is helpful because it sheds light on how older practices "lose their familiarity," leading them to become "problematized." Analytically, this seems to me particularly pertinent in relation to criminal investigations because in this context oral testimony as to origin or "ethnicity" is a common variable of physical appearance. Indeed, origin is the descriptor most frequently used in eyewitness testimony (Fox, 2010). My first hypothesis is that the problematization of genetic tests of origin in France compared to eyewitness testimony is *heuristic, in other words it sheds light on changes* ("a loss of familiarity") with respect to origin. In a broader sense, Foucault (1988, p. 257) defines problematization as "the totality of discursive or non-discursive practices that introduces something into the play of true and false and constitutes it as an object of thought whether in the form of moral reflection, scientific knowledge, political analysis, etc." This quotation demonstrates how studying problematization can allow us to take account of the scientific as well as the political and moral aspects of a practice. Nevertheless, Foucault explains that depending on the questions, one or other of these aspects will be more to the fore (in his own research the scientific aspect with respect to madness, the political dimension with respect to security, and the moral aspect in relation to sexuality). Thus while it takes all three of these aspects into serious consideration, this frame of analysis invites us to focus particularly on the political dimension of issues relating to security. Finally, toward the end of his life, Foucault (1981) expanded the concept of "problematization," focusing on the way sexuality was considered a moral problem. In doing so, he raised important questions about how we "manage our own behavior" as "subjects" (Gros, 2014). My second hypothesis is that problematization *reveals the type of "subject" produced*: a given actor may problematize a question in various ways by placing the emphasis on one or other aspect (scientific, political, moral, etc.). These three elements (problem, science/politics/morality, subject) that constitute problematization are also useful analytical tools for the study I present here.

Secondly, there are certain historical and contextual elements that need to be borne in mind. In France, the Declaration of the Rights of Man and of the Citizen in 1789 marked – at least on paper – the end of any form of segregation based on race, religion, or ethnic origin (Noiriel, 1996). In contrast to the United States, for example, where a melting-pot policy of ethnic/racial pluralism has reigned since the 1960s, being French has traditionally been considered a political adherence to the nation, theoretically indifferent to skin color and the polar opposite to any racialized concepts (Ndiaye, 2006). This explains why in France today few or no racialized data are collected or used by the state, and why the principle of non-discrimination, equality of rights between individuals, unity and indivisibility of the nation figure strongly in the legal system and constitution

(Canselier and Desmoulin-Canselier, 2011). More broadly, it should be remembered that in Europe, and particularly in France, the terms used to indicate alterity are often nationality, ethnicity, culture, or migration status, and hence for our purposes "origin" rather than "race" (Dixon and Telles, 2017). By way of example, the French population census includes a question on individuals' country of birth and any previous nationality, but not on "race." There is still heated debate around "ethnic" statistics, the desire to evaluate discrimination conflicting with the drive to maintain social cohesion and the French culture of universalism, which does not recognize separate communities within the Republic. However, this should not blind us to the fact that the republican model reflects only one aspect of the country's history, for "the tension between principles of inclusion and practices of exclusion [has] informed the republican project since the Revolution" (Chapman and Frader, 2004, p. 3). The republican ideal on which belonging to the country was founded was ambiguous from its inception, since in theory it applied to all, but in practice it was restricted owing to practices of discrimination. Over centuries, the two main forms of racism in Europe, anti-Semitism and prejudice against "non-whites" (Chapman and Frader, 2004), developed in France as elsewhere. Historian Pap Ndiaye (2006, p. 46) points out that over the centuries "the French Empire [...] developed by subjugating populations defined as non-white [...] who were denied citizenship. [...] [In the colonies], to be French was to be white." Furthermore, he explains, with the arrival of half a million black soldiers and workers during World War One, the fear of racial mixing, as it was described at the time, shifted from the colonial world to the motherland, and there was a rise in racial anxiety. It was only during the 1930s that the word "race" became widely rejected among the upper echelons of the French republican establishment. The first law against racism was adopted in 1972, marking the end of the French republican tradition of non-intervention in questions of race (Noiriel, 2006). In short, questions of "race" have never been absent, and they are increasingly being expressed in the public arena in France, despite the country's symbolic position of "color-blindness" inherited from the Revolution (Fassin and Fassin, 2006).

The production of categories and the deconstruction of problematization (2006–2007)

Problematization is not just a set of ideas or mental images; it emerges from practices (Bacchi, 2012). In response to the questions raised above, this section focuses on the launch of origin tests in France. This will enable me to analyze both the preconditions for problematization, through the production of categories of origin that were controversial at the time, and the factors that, conversely, deconstructed this problematization.

The roots of problematization

Biotechnology company [X],[5] most of whose staff were biologists, was one of the first to offer genetic analysis for the purposes of criminal investigation in France, in the 1990s. In the years that followed, the company grew rapidly and is now one of the main private companies operating in this sector in France. The founder of the company, [Y], who died in an accident shortly after I began my research, was a highly regarded physician and microbiologist. In his view, France was "very unadventurous" in the field of genetics, as he told the media. Nevertheless, this man and the company he led were more or less uncontroversial, even among the judges who contributed to the problematization of the origin tests proposed during the 2000s, as I note below.[6] More generally, company [X] has a reputation for conscientiousness, and magistrates are confident in entrusting it with their samples for analysis. However, this positive reputation could have been threatened by the fact that in late 2006 the company introduced a new test called the "geo-genetic orientation test" (test d'orientation géo-génétique, TOGG), which, as its name suggests, could be used to guide a criminal investigation by indicating the suspect's geographical origin. On the basis of DNA traces left at a crime scene, the test analyzed certain of the suspect's genetic "markers" (selected from a compilation of the scientific literature) – markers that are not specific but are more frequent in certain global populations. The genetic markers used, of which there are 34, are known as SNP (Single Nucleotide Polymorphism) and are distinct from the STR (Short Tandem Repeats) used for traditional genetic profiles, although like the latter they were chosen from among "non-coding" DNA – a fact that was to prove significant. Three populations (from Europe, sub-Saharan Africa, and East Asia) were used as references for statistical study of the distribution of variations, and the test results indicated whether an individual was "probably" of European, Asian, etc. origin. The test was also supposed to indicate whether the individual came from an "intermediate" category; in other words, someone originating from "admixtures" with a "contribution" from the three reference populations.[7] In order to illustrate what was proposed, the current CEO of the company cites a specific case:

> For example, there was the case of a young woman who had been murdered, raped and murdered. Well, we had DNA from a sperm stain. So we said that this was an individual where there was a mix of Caucasian and sub-Saharan DNA. Well, the police had a list of 500 suspects, and they took samples from all of them, whether they were white, black or yellow, but they prioritized those who came from a region where that mix might arise. So that could be North Africa, or it could also be the Caribbean. You know, there are regions of the world like that where there are mixes, the islands, the French Caribbean, Réunion, where there is a lot of mixing of populations. And it turned out the perpetrator came from … (*She checks on her computer*). He came from Cape Verde. So from the DNA, we had

> said that it was someone who came from a place where there was a mixing of black and Caucasian populations. And we weren't wrong.
>
> *(Company executive 1)*

The perpetrator was not identified using TOGG tests but rather when his DNA, entered into the FNAEG following a conviction for domestic violence, was matched several years later with the trace left at the murder scene. Noteworthy in this interview is the heterogeneity and slippage, even within the same sentence, between classifications that are by turn geographical (Europe, Africa, North Africa, the Caribbean, Réunion), genetic (Caucasian), and by color ("black, white, yellow"). In this regard, it is worth pointing out that heterogeneity of identification, by color or geographical region, has existed since the earliest days of physical anthropology (Hacking, 2005a). Such variations in terminology constitute the seeds of a problematization because they leave themselves open to ambiguous interpretations, both geographical – thus relatively neutral – and echoing racial categories as commonly understood – hence potentially subject to polemic. On the one hand these tests form part of the basis of what sociologists call "genome geography" (Fujimura and Rajagopalan, 2011), which describes how stretches of DNA are linked to geographical locations defined as people's place of origin. It should be noted, however, that here this geography is fluid and vague ("North Africa, the French Caribbean ... Cape Verde") and quite far removed from the geneticists' stated objectives. On the other hand, as other authors note (Ossorio and Duster, 2005; Fullwiley, 2008), origin in terms of continents is liable to reanimate ideas of "race" as conceptualized in the 18th century because the notions of geography and race can be topographically overlaid on one another (see above the parallel between "Africa, Europe, Asia" and "black, white, yellow"). These categories, then, have racial connotations, euphemized through the recourse to geography. Moreover, as early as the 18th century, the same scientist could recognize the absence of clear delimitation between groups, and at the same time defend the idea that "races", as they were called at the time, had a scientific foundation (Abu El-Haj, 2007). As I discuss below, today almost all geneticists reject this latter idea on scientific grounds. Yet the initial elements in this situation constitute the roots of a problematization centered around the production of ambiguous categories, which are indeed geographical but aligned with racial classifications as commonly understood.

Moreover, as I noted in the introduction, the work of problematization is to get to grips with "true and false" to use Foucault's terminology, which here may be represented by the scientific reliability of the tests. TOGG tests were based on population studies and a statistical approach, combining the science of mathematics with the specific knowledge developed by biologists. Nevertheless, as the current CEO of the company indicated in interview, no statistical value was placed on the probable origin of the suspect: "We say 'He's probably of such and such origin, etc.' [...] We didn't give probabilities, we didn't mess around with offering statistical information. Because quite simply, we didn't have it" (Company executive 1). In a radio debate, when a geneticist warned "Any prediction made will have a very broad margin of error," the CEO of company [X] responded: "That's exactly what we're saying. It's statistical, it's a guide. We're not claiming anything more" (Company executive 2). In short, while the approach drew on statistics, it was relatively inexact or, more precisely, it was honest enough not to fall into the trap of simplistic calculations that would have given the appearance of exactness. As Troy Duster points out (2011, p. 107), "to say that someone is 85 percent African, we must know who is 100 percent African," in the knowledge that there is wide genetic variation across the African continent and that the reference population is always arbitrarily chosen.[8] Unlike biomedical research, where understanding of the precise percentage of markers is well advanced (Fullwiley, 2008), here the genomic approach generates "probable" results, but the statistics are removed from reports of the results. The views of judges we interviewed about the scientific precision of the tests, and how this can be a source of problematization, are discussed below.

How to make an origin test uncontroversial

In 2008 Doctor [Y] wrote online that he was well aware of "the explosive nature [of TOGG tests]." Paraphrasing what Roger Deacon (2000, p. 140), following Foucault, calls the "deconstruction" of problems – that is, the attempt to "subvert what has been problematized" – it can be posited that the company directors sought to deconstruct the problematization of these tests. In this spirit of deconstruction, they took care to articulate a number of points about TOGG tests.

First, the categorization the tests made possible was justified on the grounds of their utility. In a television interview, Doctor [Y] stated: "They are elements that support investigation in cases that aren't about the theft of scooters; clearly, it's major crimes, really very, very serious things" (Company executive 2). He thus draws on the pragmatic argument of utility and by emphasizing the seriousness of the crimes concerned evokes the emotions that are often, understandably, aroused by such cases. These justifications on pragmatic grounds represented a first attempt at deproblematization. More precisely, they focused on the deployment of practices and discourses as a "solution" (Foucault, 1984) to the "problem" not of genetic origin but of unsolved crime.

Second, biotechnology company executives maintained that these tests were not specific. "[The TOGG test] doesn't offer much more information than eyewitness testimony. Someone who's attacked, a person in the street, you say he was black, he was 6 foot tall [...]. We weren't providing any more information than that," one of them explained (Company executive 1). Here they deconstruct the problem of the TOGG tests by relegating the genetic approach to the background. As I discuss below, this analogy with eyewitnesses was also defended by a judge and reappears in current practices.

Third, the company executives emphasized that the information they provided related to geographical origin and not to physical appearance. The 2006 expert witness report for the above-mentioned rape and murder case clearly stated that establishing geographical origin was a genetic result and "did not prejudge nationality or phenotype." Thus these executives hoped to mute accusations that the tests would stigmatize individuals or groups, at a time when it is known that "melanin" discrimination – discrimination based on skin color – is a serious issue for societies (Ndiaye, 2006).[9] One of them argued: "We didn't say anything about the person's physical appearance. We said: he comes from this region of the world" (Company executive 1). They based this assertion on the fact that the TOGG test used "non-coding" genetic markers. In their view, because these markers did not correspond to genes, the TOGG test could give "no information on skin, eye or hair color, facial features or even potential genetic diseases," as [Y] maintained in a television interview. Yet the shift from genotype to phenotype was inherent in the logic of the approach because the aim was to provide investigators with practical indications as to the suspect's appearance. The geneticists' argument that the tests gave no indication of appearance contradicted the aim of the test itself.

Finally, these company executives took pains to produce ethically grounded "Guidelines for the use of TOGG tests," which stated that the test "does not [...] specify race, particularly given that this concept is extremely vague in human genetics."[10] The executives argued for an awareness of "origins" that did not involve race (Brattain, 2007), and in their mind there was no question of hierarchies between population groups, of the kind that had held sway under colonialism and slavery, when racial theories had been developed (Wade, 2014). More generally, it should be noted that forensic science customarily attributes human remains to categories like "Black" or "White," without necessarily subscribing to racial theories (Sauer, 1992).

In short, the "loss of familiarity" experienced with regard to geographical origin is rooted in the fact that on the one hand geneticists assert that race does not exist genetically, but on the other they are offering a scientific method of distinguishing between individuals on the basis of their origin, defined within the parameters of European, African, or Asian, and with the more or less avowed aim of providing indications as to appearance. Some authors have called this kind of ambiguity "the absent presence of race" (M'charek et al., 2014; Wade, 2014). Extending this argument, we may note the way this tension acts both to support and to deconstruct problematization. Moreover, the effects of problematization in terms of what Foucault called "true and false," in other words the scientific reliability of the test, already seem to have raised questions from actors ("the prediction will have a very broad margin of error," says the geneticist), which I shall explore below. Ultimately, considered as subjects, the promoters of these tests sought to position themselves as ethical subjects and to euphemize the categorizing aspect of their work through their guidelines, their verbal caveats about the non-existence of race, and so on.

The problematization expressed (2007–2008)

I turn now to how the problematization arising from TOGG tests was articulated in France, exploring the arguments used by both opponents and defenders of the tests. I shall show that three general positions on the tests emerged among judges interviewed in 2012–2014: those who *opposed* them for reasons linked to history, law, and reliability; those who were *doubtful* for reasons relating to utility, the law, and reliability, and those who were *in favor* on the grounds of utility.

The importance of the historical and political-moral argument

The biotechnology company began its campaign by approaching judges to inform them of the possibility of this new technique, which cost several thousand euros, and persuade them of its usefulness. In 2007, one of the company's sales executives extolled its benefits at a meeting of examining magistrates in Lyon.[11] The meeting, where a dozen judges were present, was stormy, owing particularly to one judge's vehement opposition to use of the tests, for reasons detailed below. Having previously served as national secretary of the Syndicat de la Magistrature trade union, this judge was accustomed to talking to the media and contacted a young journalist, hoping to involve the press in his attempt to prevent the sale of TOGG tests. This could clearly be described as a strategy of "external mobilization," in other words getting the public involved via the media – a tactic employed when recourse to institutions is not available (Garraud, 2004). In an interview, the judge said:

> Scientists need to have a well-rounded education and an ethics, when they introduce a procedure, and [ask themselves]: is this procedure acceptable within society's norms, or is it unacceptable? [...] I'm sorry, I'm not prepared to live in a society where we categorize the perpetrators we're looking for in terms of the color of their skin.
>
> *(Judge 4)*

Thus in 2008, an article on the online news site *Médiapart* reported that TOGG tests had been used a dozen or so times by French judges and highlighted the secrecy surrounding them – a secrecy that testified to the opposition such tests were liable to arouse, on political/moral, legal, and scientific grounds.

The first type of argument put forward by opponents was, as suggested, politically and morally grounded, in a context where some were already extremely alarmed about the major growth of databases for police and court use, which in their view were liable to encroach on personal freedoms (Mattelart and Vitalis, 2014). The primary argument, and the most important in the view of opponents of TOGG tests, was the risk of discrimination and the creation of race-based databases. In the French context, the reluctance to keep this kind of information in databases has to be understood in the light of the country's history during World War Two and the "registers of Jews" that were kept during this period. The judge at the Lyon meeting who was most vehemently opposed to origin tests in criminal investigations used the term "problem," as if echoing the problematization:

> I said [to the company sales representative who had come to promote TOGG tests]: 'You're going to create a database by default.' And he said: 'Well, yes, it'll be a database of individuals who are sought, where we'll include a certain number of elements.' And said to him: 'Have you thought about that in your lab, about the problem you're setting up, especially around discrimination, discriminatory databases?' And he said: 'Ummm, well no.' And so I told him that was appalling, that if he knew anything about history, especially about the 1939–1945 war, the register of Jews, that would remind him of something.
>
> *(Judge 4)*

For their part, the senior executives of company [X] asserted that they "would not create any data bank out of samples entrusted to them" (Guidelines for use of TOGG tests). Notwithstanding these reassurances, other senior figures in the Syndicat de la Magistrature and in human rights organizations such as the Ligue des Droits de l'Homme supported the judge's position and raised the hypothetical possibility of a more or less authoritarian government coming to power. In interviews judges said, for example: "If through [this test] they create lists or databases by population category, I have a problem with that. [...] It's a serious political question. [...] Morally, ethically, I'm against [TOGG tests]" (Judge 5). Another said: "It's easy to see how it could be used if democracy was gone and history took a tragic turn, as it already has before. Behind this, you see the deportation of the Jews" (Judge 1). While many practices concerning origins can give rise to stigmatization and discrimination, particularly in the criminal justice system (Welch, 2007), the issue of databases created by laboratories – and their potential political use – makes this a particularly acute concern here. It should be pointed out that the purpose of this putative database created by the laboratory was not clear, reflecting the fact that these practices were in their infancy. Whatever the ultimate intention, at this stage it would have existed as a bank of information retained by the laboratory rather than a national database managed by the police and would have been much more limited than the FNAEG. However, the diverging points of view with regard to the nature of DNA tests were clear. As noted above, the company executives attempted to deconstruct the problematization by making the origin test appear run-of-the-mill. By contrast, a public prosecutor said in interview:

> You get an expert opinion, they tell you: 'The guy is of such-and-such origin,' [...] it's confidential to the investigation, [...] it's not made public.

> It doesn't pose a threat to social cohesion or discrimination, [...] it's not intended to set up population categories, it's very different.
>
> *(Judge 5)*

In other words, when evidence about a suspect's origin is provided by oral testimony, it remains confined to the investigation and confidential; when it is established by a laboratory, that laboratory might organize it in databases that could be disseminated, or use it to provide scientific legitimacy for a tool of discrimination.

Interestingly, in the case of the rape and murder of a young woman in a Dutch village, which continued to occupy the media between 1999 and 2013, arguments tended in the opposite direction, as described by Amade M'charek and co-authors (M'charek et al., 2020; Jong and M'charek, 2017). In this case the use of genetic origin tests was promoted as a way of preventing discrimination against migrants, who had become the subject of unfounded suspicions. Following the murder, local residents insinuated that the perpetrator was to be sought in the center for asylum seekers not far from the crime scene, where all the residents were from the Middle East. The villagers' ire was further roused when investigators announced that a former resident of the center was a potential suspect, one of them publicly calling the center a "hive of criminal activity." Suspicion was heightened by the fact that the young woman's throat had been cut with a knife, a method the media described as "non-Western," and that the suspect had disappeared on the day of the crime. However, he was exonerated by his DNA, which did not match the trace found at the murder scene. Nevertheless, the media held onto the idea that the perpetrator came from the center. In 2003, in the face of the polemic, the Public Prosecutor asked a forensic science laboratory to analyze the suspect's geographical origin. Such analyses were still illegal in the Netherlands at that time, and the geneticist tasked with the tests stated that he saw his action as an act of civil disobedience in a good cause, that of alleviating the burden hanging over the residents of the asylum-seekers' center. In the end, the laboratory results pointed to a perpetrator of North-West European origin, removing all suspicion from the center residents. Finally, investigators turned to the area around the site of the crime, and after renewed searches the perpetrator, a local farmer whose genetic profile matched the unidentified trace, was arrested and then convicted. This case played a crucial role in the legalization of origin tests for suspects in the Netherlands, which was the first country to introduce them into law, with the option of analyzing "the sex, race or other visible external personal characteristics, to be specified by Decree." Depending on context, then, the same argument of (non-)discrimination can be applied for or against such tests.

In France, this first set of arguments against the TOGG tests invites a number of remarks. Firstly, the position of those who oppose TOGG tests needs to be resituated in the context presented in the introduction, of the prohibition on collecting "ethnic" or "racial" data, which has its roots in French republican universalism – a context quite different from that of the United

States or the United Kingdom, for example.[12] Secondly, the history of World War Two is crucial for understanding the way the problematization operates in France because the history of Nazism resulted in reinforcement of the French political culture, which rejects identification on the basis of ethnicity or race (Chapman and Frader, 2004). This subject has become even more sensitive in recent times, owing to the strong electoral performance of the far right in France. While it is recognized in a general way that scientific ethics is no longer the sole province of scientists (Fischer, 2012), this is all the more true when this ethics is located at the junction of different social spaces, such as the justice system and the media. It should further be noted that in this respect those involved pose the debate not only in ethical but also, and equally, in political terms ("it's a serious political issue. [...] Morally, ethically, I'm opposed to [TOGG tests]," said one judge). In the field of DNA databases, France, unlike the United Kingdom, does not tend to see the problems as "belonging to the domain of the expert community of bioethicists rather than being matters of politics and public interest" (Skinner, 2011, p. 61). These French social actors highlight the specific nature of DNA tests in terms of the databases that may be created but do not thereby conclude that the issues raised by such tests should be deemed either a domain reserved for bioethics experts or an apolitical issue. On the contrary, it is rather as if the judges opposed to the tests had internalized the risks of publicizing them. In the words of Victor Toom (2012, p. 152), "when jurisdiction over a body is transferred from an individual to agents of power like police and medics, those bodies transform from 'private bodies' into 'public bodies'." We can add nuance to this argument, noting that these bodies are rather semi-public (by virtue of the law and norms that frame such practices); we can also extend it by pointing out that these semi-public bodies are here placed in a current or apprehended political configuration (an authoritarian government). In other words, there was here an ethics and a politics of the use of data, or more precisely of their potential use. This is a case of political-ethical subjects who are concerned with both their role in society ("I'm not prepared to live in a society where we categorize the perpetrators we're looking for in terms of the color of their skin") and the potential for genetic tests to be used by others.

Other arguments and positions

The second, and not the least, type of argument put forward by the judge and other opponents of the tests was a legal one. As noted above, French law stipulates that the DNA tests used for traditional genetic profiles are based on "non-coding" DNA markers. According to the company executives, the TOGG technique was legal because it used markers located in this non-coding DNA. However, the tests provided information on the appearance of individuals, leading those who opposed them to see them as "circumventing the law." More fundamentally, the principles of this law relate to a particularity of DNA highlighted by a number of the people we interviewed, including this examining magistrate:

> DNA research might one day be used to find out if you are at risk of such and such a disease, or to have a more precise idea of origins, it links to intimate family information. [...] There's something internal, private about DNA.
>
> *(Judge 6)*

This consideration raises the question of the balance between the interests of the investigative process and the suspect's "right not to know" (particularly in relation to characteristics linked to health conditions) (Koops and Schellekens, 2008). For those involved, DNA raises the classic problematics of the self, identity, origins, and family, while the legal framework seeks to offer guarantees with regard to the perceived DNA-specific risk of a wider range of information being gathered.

The third argument raised by the detractors of the TOGG tests concerned reliability, and here some considerations regarding scientific credibility, mentioned earlier, may be addressed in more detail. Interviewees highlighted the fact that the test had not been validated by articles in international scientific journals: "These procedures have never been the subject of an academic article in science journals like *Nature*, where there is a peer-review committee that validates the hypotheses or results presented by the scientist who's written the article" (Judge 4), said one judge. Be that as it may, the company's commercial approach, which meant it was not in a traditional research situation subject to peer review, made it impossible to precisely evaluate its conclusions. These tests therefore sit in a context of complex epistemic debates that have contradictory effects in terms of legitimacy (a legitimacy that is scientific but incomplete). Here the rules for discriminating between true and false obeyed their own internal rules (Bacchi, 2012). Their relationship with "truth" was uncertain and ambiguous, rendering them still more problematic.

Nevertheless, as noted above, the judges were not unanimous. At the small meeting in Lyon, apart from the vocal few who opposed TOGG tests, other judges, those I have termed "doubtful," were not as concerned about the test's potentially discriminatory nature. They argued rather that they might be of little use (the tests provide little information), would be illegal, and lacked scientific reliability. One judge, for example, said in interview: "Will this really help us in the investigation? [...] I don't see how it can provide evidence that's accurate enough to guide the investigation" (Judge 7).

Two of the judges present at the meeting thought that TOGG tests could be useful in helping to identify suspects: a young man who had recently completed his studies to become a judge, and a former police officer. Another interviewee, in a senior position in the Ministry of Justice and a former public prosecutor, argued for the same position:

> When you start with: 'What did the gentleman look like?' you're going to be told he was black. Really, he was black? So what? Quite honestly, I'd like […] for us to be able to use these tests in the same way as soon as possible […]. We shouldn't deprive ourselves of these investigative and expert witness techniques.
>
> *(Judge 8)*

She gives the example of a miscarriage of justice that could have been avoided, in her view, through the use of this technique, in a case she was involved in:

> The man who was convicted, he was, let's say, Caucasian, as they call it, European, he was white. And [the culprit] was a man of color. He was black. So on the basis of the traces, could we have established that [the investigators were following a false trail]?
>
> *(Judge 8)*

However, she failed to state whether, if DNA traces were available, comparison of genetic profiles would not have been simpler and more reliable than TOGG tests. Furthermore, one of the judges at the Lyon meeting told me: "The various examining magistrates in France are in email contact, and [some] were wondering about doing [the test]" (Judge 4). Nevertheless, at this point (2012–2014) support for TOGG tests among judges was much less common than the first two positions (opposition and doubt), both in media statements and in interviews.

Regulation of tests of origin (2008–2014)

The final section of this chapter deals with what Foucault called "the development of a domain of acts, practices, and thoughts that seem to me to pose problems for politics" (Foucault, 1984, p. 384). I discuss the government's positions on TOGG tests during this period and how the tests were regulated. I show that geographical origin based on genetics was also a highly sensitive issue for the Ministry of Justice.

How to damp down a sensitive problem

Following the publication of the *Médiapart* article, which was taken up by a number of other newspapers, the Ministry of Justice quickly got wind of the affair via the media. The media thus played an important part in the growth of problematization in both the public and the institutional contexts, acting in their traditional role of gatekeepers for the emergence of problems in the public arena (Hilgartner and Bosk, 1988). Media attention threw the spotlight on practices that although not in widespread use had potentially major political ramifications. The spokesperson for the Ministry of Justice, which took this situation very seriously, immediately alerted the minister's chief of staff and called in the ministry's experts on the subject. In an interview, he explained: "This technique was sensitive, it could have caused a crisis for the Ministry of Justice [...], so we really mobilized all the senior staff and departments to formulate a properly appropriate response" (Ministry spokesperson 1). He responded to journalists' questions, weighing his words carefully: "From the information currently available to us, the law is being respected," but he added that an Interministerial Technical Committee would review the "ethical" aspects of the issue. When I interviewed him, he had two comments on this statement. The first related to the form: "Everything was weighed, calibrated ... a bit waffle-y, but calming. The idea was to calm people's anxieties. [...] The idea was also to say: in principle, there is no problem, but we're going to make sure anyway." His second comment related to the content of his statement:

> Practice has evolved and, in fact, the law had not foreseen that non-coding DNA could pose problems and could be used to determine a suspect's geographical origin. The law hadn't foreseen it, so therefore it was legally authorized [...]. But from an ethical point of view, we thought: all the same, it's not a great situation.
>
> *(Ministry spokesperson 1)*

The ambiguous suggestion, then, is first that there was no "problem," and then that there was a "problem" and ethical questions. When I asked him to say more about why the issue was "sensitive," he replied:

> It was a sensitive topic that was also subject to a lot of fantasies and irrational claims. [...] DNA, profiling, ethnic, those are three big words. [...] Ethnic origin, that's an extremely sensitive issue. There's the idea of Aryans and non-Aryans ... Who knows whether people aren't going to look at things [in DNA] that they don't have the right to look at?
>
> *(Ministry spokesperson 1)*

These tests thus clearly represented a burning topic in view of their political sensitivity, given the way they combined crime, origin (with the background context of racism), and DNA (with all that it might one day reveal). The judicial context, and problems related to the retention of non-anonymous information on entire population groups, also aggravated the situation. However, the debate died down relatively quickly. The situation appeared to become calm, and for over two years the ministry, concerned not to revive the polemic, chose not to adopt an official position: while not going so far as to deconstruct the problem, this approach sought at least to abstain from fanning the flames.

How points of problematization became a taboo

Nevertheless, origin tests remained quietly present. A number of people we interviewed confirmed that some police investigators regularly asked for these tests. An executive at company [X] told me:

> The vast majority of investigators were for, in favor, of course. [...] The proof is that we were asked for them. People were prepared to pay quite large sums for that kind of information. Of course. And we still regularly get calls asking: 'Do you do it?'
>
> *(Company executive 1)*

This explains why, in 2010, investigators, who constitute "a major lobby" according to the head of the ministerial department concerned, made an informal request to the Ministry of Justice to use these tests. In addition to such informal requests, the ministry also received a formal request from a private company that wished to offer analyses of physical characteristics of suspects, which I discuss in the next chapter. These requests prompted the ministry to take an official position, following consultation with the relevant ministerial committee. The committee members were unanimous in concluding that these methods should be considered "with the greatest caution," for the reasons discussed below. On the basis of this opinion, in 2011 the Ministry Directorate published a Dispatch – which falls into the category of what Foucault (2001 [1994], p. 1365) calls "prescriptive texts," written with the aim of setting out rules and opinions "on how to behave as one ought." This Dispatch was not strictly speaking a prohibition, but rather a strong encouragement not to use the tests, which in practice came down to the same thing. The central argument was legal in nature.[13] The Dispatch pointed out that the tests fell in the domain of examination of "genetic characteristics," rather than identification of an individual, as in the case of traditional genetic profiles, because they could provide information on the individual's "obvious features." French law permits examination of genetic characteristics solely for medical purposes or scientific research, which was clearly not the situation here. One "point of problematization," to use the terminology of my frame of analysis, is therefore the shift from identification to characterization of individuals, through physical appearance. Moreover, in less detailed form, and echoing the remarks of the judges quoted above, the Dispatch pointed out that the use of scientific databases created by a laboratory was an essential precondition of these tests, and that on the basis of the evidence provided "it [was] not possible to verify that laboratories had taken appropriate measures, particularly in relation to anonymization of data" to ensure conformity with the law.[14] In this way, primarily on the basis of law, this Dispatch put an end to TOGG practices as such, until 2014 when there was a sudden turnaround, discussed in the next chapter. In the end, TOGG tests were used 15–20 times in France during this period. The legal prohibition provided the "solution" to the problematization generated by TOGG and constituted the "ethical work" of the ministry (the way that ethics works, for example, through ethical codes or laws) (Dean 1999). It should be noted, nevertheless, that three years passed between the *Médiapart* article in 2008 and the Dispatch in 2011, despite the fact that, as the ministry spokesperson indicated, a rapid response to the article would have been possible.

There was, to be sure, a political sensitivity in the issue of geogenetic origin, but the Ministry of Justice allowed practices to continue in the absence of further debate. Thus a period of "indifferent tolerance" (Gros, 2014) preceded the prohibition, making the situation a little more complex than expected.

* * *

Without suggesting that problematizations are rare (Dean, 1999), or conversely inherent in all politics (Bacchi, 2012), I have described how the issue of genetic origin, used in the context of forensic science, was problematized in the public arena in France by various groups of actors (biologists, judges and public prosecutors, politicians). This approach paves the way for a broader consideration of how the actor "problematizes what he is, what he does and the world in which he lives" (Foucault, 2001 [1994], p. 1363): what he is as a professional, a national of a country with its particular history, and a member of a species categorized in terms of genetically-defined population groups; what he does as promoter, potential user, or regulator of tests; and the world in which he lives as a society that needs to maintain the right balance between security of the public and profiling of individuals. One of the key points here is the idea, to paraphrase Bowker and Star (1999) in relation to "racial" categories, that understanding where problematization stems from helps to shed light on the political and moral order of a society. This conclusion invites comment on three levels.

The first relates to the tensions internal to the process of problematization. The research presented in this chapter indicates that these tests sat at the intersection of two trends that were in tension with one another, creating an anthropological "knot", to use Ian Hacking's term (2005b) for a situation resulting from contradictory tendencies. The first strand of this knot is the one that deproblematizes. Here I have described the deconstruction of problematization (by the promoters of the tests), the albeit limited use of TOGG tests, or demand for them, that drew on the utility argument (by some judges, public prosecutors, and investigators), and the delay between the *Médiapart* article in 2008 and the Ministry of Justice Dispatch in 2011 (on the part of politicians). The second strand of the knot is that which produces the problematization, which is both verbal, in the form of the public positions taken by judges (on the basis of political/moral, legal, and scientific criteria), and institutional, in the form of political regulation (on the basis of political/moral and legal criteria). We can add to this a more internalized aspect of problematization, reflected in the discreet nature of the requests and uses of the tests during this period. Highlighting the existence of this knot helps us to move beyond the idea of a simple prohibition and linear processes where actors provide somewhat mechanistic solutions to problems. Nevertheless, from the point of view of effects on practices, the problematizing strand initially won out over the deproblematizing strand.

The second level of remarks relates to the transformation of origin. While the notion of origin has long existed, it is the shift in the concept that poses the problem here. The observer of these new uses of DNA has a vague sense that what we are dealing with here is not simply a resurgence of ways of thinking and acting that prevailed in past centuries, even if old forms of understanding appear to persist and combine with new modes rather than completely disappearing. Firstly, these tests support both the persistence and the evolution of a way of thinking that emphasizes differences transmitted from one generation to another, and visible in bodies. Moreover, given that it is DNA that provides information on suspects, the idea that "ethnicity" or "racial" differences are a biological given and not primarily a sociocultural construction appears to follow. Finally, I have noted that those who oppose the tests point to the danger of potential domination under a more or less authoritarian regime. What then poses a problem – one that is new – is the use and potential dissemination of databases created by laboratories, as opposed to oral testimony that remains contained within the confidentiality of the investigation. According to Peter Wade (2014), phenomena that can be described as "racial" are based partly on nature, heredity, and the way heredity is expressed in appearance, and partly on geographical and historical factors. This helps to explain why these new origins are (or were) politically and morally highly sensitive subjects, in any case much more sensitive than oral testimony. Three constitutive elements of these theories – heredity, appearance, and domination – seem (or seemed) to gain renewed potency, making the subject an explosive one. A further aspect of the transformation of origin concerns the link to the national context. Didier and Éric Fassin (2006) explain that the persistence of multiculturalism in the United States is based on the ideal of equal recognition of marginalized identities and dominated cultures. They add that in France, in their view, the key issue is to acknowledge discrimination, rather than to recognize identity: what Black and Arab people (the largest "minority" groups in France) have in common is not race but racism. What my study reveals is an evolution that reintroduces an element of identity. On the basis of molecular and statistical data, TOGG tests feed questions of group identity belonging that are to some extent reconfiguring the French situation. Although this remark is made in a particular context, it shows how, in general, the circulation of technical and scientific knowledge can influence the way social questions are framed: according to judges critical of the TOGG technique, the tests could add potential discrimination on the basis of genetic identity to more traditional forms of racism (against Black and Arab people, for example). A third aspect of the changes with respect to origin arises from what is considered scientifically reliable, in other words the "play of true and false" (Foucault, 1988, p. 257). These tests are embedded within a scientific dynamic whereby, during the 20th century, genetics became not only one of the flagship disciplines of science but also a form of knowledge that could spread to a wide public: practices and policies relating to origin have taken a genetic turn. More broadly, these tests actively reconnect with a scientific approach to issues of identity and origin that was both outmoded and never entirely absent during the 20th century (Skinner, 2006; Brattain, 2007). However, these new tests take up this issue in a different way, through the use of advanced biomedical techniques, the involvement of commercial biotechnology companies, and molecularization. Among geneticists, there is a movement between the molecular body and the visible body, and vice versa, through the medium of geography (Asia, Africa, etc.). These various political, moral, legal, and epistemic elements characterize the changes occurring in relation to "geographical," "ethnic," or "racial" origin, as revealed by problematization. The study I present here contributes to analysis of how old and new ideas of the relationship between genetics and origin are being woven together, articulated, and/or coming into conflict. It also reminds us that these questions prompt debates in which social actors other than scientists, doctors, and clients purchasing online origin tests become involved (such as individuals within the police, the justice system, the government ...). Given how research into individuals' origin is emerging beyond laboratories and clinical practice, this also invites further exploration of the social issues of use not only of tests but also of the databases that categorize people by origin. Furthermore, this chapter highlights the importance of contextualizing practices in relation to the history of individual countries, rather than over-generalizing the debates on these themes.[15]

My final set of remarks concerns the politics of the living being and the frame of analysis chosen. As noted in the introduction, this frame of analysis invites us to analyze together the scientific, political, and above all moral aspects of "biopolitics" (Foucault, 2008) and the type of subjects produced. Various types of subjects and power relations are apparent, from those who offer the tests (and seek to be considered ethical subjects, through the production of Guidelines), those who contest them (who constitute themselves as ethical and political subjects, campaigning to end use of the tests), and those who regulate them (who constitute themselves as ethical and political subjects intervening by means of legislation). Moreover, what is at stake in the TOGG tests is not only an ethics of the *self* but also an ethics and politics of *society*. It is not only the relationship to self that comes into question but also the relationship to others (who is the "Other"? what are we doing to ourselves collectively?) and a relationship to the possibility of tests being used by others – and these are undoubtedly political questions. In raising concerns about potential uses of genetic databases by authoritarian powers, the judges opposed to the TOGG tests are resisting processes of biopoliticization of identity (Foucault, 2008). In contrast to the situation described by Rabinow (1999), around the conflict between the French laboratory Centre d'Étude du Polymorphisme Humain (Center for the Study of Human Polymorphism, CEPH) and the American company Millennium Pharmaceuticals, Inc. during the 1990s, here the contestation does not come predominantly from specialists in bioethics or "repentant scientists" making a "spiritual" argument about "dignity" or the definition of the human person, because the political issue, formulated as such, is more potent. In short, going beyond the example presented in this chapter, my research invites us to focus not only on scientific categories and bioethical debates but also on the political uses of genetic tests, and not only on the scientifically defined identities of individuals tested but also on the types of subjects produced among both those who promote the tests and those who oppose them. The next chapter discusses how the situation in France altered radically in 2014.

Notes

1 Anonymous (2005, July 1). M. Aznar a "manipulé" l'enquête sur les attentats du 11-Mars. *Le Monde*.
2 Phillips, C., Prieto, L., Fondevila, M., Salas A. et al. (2009). Ancestry analysis in the 11-M Madrid bomb attack investigation. *PLoS ONE, 4*(8), 1–10.
3 Newsome, M. (2007, October 5). The inconvenient science of racial DNA profiling. *WIRED*.
4 Burchard, E. G., Ziv, E., Coyle, N., Vomez, S. L. et al. (2003). The importance of race and ethnic background in biomedical research and clinical practice. *New England Journal of Medicine, 348(12)*, 1170–1175; Collins, F. S. (2004). What we do and don't know about "race", "ethnicity", genetics and health at the dawn of the genome era. *Nature Genetics*, Supplement 36, S13–S15.
5 The main companies mentioned in this study have been anonymized.
6 In contrast to the United States and United Kingdom, judges may play a role in criminal investigations in France.
7 These tests are typical of those based on what are known as "ancestry" markers, which evaluate origin on the basis of continental categories used as references, and "admixtures" of sequences thought to derive from different continents (Fullwiley, 2008).
8 In the literature, social scientists challenge this claim to scientific accuracy (Ossorio and Duster, 2005; Fujimura and Rajagopalan, 2011; Fullwiley, 2011), and geneticists themselves emphasize the constructed nature of origin categories: see Bamshad, M., Wooding, S., Salisbury, B. A. et al. (2004). Deconstructing the relationship between genetics and race. *Nature Genetics, 5*, 598–609.
9 Despite the fact, Ndiaye (2006) adds, that there are very few studies of this subject in France.
10 These guidelines, which were available online, have since been removed from the company's website.
11 The examining magistrate oversees criminal investigations and may carry out pretrial investigations [translator].
12 See the law of July 1 1972, supplemented in June 7 1977 by articles 187–1 and 416 of the Code of Penal Procedure.
13 Dispatch CRIM-PJ no. 8–28.H5 vol. 4, of June 29 2011.
14 Law on information technology, databases and civil liberties no. 78–17.
15 In this vein, some authors have sought to contextualize the issue of genetic origin (M'charek et al., 2014; Wade et al., 2014).

References

Abu El-Haj, N. (2007). The genetic reinscription of race. *Annual Review of Anthropology*, 36, 283–300. doi:10.1146/annurev.anthro.34.081804.120522.

Aronson, J. D. (2007). *Genetic witness: Science, law, and controversy in the making of DNA profiling*. Rutgers University Press.

Bacchi, C. (2012). Why study problematizations? Making politics visible. *Open Journal of Political Science*, 2(1), 1–8. doi:10.4236/ojps.2012.21001.

Bowker, G. C., & Star, S. L. (1999). *Sorting things out: Classification and its consequences*. The MIT Press.

Brattain, M. (2007). Race, racism and antiracism: UNESCO and the politics of presenting science to the postwar public. *American Historical Review*, 112(5), 1386–1413. doi:10.1086/ahr.112.5.1386.

Canselier, G., & Desmoulin-Canselier, S. (2011). *Les catégories ethnoraciales à l'ère des biotechnologies*. Société de Législation Comparée.

Chapman, H., & Frader, L. L. (2004). *Race in France: Interdisciplinary perspectives on the politics of difference*. Berghahn Books.
Deacon, R. (2000). Theory as practice: Foucault's concept of problematization. *Telos*, 118, 127–142.
Dean, M. (1999). *Governmentality: Power and rule in modern society*. SAGE.
Dixon, A. R., & Telles, E. E. (2017). Skin color and colorism: Global research, concepts, and measurement. *Annual Review of Sociology*, 43, 405–424. doi:10.1146/annurev-soc-060116-053315.
Duster, T. (2011). Ancestry testing and DNA: Uses, limits, and caveat emptor. In S. Krimsky, & K. Sloan (Eds.), *Race and the genetic revolution: Science, myth, and culture* (pp. 95–115). Columbia University Press.
Fassin, D., & Fassin, E. (Eds.). (2006). *De la question sociale à la question raciale*. La Découverte.
Fischer, M. J. (2012). Science. In D. Fassin (Ed.), *A companion to moral anthropology* (pp. 395–412). Wiley-Blackwell.
Foucault, M. (1981). *The history of sexuality, vol. 2: The use of pleasure*, trans. Robert Hurley. Penguin.
Foucault, M. (1984). Polemics, politics and problematizations: An interview with Michel Foucault. In P. Rabinow (Ed.), *The Foucault reader* (pp. 381–390). Pantheon Books.
Foucault, M. (1988). The concern for truth, trans. Alan Sheridan. In L. D. Kritzman (Ed.), *Michel Foucault: Politics, philosophy, culture. Interviews and other writings, 1977–1984* (pp. 255–267). Routledge.
Foucault, M. (2001 [1994]). *Dits et écrits II, 1976–1988*. Gallimard.
Foucault, M. (2008). *The birth of biopolitics: Lectures at the Collège de France, 1978–1979*, trans. Graham Burchell. Palgrave Macmillan.
Fox, D. (2010). The second generation of racial profiling. *American Journal of Criminal Law*, 38(1), 49–79.
Fujimura, J. J., & Rajagopalan, R. (2011). Different differences: The use of "genetic ancestry" versus race in biomedical human genetic research. *Social Studies of Science*, 4(1), 5–30. doi:10.1177/0306312710379170.
Fullwiley, D. (2008). The biologistical construction of race: "Admixture" technology and the new genetic medicine. *Social Studies of Science*, 38(5), 695–735. doi:10.1177/0306312708090796.
Fullwiley, D. (2011). Can DNA 'witness' race? In S. Krimsky, & K. Sloan (Eds.), *Race and the genetic revolution: Science, myth and culture* (pp. 116–126). Columbia University Press.
Garraud, P. (2004). Agenda. In L. Boussaguet, S. Jacquot, & P. Ravinet (Eds.), *Dictionnaire des politiques publiques* (pp. 51–58). Presses de Sciences Po.
Gros, F. (2014). Problématisation. In J.-F. Bert, & J. Lamy (Eds.), *Michel Foucault: Un héritage critique* (pp. 125–126). Éditions CNRS.
Hacking, I. (2005a). Why race still matters. *Daedalus*, 134(1), 102–116. doi:10.1162/0011526053124460.
Hacking, I. (2005b). "Façonner les gens". [Seminar]. Collège de France.
Hilgartner, S., & Bosk, C. L. (1988). The rise and fall of social problems: A public arenas model. *American Journal of Sociology*, 94(1), 53–78.
Jong, L., & M'charek, A. (2017). The high-profile case as "fire object": Following the Marianne Vaatstra murder case through the media. *Crime, Media, Culture*, 14(5), 1–17. doi:10.1177/1741659017718036.
Koops, B.-J., & Schellekens, M. (2008). Forensic DNA phenotyping: Regulatory issues. *Science and Technology Law Review*, IX, 158–202. doi:10.7916/stlr.v9i0.3818.

Mattelart, A., & Vitalis, A. (2014). *Le profilage des populations: Du livret ouvrier au cybercontrôle*. La Découverte.

M'charek, A. (2008). Silent witness, articulate collective: DNA evidence and the inference of visible traits. *Bioethics*, 22(9), 519–528. doi:10.1111/j.1467-8519.2008.00699.x.

M'charek, A. (2013). Beyond fact or fiction: On the materiality of race in practice. *Cultural Anthropology*, 28(3), 420–442. doi:10.1111/cuan.12012.

M'charek, A., Schramm, K., & Skinner, D. (2014). Technologies of belonging: The absent presence of race in Europe. *Science, Technology, & Human Values*, 39(4), 459–467. doi:10.1177/0162243914531149.

M'charek, A., Toom, V., & Jong, L. (2020). The trouble with race in forensic identification. *Science, Technology & Human Values*, 45(5), 804–828. doi:10.1177/0162243919899467.

Ndiaye, P. (2006). Questions de couleur: Histoire, idéologie et pratiques du colorisme. In D. Fassin, & E. Fassin (Eds.), *De la question sociale à la question raciale* (pp. 37–54). La Découverte.

Noiriel, G. (1996). French and foreigners. In P. Nora (Ed.), *Realms of memory: The construction of the French past, vol. 1: Conflicts and divisions* (pp. 275–379). Columbia University Press.

Noiriel, G. (2006). "Color-blindness" et construction des identités dans l'espace public français. In D. Fassin, & E. Fassin (Eds.), *De la question sociale à la question raciale* (pp. 158–174). La Découverte.

Ossorio, P., & Duster, T. (2005). Race and genetics: Controversies in biomedical, behavioral, and forensic sciences? *American Psychologist*, 60(1), 115–128. doi:10.1037/0003-066X.60.1.115.

Rabinow, P. (1999). *French DNA*. University Chicago Press.

Sankar, P. (2010). Forensic DNA phenotyping: Reinforcing race in law enforcement. In I. Whitmarsh, & D. S. Jones (Eds.), *What's the use of race? Modern governance and the biology of difference* (pp. 49–61). MIT Press.

Sauer, N. J. (1992). Forensic anthropology and the concept of race: If race don't exist, why are forensic anthropologists so good at identifying them? *Social Science & Medicine*, 34(2), 107–111. doi:10.1016/0277-9536(92)90086-6.

Skinner, D. (2006). Racialized futures: Biologism and the changing politics of identity. *Social Studies of Science*, 36(3), 459–488. doi:10.1177/0306312706054859.

Skinner, D. (2011). Mobile identities and fixed categories: Forensic DNA and the politics of racialized data. In K. Schramm, D. Skinner, & R. Rottenburg (Eds.), *Identity politics and the new genetics: Re/creating categories of difference and belonging* (pp. 53–78). Berghahn Books.

Skinner, D. (2020 [2019]). Forensic genetics and the prediction of race: What is the problem?, *BioSocieties*, 15, 329–349. doi:10.1057/s41292-018-0141-0.

Toom, V. (2012). Bodies of science and law: Forensic DNA profiling, biological bodies, and biopower. *Journal of Law and Society*, 39(1), 150–166. doi:10.1111/j.1467-6478.2012.00575.x.

Vailly, J. (2017 [2016]). The politics of suspects' geo-genetic origin in France: The conditions, expression, and effects of problematisation. *BioSocieties*, 12(1), 66–88. doi:10.1057/s41292-016-0028-x.

Wade, P. (2014). Race, ethnicity, and technologies of belonging. *Science, Technology, & Human Values*, 39(4), 587–596. doi:10.1177/0162243913516807.

Wade, P., Deister, G., Kent, V., Olarte Sierra, M. F. *et al.* (2014). Nation and the absent presence of race in Latin American genomics. *Current Anthropology*, 55(5), 497–522. doi:10.1177/0306312715623108.

Welch, K. (2007). Black criminal stereotypes and racial profiling. *Journal of Contemporary Criminal Justice*, 23(3), 276–288. doi:10.1177/1043986207306870.

Wienroth, M. (2018). Governing anticipatory technology practices: Forensic DNA phenotyping and the forensic genetic community in Europe. *New Genetics and Society*, 37 (2), 137–152. doi:10.1080/14636778.2018.1469975.

4

THE ACCEPTABILITY OF SUSPECT APPEARANCE TESTS

Between October 2012 and January 2013, five young women were sexually assaulted in a student neighborhood of the city of Lyon. The attacks showed escalating levels of violence; the perpetrator wore a ski mask and gloves and carried a knife. These serial attacks caused great alarm in the city. The attacker's DNA, which was detected on the victims' clothing, did not match any profile known to the police. In 2013 the examining magistrate overseeing the case commissioned a private laboratory to provide "all useful evidence regarding the suspect's visible morphological characteristics" on the basis of his DNA. The laboratory submitted an expert report indicating that the attacker had dark brown eyes, olive skin, and mid- to dark brown or black hair. It should be noted that no reference was made to origin in this case. Given that a 2011 Ministry of Justice Dispatch had banned this type of test, the Ministry judged that the magistrate had contravened its ruling and informed the Public Prosecutor in the city where the tests had been performed that, in its view, this amounted to illegal examination "of an individual's genetic characteristics." The Public Prosecutor began proceedings against the CEO of the laboratory that had carried out the analysis but ultimately took no action in view of the subsequent turn of events. The Lyon examining magistrate, who wished to ensure that his procedure would not be challenged, himself requested that the Investigation Chamber[1] rule on the legality of the expert report. The procedure eventually went as far as the Court of Cassation, the country's highest court. In an extremely laconic judgment, the Court ruled in 2014 that provided the procedure was restricted exclusively to revealing "the visible morphological characteristics" of the unknown perpetrator of a crime on the basis of DNA left at the scene it was valid, without specifying what it meant by "visible characteristics."[2] The attacker was eventually arrested not as a result of this technique but caught in the act of assaulting another young woman in January 2014. Nevertheless, the affair had

DOI: 10.4324/9781003456056-7

significant consequences because the case law opened the way to the use of this type of test in France.

This case, briefly summarized here, reignited debate in France around tests predicting the appearance and (though it was not part of the analysis carried out in this case) the geographical origin of a suspect for the purpose of criminal investigations. Other examples also testify to the recent expansion of such approaches. The Department of Genetic Identification at Erasmus University in the Netherlands launched a website which could be used by anyone with access to the appropriate genetic data and would provide information on hair, eye, and skin color on the basis of DNA.[3] In a similar vein, a European research project called VISAGE was set up with the aim of

> allow[ing] the construction of composite sketches of unknown trace donors directly from their crime scene traces. [...] The VISAGE Toolkit will include analysis prototype tools based on massively parallel sequencing for genotyping the large number of DNA predictors for appearance, age, and ancestry established within the Project [...][4]

Geneticists and private companies are also seeking to develop a technique, as yet unavailable, that would link biometric information on facial features to genetic markers, taking origin into account.[5] The US company Parabond NanoLabs claims to offer services of this type, but its results, which have not been published, are strongly contested in the scientific community. In 2015 the company was even selling phenotyping tests based on traces taken from litter (cigarette butts, drink cans, etc.) illegally discarded on the public highway in Hong Kong. What were claimed to be portraits of supposed offenders, drawn up on the basis of DNA, were displayed in the streets as a way of encouraging people not to litter. Finally, in a different context, but one that needs to be seen in the context of other developments, in China hundreds of DNA samples from the minority Uighur Muslim population were collected in the camps or on the pretext of preventative healthcare, with the ultimate aim of establishing a relationship between DNA, origin, and facial features. This Chinese study was criticized in the media, including *The New York Times*, and the two scientific journals that published it later retracted the articles, on the grounds that the people from whom samples were taken had not consented to the research.[6]

In this chapter, I show how this visual representation established on the basis of biological data is debated and problematized by social actors concerned about respect for privacy. For the majority of geneticists, bioethicists, and institutions, the right to privacy has been one of the most serious issues raised by the use of genetics since the 1990s, given the amount of information now available from DNA.[7] As I have noted, France has already come up against this question, when the European Court of Human Rights (ECHR) ruled against it in 2017 for "disproportionate interference with a suspect's right to respect for private life" (the study of DNA *comparisons*).

One of the tasks of social science researchers is to analyze the social contexts in which a selection is made between those actions considered acceptable and those that are not, and to study the social norms – such as privacy – on which this selection is based. The concept of privacy has long been a subject of research for social scientists, who have shown, for example, how different societies protect secrets or access to certain rituals (Kulick, 2015; Hernann, 2017). While the ubiquity of the concept of privacy leads to huge diversity in the range of themes studied, particularly in the fields of religion, social networks, health, and the body (Engelke, 2012; Scorgie et al., 2016; Horstmann, 2020), the question of privacy in the field of genetics is particularly a concern for bioethics. In this chapter, I devote considered attention to the question of privacy, as it is formulated by senior judges and professionals directly involved in these practices. Tests that seek to establish the visible characteristics raise questions such as: what are the consequences of a framing in terms of privacy, and what does it protect? In a world that is constantly changing with scientific and technological advances, how is this concept redefined in interaction with technology? What social and political relations are exposed or elided by the issue of privacy? In short, we need to examine the effects of conceptions of privacy when corporeal information moves into a semi-public domain through the operation of technologies implemented by agents of the state.[8] In this chapter, I show that not only does technology change normative frameworks but that the frameworks themselves are altered by the existence of new technologies. My key aim is to show that the availability of new tests of appearance, and the focus on the visible, *renders tests that combine crime, origin, and DNA acceptable by depoliticizing them*, and by concealing the process of racialization (Vailly, 2022).

Privacy: a political issue

The evolution of technology, lifestyles, institutions, and norms is continually transforming the concept of privacy. There is a proliferation of formal recognitions and legal texts regarding privacy, leading to what has been called its "irresistible rise" within the hierarchy of norms (Mazeaud, 2015). Despite or because of its recurrent appearance in public debate, there is no single unified definition of privacy. For the purposes of this book, I adopt the following: "a right to privacy is a right to control access to places, bodies, and personal information, and their use" (Katell and Moore, 2016, p. 3). This definition, which places significant emphasis on information, is linked to the growing use of digital data (Steijn and Vedder, 2015). As I pointed out in the introduction, daily invasions of privacy can be observed in the form of new digital technologies, or facial and biometric recognition. Similarly, the ECHR's ruling against France illustrates a conception of privacy increasingly oriented toward *data* and digital information, rather than spaces, relations, or personal decisions. The metaphor of genetic *information*, as conceptualized by geneticists some decades ago, has become a reality that can be stored, used, and revealed, like any other information, and all the more when these data are translated into digital form. However, references to privacy in French law are outdated, being found, for example, in the 1868 law on the press that protected "family secrecy" and the "honor" of individuals (Halpérin, 2015). The aim even then was to control information, but in the older sense of information about an individual published in the press.

The concept of privacy has a long history in philosophical debate, starting with Aristotle, who distinguished public life, associated with political activity, from the private sphere, associated with family and domestic life. Today many studies focus on the individual interests that privacy ought to protect (autonomy, choice, etc.), while a few emphasize the need to take into account social values relating to this issue (Regan, 1995; Solove, 2002; Roessler and Mokrosinska, 2015). Understood in this way, privacy is not only an individual prerogative but also one of the values that we collectively feel should be protected (Solove, 2002).

The aspect of privacy that is not only collective but also political is often overlooked in studies of the subject. It emerges in a context where, notwithstanding claims that technology is objective and apolitical, social scientists have long shown that this is not the case (see especially Schramm et al., 2012). In the context of genetic profiling, privacy becomes a political concern in two ways. Firstly, privacy may be linked to political life when groups of people of a given "origin," rather than individuals, are targeted by police investigations, thereby raising a question for regulation in this field. In this respect, Hannah Arendt (2005, pp. 93, 94, 96) defines politics as follows:

> Politics deals with the coexistence and association of different men. [...] Man [...] exists – or is realized – in politics only in the equal rights that those who are most different guarantee for each other. [...] From the very start, politics organizes those who are absolutely different with a view to their relative equality and in contradistinction to their relative differences.

From this point of view, one thread of the work I present here will be to show that the concept of privacy is coherent and useful, but that it is interwoven with other important concepts arising in political life, such as discrimination and equality of treatment between individuals. In this sense, I do not follow those who critique the notion of privacy on the grounds that it is not a distinct concept and can be reduced to other concepts such as property or freedom (DeCew, 2018).

The second thread relates to the principle of proportionality, which the ECHR advocated should be properly taken into account in the administration of criminal justice. Proportionality is a method applied in many constitutional jurisdictions throughout the world (Tsakyrakis, 2009). More specifically, the majority of constitutional courts, like the ECHR, use a definition that divides the principle into three sub-principles. The first is suitability, according to which the measure considered should be more or less suitable for achieving its objective. The second is necessity, according to which, among all the suitable means, the one that least restricts the right or freedom concerned should be selected. The third is proportionality in the strict sense, which argues that the weight of the two opposing sides should be reasonably evaluated: the greater the infringement of a right or freedom, the greater should be the importance of the objective that justifies it. In short, the proportionality of any measure presumes that it is suitable, necessary, and measured in relation to the infringement of rights (Tsakyrakis, 2009). The aim, then, is to find a balance between the imperatives of privacy and other interests, such as crime prevention and public safety. This leads me to consider how the relationship between the imperative of privacy and the need to maintain public safety is discussed in society and implemented. The political dimension becomes apparent when we remember that this balance is a marker of democratic societies and that the principle of proportionality is a principle of moderation of power. In the words of Priscilla Regan (1995, p. 213), "privacy is [...] a public value in that it has value not just to the individual as an individual or to all individuals in common but also to the democratic political system." These remarks having been made, I now turn to consider the *effects of depoliticization of privacy.*

Between secrecy and a vector of equality

In Chapter 3 I described how the issue of genetic origin, used in the context of criminal investigations, was "problematized" in the Foucauldian sense (Foucault, 1988) in the public arena in France. As noted, this culminated in the publication in 2011 of a Ministry of Justice Dispatch prohibiting tests to determine suspects' origin or physical characteristics – a regulation that was overturned by the Court of Cassation in 2014. At a conference, one senior executive of the company that sold the TOGG tests remarked on this subject: "There were high-minded people who wrote newspaper articles [about TOGG tests] and raised a huge public outcry. And today nobody sees it that way" (Company executive 1). One of the questions that arises is therefore what distinguishes the TOGG tests from tests of "visible morphological characteristics," which aroused no serious controversy.

Current practice and how appearance tests became standard

I turn, then, to the current situation. A number of laboratories offer tests of this type in France: two private labs I shall call [Z] and [X], and the National Forensic Police Service (Service national de la police scientifique, SNPS).[9] It was laboratory [Z] that carried out the analysis in the Lyon case, and laboratory [X] that offered the TOGG tests in 2006; the SNPS is, as its name indicates, the state police laboratory. Since 2016–2017, the national gendarmerie's criminal research laboratory has also been working on establishing physical characteristics on the basis of a suspect's DNA. There is one other laboratory that very occasionally offers such analysis, working with old DNA, because the technique is used in paleogenetics to deduce the appearance of prehistoric people. Depending on which laboratory is asked to provide the expert analysis, various indications may be given, including the individual's hair, eye, or skin color, or their "biogeographical origin" (sometimes called "ancestral origin" because it is deduced from what are known as ancestry-informative markers, as I discuss below), defined on a continental or sub-continental level (e.g. Europe, sub-Saharan Africa, South-East Asia, America, or Oceania), as well as predisposition to premature baldness in men, and to freckles. Since the term "origin" is the one most frequently used by social actors, I adopt it here unless otherwise specified. The European VISAGE consortium recently developed other approaches that might eventually be offered, such as eyebrow color, hair texture, and geographical origin for the paternal line. As aging is associated with modifications generated by molecules that attach to DNA (known as epigenetic modifications to distinguish them from modifications of DNA sequences), the individual's age, detected from blood, saliva, sperm, and bone tissue, may be added to this list.[10] Some academic research has shown that in certain cases it is possible to detect epigenetic changes due to habits of consumption, particularly of tobacco, alcohol, or drugs, but these preliminary results are not sufficiently well supported to be used routinely in forensic science and have yet to be regulated by law or ethical guidelines. In the future, the new generation of rapid DNA sequencing, development of which is well under way, should provide still more genetic and phenotypical information, including data relating to health. This will surely raise thorny questions about the regulations that need to be put in place. In 2021, almost three-quarters of European forensic science laboratories already possessed a rapid sequencer, or were planning to buy one within the following two years.[11]

At the time when I conducted my research, the SNPS was processing on average one test of this type per month, with requests almost equally split between judges and police officers; laboratory [Z] was processing one per week, and laboratory [X] a smaller number. In September 2021, the SNPS carried out a total of 65 analyses of this type, 40% in cases of rape, 30% for murder, 9% for armed robbery, just under 8% for identification of bodies, and 14% for other reasons not specified. Depending on the laboratory, the service for testing ready-purified DNA costs between 1,000 and 2,000 euro for hair, eye, and skin color and origin.

By way of a broader overview, in late 2019 the VISAGE consortium drew up a table of the use of these tests in various European countries (Schneider et al., 2019). It revealed three possible situations: in some countries they were authorized by law, in some they were not formally prohibited and were considered to be permitted, and in the remainder they were explicitly or implicitly prohibited. The countries where use was explicitly authorized by law were the

Netherlands (the first to have authorized them) and Slovakia; those where they were conducted in conformity with existing law were Austria, Poland, the Czech Republic, Sweden, Hungary, Spain, and the United Kingdom. Following a change in the law in 2019, Germany now authorizes tests for skin, eye and hair color, and age, but not for origin. In Switzerland the law banned these techniques, but it is currently under review. In Finland legislation is planned, and the situation in France is as discussed above. In Greece, Luxembourg, Portugal, and Slovenia, the tests are banned.

One important point to note is that while laboratories differ in their opinions on which features are appropriate to analyze there is an idea widely shared in France and beyond, and suggested by the Court of Cassation's judgment, that the issue of privacy should be considered from the point of view of *appearance and visibility*: all visible information is public, all non-visible information is private. Thus all the physical morphological characteristics that it is possible to observe in an individual, either in the street or in a photograph, may be analyzed because they are not intrusive. As the examining magistrate in the Lyon rapist case explained: "Everyone knows I have an olive complexion, it's hardly a revelation, it's not something personal in the sense of it being secret or intimate. It's something that's clear for everyone to see" (Judge 9). This assertion, which appears self-evident, calls for some comment.

Courts throughout the world regularly articulate the reasoning that once a fact is divulged in public, however limited or narrow the disclosure, it can no longer remain private. Thus according to a judgment rendered in the United States, "what a person knowingly exposes in public" cannot give rise to expectations of constitutional privacy (Fox, 2010, p. 59).[12] In a general sense, this conception of privacy, which is shared by a majority of those concerned in France, and was suggested by the Court of Cassation, assimilates it to complete secrecy of information, the opposite of "everything that is visible is public" (Solove, 2002). Privacy as understood in this sense sits alongside the notion of "intimacy" ("something personal in the sense of it being secret or intimate," says the judge), which, by definition, is not something to be shared with all and sundry. It is worth pointing out that this position passes over the fact that people may wish to keep information private from some people and not others, but also at some times and not all the time. As Solove (2002) argues, the books we read, the people we associate with are not often thought of as secret, but we generally see them as private matters.

Aside from the shared outlook on visibility, one question left unexamined by the Court of Cassation's succinct ruling is whether people's geographical origin forms part of their visible characteristics. In the absence of any more specific legislative framework, each laboratory creates its own standards in this respect, and some divergences are apparent. Like most people we interviewed, the heads of SNPS and laboratory [X], which offered the TOGG tests, include origin among the visible characteristics. As with other detectable characteristics, a parallel is often drawn with everyday eyewitness testimony. One example was given by a gendarme, who represented the test as run-of-the-mill, arguing that it would not provide any information different from what an eyewitness might offer: "You pass a Black man in the street, you say: he's black. I don't see the problem, as long as you keep to what's visible" (Gendarme 4). This analogy with eyewitnesses is also argued by geneticists in the biomedical literature, thereby drawing the focus away from the genetic approach.[13] Recalling the arguments of those who promoted the TOGG tests, and presented as a simple piece of evidence devoid of racism, this datum is portrayed as neutral and not aimed at targeting any particular group. In this way, my interviewees establish a connection between appearance and racial categories as commonly understood ("Black"), trying to leave genetics temporarily aside despite the fact that this is impossible because these categories are established on the basis of genetics. Like TOGG tests, these genetic appearance tests that include origin place it in relation to appearance, racial categories as commonly understood and, whether explicitly or not, with genetic ancestry.

Interviewees put forward a number of other arguments to support their position in favor of origin tests. First, police officers and examining magistrates emphasize the unreliability of eyewitnesses, who often have an emotional reaction to violence. Their other argument stems from their desire to move their inquiry forward, the imperative to arrest perpetrators of serial crimes, and to position themselves firmly "on the side of the victims." In this way, they adopt a pragmatic point of view that emphasizes the everyday, routine aspects of criminal investigation and the need to make use of all information at a crime scene (Williams and Johnson, 2004). Finally, geneticists who study origin argue that their analysis will be better if they are allowed to supplement their results with this information, rather than stopping at information on skin color, for example. This position is not an outcome of their professional activity, because its supporters are to be found among both geneticists and police officers and judges.

An alternative view: the problem of stigmatization

The point of view described above is contested by an alternative position, which argues that the conception of privacy is shaped not only by legislation and case law (precedents involving visible features), and technology (DNA tests), but also by extra-legal norms, such as those upheld by the CEO of laboratory [Z]. In the 2000s, he had applied to the Ministry of Justice for authorization of the study of "the physical characteristics of suspects" – a request that was refused by the 2011 Dispatch. Having defied the ministry's ban by carrying out the genetic analysis of eye, hair, and skin color in the Lyon case but no doubt wary following the experience of the TOGG tests, this executive argued for a restrictive definition of visible characteristics: in his view, origin deduced from ancestry markers should not be examined in the search for suspects. "A person's ancestral origin, that's part of private life, of the person's history, so I don't work on that" (Company executive 3), he stated at a hearing the National Consultative Committee on Human Rights (Commission nationale consultative des droits de l'Homme, CNCDH) held on this issue. As if in echo to the TOGG controversy, he added that as a biologist he was "a prisoner of the culture and history of my country," citing the tragedies that Europe had suffered and alluding indirectly to the registers of Jews during World War Two. Thus he positioned himself as an "ethical subject" (Foucault, 1997) concerned with moral problems. Given that he was equally concerned for the image of his company, his position should not lead us to forget that entrepreneurs' statements about privacy are designed to contribute to shaping public perceptions of the technology they develop and making it acceptable (Kudina and Verbeek, 2019).

This entrepreneur was not the only person in France who saw origin tests as a problem. Some senior judges involved in the debate expressed strong reservations about them, and indeed sometimes about other tests of skin or hair color. These judges, though few in number – and distinct from those who argued against the TOGG tests but did not participate in public debate around tests of visible characteristics – saw the new tests as dangerous. One of them, a leading French judge, defined criminal investigation procedure as a set of limitations on the rights of the judge (and, we might add, of the police officer) to enter the home and telephone records of individuals but also their body, their thoughts, and their DNA. He stressed the need for an institution that would place limits on such intrusion, particularly in the domain of DNA, which, he said, touched on "people's essence." The essentialization at work here illustrates DNA's position as "cultural icon" (Nelkin and Lindee, 1994), although most geneticists in the world today have a more measured perception of the relative importance of genetics and environment (Lock, 2013). Nevertheless, such essentialization is still today one of the reasons that the study of DNA remains a "sensitive" question, in the view of these judges, particularly any analysis that seeks to predict the population group to which the suspect belongs. As one of them put it in interview: "If in a rape case, like this one, they say: 'the perpetrator is black', that poses a serious ethical problem. The entire black population is thereby stigmatized" (Judge 10).

This position invites comment on two fronts. First, the problem is once again expressed in terms of a commonly understood racial category, but this time with the added risk of stigmatization. As noted above, in the view of Peter Wade (2014; see also Sen and Wasow, 2014), phenomena that can be described as "racial" are based partly on nature/heredity and the way it is expressed through appearance, and partly rooted in geographical and historical circumstances characterized by domination. Thus, as in the case of the TOGG tests, these interviewees indirectly raise the problem of racialization through three elements constitutive of racial theories as outlined by Wade – nature/heredity (today reformulated as genetic ancestry), appearance, and domination/stigmatization. Secondly, the concern formulated with regard to these tests is that even if they are applied to the perpetrator of a particular offense linked to specific criminal acts, they target the *population* she/he represents. This once again raises the fact that the question of privacy concerns not only interpersonal relations but also groups and communities: personal information rarely belongs to a single individual and is often formulated in relation to other individuals (Anthony et al., 2017). From this point of view, it is worth remembering that in France, in the United States, and elsewhere, among racialized populations the individual always represents the collective, whereas the privilege of "whiteness" is to be perceived as a simple individual and not as the representative of a population. More generally, it is impossible to analyze these questions without taking into account unequal, and therefore discriminatory, treatment based on skin color and appearance in the criminal justice system, regardless of genetic definitions: the probability of being stopped by the police, of receiving a prison sentence, etc. (Alexander, 2010; Fassin, 2013). One study in France showed that where all other things are equal, minorities are stopped more often than white people on the basis of appearance, which combines sex, age, type of bag carried, clothing, and skin color (Jobard et al., 2012). In the United States, Sheldon Krimsky and Tania Simoncelli (2011) showed that racial disparities are well established at various levels of the criminal justice system, particularly with regard to arrests but also prosecutions and convictions. It could, of course, be pointed out that traditional police searches were already discriminatory, and that these tests are nothing new in this respect. I shall return to this point in the final part of this chapter.

To sum up this section, there is a tension between the majority position that genetic tests should become standard procedure, on the basis that they deal with visible characteristics, and the "sensitive" question of commonly understood racial categories. While the polysemy of the term "privacy" means that different authors conceptualize it differently, here my interviewees associate it in one case with what is *secret* (the opposite of "all that is visible is public") and in the other with the absence of discrimination and stigmatization, in other words with *equality*. How are these two positions to be further analyzed? My aim is not to homogenize opinions and the social positions of those who hold them, which as we have seen are diverse, but to analyze their meaning. Sociologist Mark Brown (2015) argues that situations become political when people contest the power relations associated with them, and become non-political when such contestations are eliminated or transformed into relations based on routine or habit. This corresponds to the two positions observed in my research. While the majority conception of privacy *touches* on a political domain (security as instigated by agents of the state), it *is* depoliticized in the sense that it ignores the questions of equality and diversity between individuals of diverse "origins" (remembering Arendt's phrase, "Politics deals with the coexistence and association of different men. [...] Man [...] exists – or is realized – in politics only in the equal rights that those who are most different guarantee for each other"). In other words, even though the notion of privacy is widely articulated in public policy and legislation, the majority *conception* of it ignores its political effects. The euphemization and evasion of controversy rests on tests that are deemed to provide only known, neutral details, avoiding power relations and racism. Moreover, it aligns with the notion of "intimacy" and being hidden from *view* (what can be seen by others). This can be compared with Arendt's view (1998 [1958], pp. 62, 69) that what today we call "private" is in fact reduced to "intimacy," which seems a flight from the outer world, a refuge sought by individuals, sheltered from the prying eyes of others.

By contrast, the minority conception of privacy makes space for power relations and articulates the political concerns of risk of discrimination and stigmatization raised by this practice. Associating the risk of stigmatization with appearance and heredity, it indirectly highlights issues of racialization. The burden therefore weighs more heavily on the discriminated or stigmatized group than on the criminal. In other words, there is indeed an issue of privacy, but it is articulated with other questions such as equality and discrimination. Privacy, in this sense, is not only an individual value but is also involved in relations that enable societies to function by limiting discrimination. In short, adopting a conception that takes into account the political dimension of privacy, as suggested by my frame of analysis and as the minority position does, allows us to grasp the issue of racialization. Taking this argument further, the following sections reveal the process of racialization linked to a relatively depoliticized understanding of privacy, first in the domain of science and then in the dissemination of information.

The norm defined in terms of the visible: unanswered questions

The approach formulated in terms of visible appearance is shared by other countries such as the Netherlands, where an amendment to the law in 2003 authorized the identification of "externally observable characteristics," including "race" (according to the official terminology).[14] "Phenotyping," the term often used for these techniques, which may or may not include so-called "origin" tests depending on the author, suggests the same idea because the phenotype is by definition the set of observable characteristics of an individual or an organism. Given that the visible is central in accounting for how privacy is understood, in this section I address how the visible (viewed as public) and origin (viewed by some as public, by others as private) are articulated. On this basis, I reveal the scientific ground on which racialization is produced by a conception of privacy that focuses on appearance.

The visible and DNA

First of all, I describe the technical details of how this circulation between what is visible, materialized by the exterior of the body, and DNA, representing the interior, actually operates. Geneticists use different genetic markers, some variations of which may be associated with the trait being studied. Analysis of several regions of DNA helps to establish a statistical prediction for each of these characteristics: a probability of belonging to a group of individuals who, for example, have black eyes. On the basis of this probability, the individual can be placed on a scale of skin, eye, and hair color, in a more or less standardized and measurable form. It may be noted in passing that analysis of eye, skin, and hair color is based on SNP (Single Nucleotide Polymorphism) markers that are located in coding DNA, or sometimes in non-coding DNA. In other words, coding or non-coding DNA is no longer a subject of concern when it comes to phenotyping, despite the scientific and political debates around it with regard to genetic profiling, discussed in earlier chapters. In the most widely used model, HIrisPlex, geneticists use 6 markers for eye color, around 20 for hair color, and about 40 for skin color (the number and nature of the markers used varies from one laboratory to another). Since the analytical method is based on statistics and probabilities, some uncertainty, which geneticists strive to reduce to a minimum, remains. While the stated reliability of tests may be high (between 70 and 95%), prediction of blue or black eyes in particular is more reliable than that of intermediate colors, since the reliability of a predictive test depends on a number of factors (the more or less heritable nature of the trait analyzed, the choice and number of SNPs, the statistical model used). For hair color, the predicted color relates to color in childhood and cannot establish whether an individual's hair has darkened in adolescence, changing from blond to brown, for example.

In the case of origin, analysis focuses on ancestry markers, most of which are located in non-coding DNA. These usually show variations that are not specific but more common in certain world populations, with an accuracy on the continental or occasionally sub-continental level, although some, which are more genetically informative, are specific to certain continents or populations. The SNPS geneticists, for example, use 46 genetic markers (including those known as InDel) developed by researchers at the University of Compostela and an algorithm for statistical analysis of the results. On this basis they position the suspect's DNA in relation to a system of scatter plots that forms a graphic representation of the reference populations – African, European, Asiatic, Oceanian, and Amerindian. In these scatter plots, each point color represents a "biogeographical origin" (bearing in mind, for example, that a "white" North American or Australian would be considered European). The test has a stated reliability of 95%, although people of mixed heritage are harder to interpret. The VISAGE consortium has developed a tool with 225 markers (mostly SNPs). It uses seven reference populations because it distinguishes Middle Eastern populations and divides Asiatic populations into two groups, East Asians and South Asians. The issue of reference populations is complex because the research and the reference groups are often drawn from European populations. In order achieve greater accuracy, geneticists are working to create diagrams of populations defined more narrowly than at continental level but in 2021 still said they did not have enough individuals for each given region. One geneticist told me: "The concern is […] that some regions of the world are not covered at all by these references" (Geneticist 2). She added: "And even leaving that aside it's still complicated because what does 'reference population' mean?" given that there is wide genetic variability within continents and that the population used as a reference is always an arbitrary choice. The scientific limitations of this approach are thus evident. Nevertheless, when the DNA tested sits in the middle of the scatter plot, according to the geneticists it indicates a very strong probability that the person originates from the corresponding region. If the DNA sits in an intermediate position between two or more plots, visible in a three-dimensional representation, this indicates that it is a mix. However, complex mixes are difficult to interpret. Moreover, geneticists point out that they cannot determine when the mixing took place, and therefore cannot know whether it occurred in the preceding generation or is the product of an ancient mix of populations in a region of the world where such admixtures are frequent.

Through analysis of the relationship between the visible and DNA, we gain a clearer sense of the place of vision in the concept of privacy and in racialization. On a broader level, Rebecca Coleman and Liz Oakley-Brown (2017, p. 11), explain how "the visible outside part of a body" gave rise to the word "surface" in France in the 14th century. Moreover, if vision and surfaces are mutually articulated, the molecularization of appearance and origin leads both to a transition from phenotype (the visible, surface) to genotype (DNA, interiority), as has been described in the field of biomedical research (Abu El-Haj, 2007), and to an inverse movement from genotype to phenotype. In other words, what we are concerned with is not "a surface [that] presents a form" but rather "an interface [that] performs a shaping" (Hookway, 1988, p. 14), or with "folds" between exterior and interior (Coleman and Oakley-Brown, 2017). Understanding the role played by vision as new ways of using DNA are developed thus invites us to step beyond the traditional dichotomies between interior and exterior, visible and invisible, because the surface may operate not only as a line of demarcation but also as a fold between exterior and interior. Visible appearance as deduced from DNA, then, reveals the complexity of the relationship between public life and privacy when it is perceived through appearance, as the following section illustrates.

Relationships between appearance and origin

One question faced by all specialists studying origin is that of how far it is possible to assert that origin is visible and, inversely, that what is visible gives an indication of origin. With regard to the visibility of origin, one aspect appeared to be self-evident to those we interviewed – what academics call "somatic norms" (Skinner, 2020 [2019]): "The morphotype is visible from the outside, if you take it on a basic level, when I see an Asian, I know they're Asian," says one gendarme (Gendarme 4). Where information on appearance and origin match, the specialists' job is made easier. One geneticist described the "easy" example of a "true Breton, really of West European origin, the western coast of France [or] the British Isles, generally with brown hair, brown eyes, but pale skin" (Company executive 1).

Nevertheless, the geneticists also offered examples where there was a mismatch between origin and phenotype. One cited the case of a woman from

Réunion "who looked like a typical Réunion woman" but whose DNA revealed a genetic profile situated in the center of the European cluster. Another example was that of a Melanesian population, 10% of whose members are light-skinned blonds. This is due largely to the fact that the ancestry markers, located in "non-coding" zones of DNA as I noted above, represent complex historical traces of evolution and population mixing and are not all related to visible characteristics (Abu El-Haj, 2012). Clearly, then, at molecular level, some elements of origin may overlap with aspects of appearance but others not. This is why basing the norm on the visible, while using ancestry markers that are by no means all related to appearance, is not a valid approach.

Conversely, with regard to how appearance indicates origin, one judge we interviewed pointed out that the type known as "Indian" is found in various regions of the world including Bali, Madagascar, Réunion, and Mauritius. Backing up this comment, a geneticist working with the forensic police explained that genetic markers located in genes that code for the skin pigment melanin may be the same in Africans, Malagasy people, and Indians. Indeed, an article on genetics published in the prestigious journal *Science* notes that virtually all of the variants associated with dark pigmentation among Africans are identical to those found in South Asia and in Australo-Melanesian populations.[15] This article notes both a molecular convergence between the populations of various countries in the world through adaptation to the environment, and inheritance of genetic variants associated with dark pigmentation, probably brought long ago by people who migrated from Africa. One of the researchers at the center of this research in the Netherlands argues:

> the assumption that the geographic region(s) where the genetic ancestors of a person originate is manifested in the person's appearance does not always hold true. [...] Extrapolating human appearance information from DNA-based biogeographic ancestry information is very difficult, if not impossible, for people of mixed genetic origins (with ancestors from different regions). Currently, there is no scientific understanding about the relationship between genetic admixture and appearance trait manifestation whatsoever.[16]

Taking a more sociological approach, we can expand on Simmel's argument (1955 [1922]) that the individual affiliated with several groups thereby at the same time *escapes* these groups: the person with brown skin sits at the intersection of several groups and escapes geographic categories. Moreover, being part of a group becomes simultaneously a confrontation with that group when there is a mismatch between origin and visible characteristics (a person from Réunion located in the European cluster). The fact that individuals escape categories weakens the existence of those categories, making their boundaries porous. In what follows, I examine some of the consequences of this in terms of racialization.

To sum up, on the one hand the division between interior and exterior is far from simple when we consider diverse regions of DNA; on the other, origin and appearance often match, but not always, introducing a further level of complex interrelation between DNA and the visible. Defining privacy in terms of the visible therefore encounters problems, and indeed contradictions, because it ignores the fact that in this situation the visible is constituted by its relationship to technology (Coleman and Oakley-Brown, 2017). This makes it difficult to maintain the position outlined above, which links privacy with the secret and the norm of good practice with appearance. Once the interior is visible and the visible does or does not match the interior it becomes difficult to restrict DNA analysis to appearance.

The fact that there is no automatic correspondence between appearance and origin, and the existence of individuals who escape groups, ought to support a process of deracialization, since the link between appearance, origin, and genetics (and leaving the issue of stigmatization aside for the moment) becomes more elastic. Yet despite these examples of mismatches, geneticists continue to try to differentiate populations. One forensic police report states, almost in a tone of regret: "It is important to point out that human populations originating from North Africa and the Middle East are genetically very close to European populations. They cannot be differentiated using this method." Another geneticist says: "the more people get on, the worse it is for geneticists: people mix, that's fantastic, but for us it's really complicated" (Geneticist 2). Here science seems to rest on the assumption that in the past there was no contact between human populations living on different continents, whereas it is known that populations have been mixing since the dawn of time (Marks, 2013), as demonstrated by the issue of variants of dark skin discussed above. On the one hand, geneticists' scientific analysis sometimes seems to bring populations closer together when they struggle to differentiate them genetically; for example, people from North Africa or the Near East in relation to European populations. However, these studies more often rigidify populations by seeking to define their boundaries more precisely and differentiate them through DNA. Importantly, too, their analytical categories are still at continental level and thus, like the TOGG tests, help to perpetuate imaginaries of "race" because of the way geographical and racial concepts can overlap topographically (Africa/Black, Europe/White, etc.). Globally, despite substantial scientific evidence to the contrary, geneticists' continued efforts to demarcate populations, and their use of continent-level categories, contribute to processes of racialization. Thus the approach that addresses privacy in terms of the visible but includes origin offers an arena for deeper investigation of, in Didier Fassin's words (2011, p. 421), "how bodies become racialized" (transposed to the present case, this would relate to the visible, which often, but not always, indicates continent-level origin) and how "origin is embodied" (which here could be translated in terms of a continent-level origin, which is often, but not always, inscribed in the visible). Fassin's study focuses on domains outside of science, and therefore not linked to genetics, exposing what he calls the "basic structures of racial embodiment." The following section shows how this process persists when we move beyond the scientific arena, particularly in the absence of safeguards in terms of proportionality.

Communicating information about origin

The political dimension of privacy discussed above is amplified by the *communication* of information about an individual. The information that needs to be considered here varies not only with the shift from one group of individuals to another (from the average citizen to the criminal) but also when the frame of reference shifts from one context to another (from the world of science to that of criminal investigation or the media) (Baghai, 2012). This raises the question of how the results of genetic analysis are communicated internally (within the police and justice system) and externally (particularly through the media), in other words to anyone who is observing, commenting on, and interpreting the data provided.

Internal communication

The first of these is the police officer or judge who commissioned the analysis. An SNPS geneticist we interviewed spoke of the need to make a very precise choice of terms when professionals are communicating with one another or with those on the outside. He makes a link between communication of results and his efforts to persuade the police officers he is in contact with to stop referring to "races":

> That's why I try to re-educate police officers about the term race, because it horrifies me. [...] Sometimes I have officers who call me for information about a genetic photofit and say: 'his race is black.' I try to give them a bit of genetics and populations 101, that there are no such thing as races, we are one human race, but it's ingrained in their subconscious and it's complicated to explain.
>
> *(Geneticist 3)*

As in the case of TOGG tests, and like other geneticists throughout the world (Fujimura and Rajagopalan, 2011; Abu El-Haj, 2012), French genetics experts argue for a form of taking genetic "origins" into account that does not involve race. This also highlights the difference between the point of view of the SNPS geneticist and the police officers who readily talk about race. And the way police officers understand, see, and speak of suspects shapes racial identities. The everyday practices of police officers reinforce the routinized idea of race, as one detective suggests:

> In a genetic profile, if the people are wearing hoods, I'm not really shocked if I'm told they're black.
>
> (Interviewer): You mean, in everyday practice, that's information that's already used?
>
> Yes, and what's more it's explicitly permitted. It's even semantically labeled, so you can say 'North African,' you can say 'of black race,' you

> can say 'Asian,' [...]. There are types that are referred to and you can use those terms specifically.
>
> *(Police officer 9)*

The position expressed by this detective calls for a number of remarks. First, these statements are corroborated, in different terms, by the fact that the Traitement d'antécédents judiciaires (Criminal Records Database, TAJ), which contains around 19 million records of individuals questioned under caution or charged in criminal investigations, victims, and missing persons, "may include information on origin, as a description."[17] Second, this position articulates a slippage from the term "origin" to that of "race," despite the often sensitive nature of this term in France. By making the term routine, it seeks to deconstruct the problematization posed by the geneticist cited above. It reintroduces a familiarity of use, contrasting with the "loss of familiarity" (Foucault, 1984), in other words the novelty of these genetic tests. In doing so, it fails to analyze the place of science in these practices and the way it can lend legitimacy to a scientific connection between appearance, continent-level origin, and heredity. Furthermore, it passes over the way the information is gathered. In fact, when the information is gathered in the street on the basis of verbal testimony, the relationship to privacy is different from when it is sourced from DNA. The technique that seeks to determine facial morphology on the basis of DNA, which the SNPS claims to be following "with great interest," makes this clear. If it one day became possible to reconstitute a face on the basis of DNA that could be detected *anywhere* and *at any moment in time*, wherever an individual has been (given that DNA is relatively stable over time), such an extension of genetic appearance tests would suggest that privacy also depends on *accessibility* of information. Then there might also be situations where DNA found at a crime scene proved to be that of a different, non-suspect individual, who would be subjected to an intrusion into their genome. A form of "genetic transparency," by analogy with "digital transparency" (Harcourt, 2020 [2015], p. 29, see also M'charek, 2020), would appear to be the goal. From this point of view, it is interesting to note that in the United States, for example, there is no federal law against undeclared gathering of DNA. Only a handful of states forbid the analysis of DNA outside of criminal investigations without the consent of the individual concerned: in other words, in most US states, in contrast to France, unauthorized individuals may gather and analyze the DNA of other individuals without informing those concerned.[18] Finally, this viewpoint ignores the issues of communication and use of these data.

Dissemination in the media

A further aspect of privacy relates to dissemination of information to the outside, particularly via the media, which contributes much to blurring the boundary between public and private. Like the SNPS geneticist quoted above, a number of those we interviewed who were in favor of appearance tests are quite attentive to the question of external communication of results (at least two of them clearly expressed this). Nevertheless, the difficulty of controlling such information can be gauged from the high level of media interest in this approach. As early as 2009, a national television channel reported on its prime-time news bulletin:

> Using a single hair or a drop of dried blood, a DNA trace, it is possible to establish an individual's region of origin in the world, and therefore to know their eye or skin color. [...] Depending on whether you come from Europe, Africa, Asia, or America, you will have more of certain markers than others, making it possible to determine the origin of an individual, or actually of their ancestors. [...] A test that was used [...] in the case of Coulibaly [the photo of a young black man appears], a serial rapist.
>
> *(France 2, 8.00 pm news bulletin)*

Here the link between region of origin and skin color is presented as self-evident, contrary to the evidence presented above and feeding the process of racialization ("and *therefore* to know their skin or eye color"). This raises questions not so much about the information provided but about what it implies for public understanding of the relationships between appearance, origin, heredity, and crime. It shows once again that the problem of privacy arises when an event in a given social world is communicated to another world; for example, when individuals' origin moves from a scientific arena to that of the police and justice system, and then to the media. Whether a question is public or private is not only a matter of its content but also of its pertinence in the social world in question – and a complete separation between social worlds is impossible (Baghai, 2012). Here, for example, the journalist publicizes the principle, use, and result of the test, as well as the name and photograph of the perpetrator of crimes, giving the process a public life.

This process is further fueled by the second problem that such appearance tests raise for human and social sciences concerned with political issues – the question of *proportionality* between invasion of privacy and the objective of maintaining security. In the first place, while it does not encompass the complexity of the issues, the question of how useful the technique really is in investigations remains, given that in various cases where it was used in France the perpetrators were often identified by other investigative techniques. However, in some cases, the use of origin tests has helped to whittle down the number of potential suspects, has made it possible to identify the group to which an unidentified body belongs, to close down a false trail, or has validated results after the event. One detective told us how in one case it acted as "a filter," allowing them to reduce the number of suspects from 600 to 13 individuals of a given "biogeographical origin." However, overall this approach today appears to represent a promise or hope rather than being fully backed up by experience. As the head of one biotechnology laboratory told us: "the number of cases where this technology is applicable is not large" (Company executive 1). Furthermore, one way of retaining a degree of proportionality and curbing potential excessive interference in privacy is – at the very least – to regulate the use of such tests through the law or ministerial guidelines. Most of those we interviewed advocate for the tests to be used within a regulatory framework specified in law, and they pointed to a number of aspects that need to be regulated. The first concerns the methods of gathering, processing, and storing samples and data from expert analysis – an aspect that may be aligned with the communication of information, as discussed above. The second aspect concerns the offenses to which such a measure should be applied, in the concern to ensure a degree of proportionality between intrusion into the genome and the importance of identifying a suspect. Our interviewees broadly shared the idea that this technique should be reserved for the most serious crimes (rape, murder, armed robbery), rather than being used to identify the perpetrator of a simple theft. In this view, preservation of privacy involves ensuring that personal information is used within the regulations and in relation to the perceived importance of the objective. Today, however, the legal basis for use of these tests in France rests purely on the Court of Cassation ruling, which authorizes them without specifying any safeguards or criteria of proportionality with regard to any resulting invasion of privacy. The Court has not ruled on criteria of appropriateness or necessity, still less on proportionality in the strict sense discussed above, or on the relationship between public safety and civil liberties. Yet rejecting proportionality exposes France once more to ECHR judgments against it on grounds of infringement of the right to private life, following those relating to the FNAEG, the FAED, and police telephone tapping.[19] More generally, in the digital domain, private companies' use of data is often for commercial purposes, and Harcourt's remark (2020 [2015]) that an economic cost-benefit logic prevails seems entirely justified. In the domain of genetic tests used by the police, one of the key issues of proportionality is, rather, in my view, that of democratic balance, an issue the Court of Cassation ignores. In this sense, the Court obscures the political dimension addressed in the early part of this chapter, of the proportionality of practices in democratic societies. This lack of a regulatory framework means that tests can be used without any restriction apart from appearance, thus fostering the process of racialization.

* * *

As a general rule, emergent technologies, with the hopes and fears they bring with them, often raise new debates and shed unaccustomed light on norms that seem to go without saying (Kudina and Verbeek, 2019). In this situation, the reverse is the case because there is a lack of debate, and an emerging technology is rendered invisible as it becomes routine. Furthermore, comparison of the TOGG tests, which provoked controversy, and tests of visible characteristics, which have been validated by the Court of Cassation and are being developed without giving rise to any marked public opposition, speaks volumes. It helps to clarify the dynamics and effects of interaction between technology and normative frameworks, as represented in particular by case law from the Court of Cassation. Here we see that not only does technology change normative frameworks (from the ban in the 2011 Dispatch to authorization under the Court's ruling), but also the frameworks are themselves modified by new technologies. The fact that new tests of appearance are available, and focusing on the visible, *renders tests of origin acceptable, without the combination of crime, DNA, and origin being as controversial and explosive as it was in the case of TOGG tests*. The principles forming the basis for evaluation of these tests are coproduced by scientific approaches that purport to reveal only appearance, and by the familiar use of descriptions of suspects in terms of skin color, for example. By retracing these dynamics and shifts, I have shown how an understanding of privacy rooted in "visible characteristics" has been reinvented in the interaction between technology, laboratories, private enterprise, the police, and the justice system. This allows for a critical analysis of the political and "moral mediation" enabled by these technologies – in other words, the implications of technologies for practices, how they are perceived, and the normative frameworks regarding privacy that govern their use (Kudina and Verbeek, 2019).

Such technological mediation of information based on appearance is made possible by a majority conception of privacy that elides both stigmatization and racialization, and the idea of proportionality. With regard to stigmatization and racialization, there are contradictions in the relationship between origin and appearance: basing the norm on the visible by using ancestry markers that are by no means all linked to appearance is not a valid approach. Despite this paradox, and the fact that geneticists deny the existence of race, these tests, like the TOGG tests, help to perpetuate and expand ways of thinking that insist on differences passed down through generations and visible in bodies, aligned with continental categories. In so doing, they disseminate the idea that "racial" differences are a biological given rather than a "bundle of sticks" (Sen and Wasow, 2014) made up of ideas of heredity, appearance, power relations, and geographical and historical inheritance. Moreover, this majority conception of privacy operates in a country that makes equality one of its cornerstones, apparently working from the principle that everyone enters the justice system on an equal footing, when this is not the case (Alexander, 2010; Fassin, 2013). Interestingly, these lines are being drawn at a time of raging controversy over racist practices and discourses within the police, in both France and the United States.[20] These debates remind us that tests of origin and appearance are set against a background of frequent tension between the police and people subject to racism, even if this is denied by the vast majority of police officers and the social world of the police is broadly heterogeneous.[21] As Dorota Mokrosinska (2015, p. 189) points out, "the integrity of liberal politics presupposes a domain of privacy that removes from the collective attention material that is incompatible with the commitment to equal freedom, such as racism [...]." The minority position that highlights the risks of stigmatization is virtually erased from public debate. In light of these various considerations, we may hypothesize that

France is a country living under the illusion that equality prevails, partly preventing it from considering the problems raised by such genetic tests.

However, it is worth pointing out that in some countries origin tests are beginning to be conducted at the sub-continental level (Eastern Europe, South Asia, etc.). Will this undermine some of the foundations of the claimed biological origin of "races" in society? It will evidently not prevent stigmatization, as the following example shows. In Germany, an origin test conducted after a series of murders established that the perpetrator was probably from Eastern Europe. Added to the evident mobility of the perpetrator, this was interpreted by the police and reported by the media and in public discussion as a sign of crimes committed by an individual from the community of "gypsies" or "Travelers" from Eastern Europe, stigmatizing this group. In 2012, when the trace was shown to be an artifact from an employee of the company that made the cotton buds used for sampling, who came from Eastern Europe, the Interior Minister of the state of Baden-Württemberg apologized to the Sinti and Roma communities for the erroneous interpretation of the DNA trace (Lipphardt et al., 2017). This reveals the tendencies that nevertheless do not lead to radically different techniques or to elimination of the risks of stigmatization.

By highlighting the process of racialization and stigmatization, we can grasp and evaluate what is at stake in assessing the proportionality of a practice, between infringement of privacy and its effects and the search for offenders and protection of public order. The second issue elided by the Court of Cassation is that of proportionality. This elision leads to a lack of legal safeguards around retention and gathering of data and the conditions under which these tests are used, thus supporting their more widespread application. As a general rule, privacy norms depend on a range of contextual factors such as the individual's characteristics, the level of perceived threat to society, the objective pursued, and the way the information is used. Crimes are, by definition, acts of deviance that in themselves violate legal norms. In this context, it appears that privacy as conceived by the Court of Cassation, and its corollary, the risk of stigmatization and racialization, is being exchanged for technical tools to be used by the police and justice system. According to Adam Moore (2000), opinions that trade respect for privacy in exchange for security set up a false balance and, in many cases, erode both privacy and security. To go further, it is worth emphasizing that a broader conception of privacy that takes proportionality into account raises questions in terms of "weight" or "measure" of the interests involved (in justice, the symbol of the scales itself conveys a quest for precision in judgment). What is measured (interests, principles, rights ...)? How is it measured (with what instrument)? Who should carry out this measurement (the judge, the legislator ...)? Some authors raise the problem of how values and rights that are in conflict can be measured using a common metric, when they are incommensurable (Tsakyrakis, 2009). I would argue for a degree of measurability that takes note of the absence of a common metric to measure proportionality but makes it possible, at least in the case I focus on here, to place values and rights in relationship with one another (the problem of racialization and stigmatization above an investigation technique). In short, this notion of proportionality helps to outline a broad conception of privacy that takes into account its impact on the functioning of societies. While much research into privacy focuses on the effects on individuals, the work described here emphasizes the consequences changing privacy norms may have for the political functioning of societies.

Notes

1 *La chambre de l'instruction* – a division of the Court of Appeal that rules on decisions made by examining magistrates and sentencing judges [translator].
2 Judgment no. 3280 of June 25 2014.
3 See https://hirisplex.erasmusmc.nl/ (accessed June 21 2019).
4 This consortium, of thirteen partner organizations from various European countries, aimed to harmonize methods of analysis in European laboratories and to offer them tools validated by scientific articles and developed in active collaboration with universities. See https://cordis.europa.eu/project/id/740580 (accessed August 4 2023).
5 Claes, P., Hill, H., & Shriver, M. D. (2014). Toward DNA-based facial composites: Preliminary results and validation. *Forensic Science International Genetics, 13*, 208–216.
6 Wee, S.-L., & Mozur, P. (2019, December 3). China uses DNA to map faces, with help from the West. *The New York Times*, and Wee, S.-L. (2021, September 9). Two scientific journals retract articles involving Chinese DNA research, *The New York Times.*
7 As early as 1996, a group of bioethicists in the United States published a report titled *The genetic privacy act: A proposal for national legislation*, which can be found today on a website that lists research into protection of genome privacy. See https://genomeprivacy.org/ (accessed May 16 2019).
8 This discussion does not address the issue of medical information.
9 The Service national de la police scientifique was formed in 2021 by the merger of the Institut national de la police scientifique (National Institute of Forensic Police, INPS) and the Service central de la police technique et scientifique (Central Technical and Forensic Police Service, SCPTS).
10 Today geneticists estimate the average margin of error in such age evaluations to be around four years, though with wide variability of error possible, depending on the individual and assuming the availability of a substantial quantity of tissue.
11 Gross, T. E., Fleckhauss, J., & Schneider, P. M. (2021). Progress in the implementation of massively parallel sequencing for forensic genetics: Results of a European-wide survey among professional users. *International Journal of Legal Medicine, 135*(4), 1425–1432.
12 Katz v. United States, 389 U.S. 347, 351 (1967).
13 Kayser, M. (2015). Forensic DNA phenotyping: Predicting human appearance from crime scene material for investigative purposes. *Forensic Science International Genetics, 18*, 33–48.
14 Besluit DNA-onderzoek in strafzaken. Available at https://wetten.overheid.nl/BWBR0012791/2020-11-01 (accessed October 19 2021).
15 Crawford, N. G., Kelly, D. E., Hansen, M. E. B., Beltrame, M. H. et al. (2017). Loci associated with skin pigmentation identified in African populations. *Science, 358* (*6365*): eaan8433.
16 Kayser, M. (2013). Forensic DNA phenotyping: DNA testing for externally visible characteristics. *Encyclopedia of Forensic Sciences, 1*, p. 369.
17 Ligue des Droits de l'Homme (2014). Fichage institutionnel: Quel risque pour le citoyen?, p. 2, see https://www.ldh-france.org/wp-content/uploads/2014/05/Monographie-France-DEF1.pdf (accessed March 27 2022).

18 DeFrancesco, L. (2018). DNA makes an appearance. *Nature Biotechnology, 36(1)*, 14–17.
19 See in particular M. K. v. France (Application no. 19522/09), judgment of April 18 2013, and Vetter v. France (Application no. 59842/00), judgment of May 31 2005.
20 Jobard, F. (2020, June 12). L'institution policière est extrêmement perméable au racisme. *Le Monde*; Mahad, I. (2020). Gardiens de la paix. Arte Radio, https://www.arteradio.com/son/61664080/gardiens_de_la_paix (accessed July 13 2020).
21 Chapuis, N., & Bénézit, J. (2020, June 10). Les policiers "en colère" après que l'exécutif a durci le ton contre le racisme et les violences. *Le Monde*.

References

Abu El-Haj, N. (2007). The genetic reinscription of race. *Annual Review of Anthropology*, 36, 283–300. doi:10.1146/annurev.anthro.34.081804.120522.

Abu El-Haj, N. (2012). *The genealogical science: The search for Jewish origins and the politics of epistemology*. University of Chicago Press.

Alexander, M. (2010). *The new Jim Crow: Mass incarceration in the age of colorblindness*. The New Press.

Anthony, D., Campos-Bastillos, C., & Horne, C. (2017). Toward a sociology of privacy. *Annual Review of Sociology*, 43, 249–269. doi:10.1146/annurev-soc-060116-053643.

Arendt, H. (1998 [1958]). *The human condition*. University of Chicago Press.

Arendt, H. (2005). *The promise of politics*. Schocken Books.

Baghai, K. (2012). Privacy as a human right: Sociological theory. *Sociology*, 46(5), 951–965. doi:10.1177/0038038512450804.

Brown, M. B. (2015). Politicizing science: Conceptions of politics in science and technology studies. *Social Studies of Science*, 45(1), 3–30. doi:10.1177/0306312714556694.

Coleman, R., & Oakley-Brown, L. (2017). Visualizing surfaces, surfacing vision: Introduction. *Theory, Culture & Society*, 34(7–8), 5–27. doi:10.1177/0263276417731811.

DeCew, J. (2018). Privacy. In E. N. Zalta (Ed.), *The Stanford Encyclopedia of Philosophy*. https://plato.stanford.edu/entries/privacy/.

Engelke, M. (2012). Angels in Swindon: Public religion and ambient faith in England. *American Ethnologist*, 39(1), 155–170. doi:10.1111/j.1548-1425.2011.01355.x.

Fassin, D. (2013). *Enforcing Order: An Ethnography of Urban Policing*, trans. Rachel Gomme. Polity.

Fassin, D. (2011). Racialization: How to do races with bodies. In F. E. Mascia-Lees (Ed.), *A companion to the anthropology of the body and embodiment* (pp. 419–434). Wiley-Blackwell.

Foucault, M. (1984). Polemics, politics and problematizations: An interview conducted by Paul Rabinow. In P. Rabinow (Ed.), *The Foucault reader* (pp. 381–390). Pantheon.

Foucault, M. (1988). The concern for truth, trans. Alan Sheridan. In L. D. Kritzman (Ed.), *Michel Foucault: Politics, philosophy, culture. Interviews and other writings, 1977–1984* (pp. 255–267). Routledge.

Foucault, M. (1997). *Ethics, subjectivity and truth: The essential works of Michel Foucault, 1954–1984*. Vol. 1, trans. Robert Hurley *et al*. New Press.

Fox, D. (2010). The second generation of racial profiling. *American Journal of Criminal Law*, 38(1), 49–79.

Fujimura, J. J., & Rajagopalan, R. (2011). Different differences: The use of "genetic ancestry" versus race in biomedical human genetic research. *Social Studies of Science*, 4(1), 5–30. doi:10.1177/0306312710379170.

Halpérin, J.-L. (2015). Protection de la vie privée et privacy: Deux traditions juridiques différentes? *Nouveaux Cahiers du Conseil constitutionnel*, 48, 59–68.

Harcourt, B. (2020 [2015]). *Exposed: Desire and disobedience in the digital age*. Harvard University Press.

Hernann, A. (2017). Outside Timbuktu's divine cover: The negotiation of privacy among displaced Timbuktians. *American Ethnologist*, 44(2), 275–287. doi:10.1111/amet.12478.

Hookway, B. (1988). *Interface*. MIT Press.

Horstmann, N. D. (2020). The power to selectively reveal oneself: Privacy protection among hacker-activists. *Ethnos*. https://www.tandfonline.com/action/doSearch?target=default&ContribAuthorRaw=Horstmann,%20Nina%20Dewi.

Jobard, F., Lévy, R., Lamberth, J., & Névanen, S. (2012). Mesurer les discriminations selon l'apparence: Une analyse des contrôles d'identité à Paris. *Population*, 67(3), 423–451. doi:10317/popu.1203.0423.

Katell, M., & Moore, A. D. (2016). Introduction: The value of privacy, security and accountability. In A. D. Moore (Ed.), *Privacy, security and accountability* (pp. 1–18). Rowman & Littlefield.

Krimsky, S., & Simoncelli, T. (2011). *Genetic justice: DNA data banks, criminal investigations and civil liberties*. Columbia University Press.

Kudina, O., & Verbeek, P.-P. (2019). Ethics from within: Google Glass, the Collingridge dilemma, and the mediated value of privacy. *Science, Technology, & Human Values*, 44(2), 291–314. doi:10.1177/0162243918793711.

Kulick, D. (2015). When privacy and secrecy collapse into one another, bad things can happen. *Current Anthropology*, 56(12): S241–S250. doi:10.1086/683675.

Lipphardt, V., Lipphardt, A., Wienroth, M., Surdu, M. *et al.* (2017). Open letter on critical approaches to forensic DNA phenotyping (FDP) and "biogeographical ancestry (BGA)". *ResearchGate*. https://www.researchgate.net/publication/316527261_OPEN_LETTER_ON_CRITICAL_APPROACHES_TO_FORENSIC_DNA_PHENOTYPING_AND_BIOGEOGRAPHICAL_ANCESTRY.

Lock, M. (2013). The epigenome and nature/nurture reunification: A challenge for anthropology. *Medical Anthropology*, 32(4), 291–308. doi:10.1080/01459740.2012.746973.

Marks, J. (2013). The nature/culture of genetic facts. *Annual Review of Anthropology*, 42, 247–267. doi:10.1146/annurev-anthro-092412-155558.

Mazeaud, V. (2015). La constitutionnalisation du droit au respect de la vie privée. *Nouveaux Cahiers du Conseil constitutionnel*, 48, 7–20.

M'charek, A. (2020). Tentacular faces: Race and the return of the phenotype in forensic identification. *American Anthropologist*, 122(2), 369–380. doi:10.1111/aman.13385.

Mokrosinska, D. (2015). How much privacy for public officials? In B. Roessler, & D. Mokrosinska (Eds.), *Social dimensions of privacy: Interdisciplinary perspectives* (pp. 181–201). Cambridge University Press.

Moore, A. D. (2000). Employee monitoring and computer technology: Evaluative surveillance v. privacy. *Business Ethics Quarterly*, 10, 697–709. doi:10.2307/3857899.

Nelkin, D., & Lindee, S. (1994). *The DNA mystique: The gene as cultural icon*. W. H. Freeman & Co Ltd.

Regan, P. (1995). *Legislating privacy*. University of North Carolina Press.

Roessler, B., & Mokrosinska, D. (2015). *Social dimensions of privacy: Interdisciplinary perspectives*. Cambridge University Press.

Schneider, P., Prainsack, B., & Kayser, M. (2019). The use of forensic DNA phenotyping in predicting appearance and biogeographic ancestry. *Deutsches Ärzteblatt International*, 116, 873–880. doi:10.3238/arztebl.2019.0873.

Schramm, K., Skinner, D., & Rottenburg, R. (2012). Ideas in motion: Making sense of identity after DNA. In K. Schramm, D. Skinner, & R. Rottenburg (Eds.), *Identity politics and the new genetics: Re/creating categories of difference and belonging* (pp. 1–29). Berghahn Books.

Schramm, K., Skinner, D., & Rottenburg, R. (Eds.). (2012). *Identity politics and the new genetics: Re/creating categories of difference and belonging*. Berghahn Books.

Scorgie, F., Foster, J., Stadler, J., Phiri, T. *et al.* (2016). "Bitten by shyness": Menstrual hygiene management, sanitation, and the quest for privacy in South Africa. *Medical Anthropology*, 35(2), 161–176. doi:10.1080/01459740.2015.1094067.

Sen, M., & Wasow, O. (2014). Race as a "bundle of sticks": Designs that estimate effects of seemingly immutable characteristics. *Annual Review of Political Science*, 19, 499–522. doi:10.1146/annurev-polisci-032015-010015.

Simmel, G. (1955 [1922]). *Conflict and the web of group-affiliations*. The Free Press.

Skinner, D. (2020 [2019]). Forensic genetics and the prediction of race: What is the problem? *BioSocieties*, 15, 329–349. doi:10.1057/s41292-018-0141-0.

Solove, D. J. (2002). Conceptualizing privacy. *California Law Review*, 90(4), 1087–1156.

Steijn, W. M. P., & Vedder, A. (2015). Privacy under construction: A developmental perspective on privacy perception. *Science, Technology, & Human Values*, 40(4), 615–637. doi:10.1177/0162243915571167.

Tsakyrakis, S. (2009). Proportionality: An assault on human rights? *International Journal of Constitutional Law*, 7(3), 468–493.

Vailly, J. (2022). Appearance and origin: The depoliticization of genetic privacy in France. *Current Anthropology*, 63(6), 637–659. doi:10.1086/722354.

Wade, P. (2014). Race, ethnicity, and technologies of belonging. *Science, Technology, & Human Values*, 39(4), 587–596. doi:10.1177/0162243913516807.

Williams, R., & Johnson, P. (2004). "Wonderment and dread": Representations of DNA in ethical disputes about forensic databases. *New Genetics & Society*, 23(2), 205–223. doi:10.1080/1463677042000237035.

PART 3

Genetic suspects: new frontiers

5

DNA EVIDENCE AND ITS NEW REGIMES OF PRACTICE

The innovations discussed throughout this book raise a number of important questions around regimes of truth and the place of science in the production and management of criminal evidence. These questions include the probative value to be ascribed to certain scientific evidence to ensure correct procedure in criminal investigation and the interaction between science and the law. What are the knowledges, the methods of examination and calculation, and the rationalities articulated in this particular activity of government? How far is it permissible to go in the search for evidence while remaining within the bounds of acceptability in contemporary societies? What might be a correct ("*juste*" in French) use of DNA in the puzzle the investigator must piece together? Raising the question of the *correct* use of DNA invites consideration of the three senses of the word. Here "correct" connotes at once precisely adjusted (it corresponds to the method's actual capacities), legal (it conforms with the law), and equitable (it conforms with values). As Sheila Jasanoff (2006) suggests, there is value in considering the reliability and the extension of DNA evidence from the point of view of the human and social sciences: the question is not only one of whether genetic analysis can, in theory, provide incontestable evidence but also whether societies are capable of generating genetic evidence free from both error and abuse.

Among these various conceptions, the production of truth within a judicial procedure is thus central. After all, evidence is, in the dictionary definition, "information tending or used to establish facts" (Oxford English Dictionary). But while this conception may fuel reflection on the place and use of evidence in professional practice, it cannot be normative and confused with the question of whether the law and science reach "the" truth in its abstract and supreme form. The truth that I am interested in here is defined, rather, in Foucault's terms (2001 [1994], p. 158) as the set of rules and procedures that make it possible to utter or bring into play statements that people, at a given moment, consider to be true.

DOI: 10.4324/9781003456056-9

Because police and court practice today aspires to be evidence-based, the study I present here takes up the challenge of both opening up the "black box" of science (Latour and Woolgar, 1986 [1979]) and examining the broader context within which scientific objects evolve. As a prelude to this chapter, I highlight some of the dividing lines in terms of what constitutes "truth" for sociologists and anthropologists of science, before moving to a more specific review of the literature on aspects of DNA evidence as used in the context of criminal investigation. I then address the various facets of this evidence as they emerge in new developments of the technique, particularly in relation to familial searching and genealogical tests. Examples of court cases help to clarify the interpretive value this evidence holds in different situations. More generally, this analysis also helps to explain how the category of suspect is evolving in relation to these new uses of DNA.

Evidence and truth through genetics

Truth in science: between rationalism and relativism

While bearing in mind that DNA evidence is not science as practiced in research laboratories, it is helpful to remember a few general points about the human and social sciences of science, which have seen substantial growth in both quality and quantity over recent decades. I shall not attempt to present all the diverse problematics and the many trends, but I will highlight some key points that help to clarify the scientific issues of DNA evidence.

Geoffrey Lloyd (2003) points out that in ancient Greece there were three groups of positions with regard to the concept of truth and that some of these can be aligned with current debates in the analysis of science. The first is objectivism, championed by Aristotle. In Aristotle's view, the true is synonymous with the authentic or the real. The contrast between what is true and appearance is fundamental: the true is truly correct, in contrast to what simply appears to be correct. The second viewpoint is that of relativism. Truth is relative because everything that has been believed or appeared to have been believed by a person is thereby real for that person. The third viewpoint is that of skepticism, according to which one should be wary of perception but also of reason. In the view of the skeptics, therefore, the best route is to suspend judgment. Today, while they distinguish themselves from philosophers and reassert that their study is firmly rooted in practices (Pickering, 1992), sociologists of science and knowledge are equally divided into two camps. Traditionally, rationalist sociologists tend to support the existence of scientific propositions whose validity is independent of social context (Vinck, 1995). Others, spearheaded by adherents of the "strong programme" in sociology of science (Bloor, 1983 [1976]), tend more toward relativism: they reject absolute criteria of rationality. According to this view, the establishment of scientific truth is always a social undertaking, situated in particular places and circumstances, and culturally embedded. In the same vein, some call for an inversion of propositions, so that reality becomes the consequence of the stabilization of a statement rather than its cause. In other words, it is because a statement is stabilized as a scientific fact that it becomes true (Latour and Woolgar, 1986 [1979]). This proposition has been vehemently contested on the grounds of its "derealization" effect, which appears to suggest that facts are entirely fictive (Bourdieu, 2004). Similarly, the question of how to explain the stability of statements constitutes a point of difference between sociologists of scientific knowledge rooted in constructivism and their opponents (Hacking, 2000): relativists and constructivists agree in preferring external explanations. That said, many researchers take a position that combines internal explanations (imputable to nature itself) and external ones (dependent on social, economic, and other factors) for the stability of science. This is the position I shall myself take, not out of a concern for balance, but because it is the one that seems to me to best account for observations. In addition to sociologists and anthropologists, historians of science are also engaged in describing how arguments deemed convincing are constructed and in highlighting the diverse contributing factors (Montel, 2004). In the field of physics in particular, studies by Michel Atten and Dominique Pestre, and by Peter Galison, trace the history of methods in the process of managing evidence (Montel, 2004). The study of DNA evidence could thus make a substantial contribution to this already abundant body of research. What distinguishes it is that it sits at the intersection between science, police practice, and the law.

Truth in the history of DNA evidence

In order to better understand how DNA evidence has won legitimacy, it is helpful to start by describing how a match between two genetic profiles is established. This is a statistical process. The biologist assesses the rarity of the profile, on the basis of databases that estimate the frequency of genetic markers in a given population (European, Asian, etc.), and then calculates the probability of the two profiles matching. The significance or weight of the match is known as the "random match probability" (RMP), a figure that expresses the probability that a person chosen at random has the same profile as the sample found at the scene. The RMP might, for example, be 1 in 7.8 billion, indicating that the profile is rare and the probability low that a person other than the suspect has a profile that matches the trace. The lower the probability, the rarer the profile, and the more significant the results. It is thus clear that judicial truth is based not only on an understanding of genetics but also on the scientific legitimacy of statistical calculations made by forensic scientists. These scientific probabilities, with their sometimes remarkable figures, grant this approach a degree of probative power.

Michael Lynch and Sheila Jasanoff, researchers in Science and Technology Studies, were among the first to take a social science approach to practices located at the interface between the law and forensic science. They focused particularly on the legal and scientific controversies around DNA sparked by certain trials in the United States in 1989 (People vs. Castro) and the early 1990s (notably the O. J. Simpson trial). In these trials, an unusual number of expert witnesses, many highly regarded, were summoned to discuss genetic analysis and raise hitherto unaired questions about the efficacy of forensic procedures, checks, and methods of estimating matches between profiles (Aronson, 2007; Lynch et al., 2008). These trials were unusual in that they became as it were a public and media forum on the credibility of DNA evidence, sites of epistemic contestation that ultimately led the US National Research Council to form a committee dedicated to the study of forensic uses of genetic profiling. Debate continued to rage within the pages of prestigious scientific journals such as *Nature* and *Science*, where methods of calculation used in matching that involved hypotheses about population genetics, and the independence or otherwise of transmission of genetic markers, were hotly criticized (Aronson, 2007). Certain biases in the establishment of matches were indeed due to the fact that individuals belonging to the same "ethnic" group share more genetic characteristics with one another than with individuals outside that group, and this could influence the statistical calculation of random matching where few or partial genetic markers were available. As Michael Lynch (2013) remarks, during this initial period of DNA evidence, the number of genetic markers studied was limited to four, five, or six, and the random match probabilities calculated were of the order of one in hundreds of thousands or one in a few million, which was not sufficient to exclude the possibility that a person other than the suspect within an urban or national population might match the profile established on the basis of DNA traces. In this way, Lynch argues, court cases blew apart the certainty of scientific evidence and the authority of scientific spokespeople.

It is worth pointing out here that while the contrasts should not be over-emphasized, this discussion is shaped by the legal traditions of different countries. In English-speaking countries with an adversarial tradition, the trial takes the form of a public and largely verbal antagonistic confrontation between prosecution and defense: each side must prove the facts supporting its case, and the judge's role is to arbitrate between the arguments and evidence of the two sides rather than to examine the facts of the case. The results of scientific tests may therefore be discussed in court and their uncertainties exposed. By contrast, in countries with a civil law system, like France, which have an inquisitorial tradition, the situation is less clear. The procedure is generally written, often conducted behind closed doors, fairly non-confrontational, and the judge her/himself is responsible for producing judicial truth. In fact, while laboratories in France must be accredited by the state and their analytical techniques validated, methods of analysis are not really discussed during the trial as they are in countries with common law systems. Without wishing to promote one judicial system over another, historians do suggest that the adversarial procedure played a role in improving the technology of DNA analysis in the United States (Aronson,

2007). Nevertheless, social scientists in English-speaking countries point out that there are often very real practical constraints on the power of individuals to contest scientific evidence during the trial (Lynch et al., 2008). In particular, socially disadvantaged defendants often lack the financial and social resources to mount a convincing defense capable of challenging the arguments of the prosecution and instilling doubt in the minds of the jury (Jasanoff, 2006). Moreover, in many cases it appears that expert testimony is accepted without being challenged by the defense. There is a need for an in-depth comparative study of common law and civil law systems, and how evidence is articulated in each of them, to help us understand how legal institutions, traditions, and values shape the production of expert testimony and evidence.

Be that as it may, it still remains that within the space of a few years genetic profiles became widely recognized as *the* benchmark of forensic police tools in a range of countries, deemed as providing "irrefutable evidence" or a "truth machine" (Lynch et al., 2008). Indeed, some authors talk of an "inversion of credibility" in the way professionals now view DNA analysis as a more reliable and robust method than physical fingerprints (Lynch et al., 2008). Lynch (2013) summarizes the conditions that enabled DNA forensic evidence to acquire the status of gold standard: a set of technical, legal, and administrative solutions that helped to gradually dampen debate about the reliability of the approach in the United States in the late 1980s and early 1990s. These solutions were primarily based on administrative recommendations for quality assurance and monitoring of how police forces and forensic laboratories managed the collection, processing, and analysis of evidence. This made it possible to establish precautions against DNA contamination and erroneous labeling, thanks to the use of barcodes to track samples. Secondly, and still more crucially, these solutions were rooted in scientific and technical developments such as the introduction of the now familiar PCR test, based on analysis of short DNA repeats, which replaced the initial analyses by RFLP (Restriction Fragment Length Polymorphism). This made it possible both to increase the number of loci studied for a profile, which rose from four to six, then to eight or more, and to choose markers that are transmitted independently of one another, increasing the statistical power of the calculation. In short, compared to older methods of analysis, the PCR technique improved the discriminatory power of the test and reduced the probability of profiles from two different individuals being identical (except in the case of monozygotic twins). Subsequently, with the advent of large databases, it became even more important to increase the number of markers studied and the minimum number required for a match, given that as the size of databases increased so did the chances of obtaining a false match with an insufficient number of markers.

Thus provided that all conditions are satisfied (the DNA is of good quality, the tests have been performed correctly and without error, and the forensic scientist obtains very convincing probabilities), the suspect is almost certainly the source of the sample analyzed. For this reason, reporters and commentators often ascribe DNA evidence an exceptional epistemic status as scientific arbiter of truth or "rock-solid fact" (Lynch and McNally, 2009, p. 296). From what judges and lawyers told us in interviews, in France as in the United States and other countries, DNA holds a significant place in the epistemic space of courts and investigations. This book too offers a number of examples where DNA played an important role in establishing judicial truth.

However, Lynch and co-authors explain that despite real and important technical advances, it would be wrong to abstract genetic evidence from its permanent reliance on sequences of operations running from the taking of samples to the production of a result. Notwithstanding the scientists' emphasis on calculations of the possibility of a random match, Lynch and co-authors argue that other sources of uncertainty should not be ruled out, in particular the contingent local practices and material transformations that precede the presentation and interpretation of the result. They conclude:

> To say this does not demean the reality of DNA testing or the reliability of its results. Instead, it provides a specific locus for the credibility of DNA evidence that tends to be obscured when commentators speak of it as unassailable, as truth derived from science.
>
> *(Lynch et al., 2008, p. 221)*

Lynch and co-authors thus foreground the concerns of sociologists of science, who take seriously the social contexts in which scientific evidence is produced, and highlight the question of the construction of evidence at all stages.

We also need to consider that DNA evidence is bound up with imperatives other than that of scientific knowledge and ultimately takes its place in a legal arena where other constraints and institutional needs apply. Although the law and science share a common vocabulary around terms such as "true," "investigation," "evidence," "fact," and "law," as Jasanoff (2006) points out, the use of scientific evidence like DNA tests brings into collaboration two institutions with substantially different objectives and normative commitments. Jasanoff identifies three major differences, each of which reflects concerns that distinguish the scientific from the legal approach. First, she argues, the legally pertinent facts are often specific to the cases they are supposed to help clarify, whereas scientific facts are presumed to have more general validity. Scientific facts are focused toward the future, enabling future scientists to draw on current research, whereas legally pertinent facts are focused on the past because they are required to retrace as accurately as possible a sequence of events that has already taken place. Secondly, the requirement for certainty is different in the scientific and legal contexts because science used in legal procedures cannot be subjected to the kind of peer review and questions of reproducibility of experiments that typify scientific research. Finally, the ethical constraints around the production and use of knowledge are different in the two institutional contexts. Although it turns to science to obtain authoritative data, the law must retain its commitment to fundamental values (a fair trial, proper administration of justice, protection of privacy, etc.). As Jasanoff concludes, in a court, science cannot be presented as a source of "transcendental truths"; more modestly, and with the appropriate safeguards applied, it can be a source of "simple evidence" (Jasanoff, 2006).

In the following section, I broaden my analysis to incorporate factors other than DNA evidence itself, in other words going beyond the fact that DNA evidence is rooted in a series of social contingencies to show how it is interwoven with other, non-genetic aspects of the investigation and trial.

A piece of evidence

Incriminating evidence and the place of the word

In some cases, statistical analysis indicates that the DNA profile of a suspect identified in an investigation, or an individual recorded in the database, matches that found at the scene of a new offense. The probative power of statistics is of a technical nature that sometimes makes it difficult to question this approach, particularly in a country like France with an inquisitorial system. Under these conditions, Katja Franko Aas (2006, p. 151) suggests, DNA matches close down all debate owing to the power of the identification produced: "Not only do biometric forms of identification minimize the need for verbal communication, they almost completely eliminate the possibilities for doubt and negotiation," she argues. As noted above, this was not true of certain highly publicized trials in the United States, which gave rise to heated debate. More broadly, in the most simple cases, DNA matches leave little doubt as to the identity of the person who left a trace, but this does not *necessarily* imply that this individual is the perpetrator of an offense (they might have left the trace when passing through the room, for example). This important reservation pre-existed genetic investigations because it is also true of fingerprints: the discovery and identification of a fingerprint similarly does not determine the role played by the individual who left it. Nevertheless, the problem is amplified today by the fact that, compared with fingerprints, a genetic trace is much more easily transported, often without the knowledge of the person transporting it: DNA is left on an object by a person who has simply touched it or, in certain conditions which are often difficult to prove, by someone who has been touched by another person who then touched the object. In other words, cells containing DNA can be transferred to an object without the person from whom the DNA originated ever coming into contact with that object. These traces, known as "touch DNA," may influence the status of this evidence among other elements in the case file. Following the development of PCR tests, discussed above, and because a tiny trace, even a single cell in certain cases, is today sufficient to provide analyzable DNA, the defense may raise all sorts of reasons why this minute quantity is present at a crime scene, unlike situations where large quantities of bodily fluids (blood, semen, etc.) are found that are more difficult to explain. This is further amplified by the fact that the forensic expert cannot determine when the DNA was deposited, which may have been prior to the offense. In France, therefore, as judges told us, debates in criminal courts center not on the match between the trace and the defendant but rather on the circumstances in which the evidence was transferred to the surface. Corroborating these remarks, forensic experts report that they are now "somewhat picked on" by lawyers who challenge their reports on grounds of the risk of contamination, DNA transfer, or the time at which the trace was left in relation to the time of the offense. To put it another way, if the body of the suspect establishes a form of truth, if it "does not lie" (Aas, 2006), it is not the only one that "speaks"; a place remains for words, both during the police investigation and during the trial. As one police chief of a large precinct in the Paris region, a former detective, declared: "If we find a trace of a person's DNA at a crime scene, [...] they have to *explain* why that trace is present" (Police officer 6). In short, when science enters the investigation, or later the courtroom, it must do so accompanied by a credible narrative. In this sense, Paul Ricœur argues (1991, p. 20), "the discourse of justice offers a perfect example of the place of argumentation, midway [...] between intellectually rigorous evidence, as in mathematics, and sophistic use of language."

The relationship between the probative power of DNA and that of other kinds of evidence is illustrated by a case dating from 2004. The body of a man who had been bound, gagged, beaten, and suffocated was found at his home in the south of France, with no apparent motive for the murder. The police questioned a man whose number was recorded in the victim's phone. Initially he denied having been to the victim's home, but his genetic profile matched traces found in the apartment. He was charged and held on remand for twenty-one months. Yet he had an alibi, no motive, and there were no witnesses. His lawyer explained that he initially lied because he was terrified of having to reveal his homosexuality. In the end, the case was dismissed because the presence of his trace did not prove that he committed the crime.[1] This case demonstrates that, as in any other field, just as the doctor must link what the tortured body reveals with the story recounted by the refugee in the assessment of an asylum application (Fassin and d'Halluin, 2005), the police officer and judge must link what the suspect's DNA reveals with what she/he says about her/his past during a criminal investigation. In fact, judges, police officers, and forensic experts are virtually unanimous in seeing genetic analysis as a *piece of evidence* that sometimes plays a more important role than other elements in the process of criminal investigation, but one that has to be placed in the context of the investigation in order to understand how it came to be at the crime scene, rather than a proof of guilt. Several of the judges we interviewed described a change in this respect, as if hindsight had done its work since the early period of DNA evidence, returning it to its rightful place. More specifically, they described a time in the past when the culture of confession prevailed, then a period when DNA reigned supreme, followed more recently by a readjustment where DNA is generally used with more caution than previously. For example:

> For a very long time, people said: confession, confession, that's the supreme evidence. We sought confession above all else. Then it really changed, and for the last 30 years, it's scientific evidence that has become the supreme evidence. In particular [...], what I've seen over the last 15 years is DNA identification, that was the pinnacle. As far as criminal evidence goes, DNA today, there's a sort of mystique that's developed around it, and there's a systematic search for scientific evidence, and especially DNA identification. [...] DNA in all that, I'm coming back to what it is that identifies, and in my view, it's a good tool, but it's not the supreme evidence. It's one tool among others. A fingerprint can be much more important than DNA identification, just as a credible witness statement can be as important as DNA identification.
>
> *(Judge 11)*

> The cornerstone is the traditional investigation; on the other side, you've got objective scientific evidence, including DNA, that is unrelated to that cornerstone. And it's when the two align that you solve a case. [...] A criminal investigation is a puzzle, so it's a piece of the puzzle, it's like you're playing poker, so DNA is one card, either in the investigation strategy or in the examining magistrate's interrogation strategy or in the public prosecutor's strategy in court.
>
> *(Judge 5)*

At a conference, a lawyer added:

> I think things are changing, but I don't think it's a recent development. We've come to realize ... [in 2012–2013], if there was DNA in a case file, it was case closed, there was no further discussion. And I have to say I've seen a few of those. Today, things are changing because we've seen that all the same there was a range of evidence ...
>
> *(Lawyer 5)*

Contrary to what some media accounts suggest, the presence of a minute bodily fragment does not supplant the alibi; it combines with both other recent tracing techniques such as GPS localization and more traditional investigative techniques like telephone tapping, and with the suspect's "explanations," to establish a form of truth. It must be examined alongside other elements in the investigation because it provides a scientific contribution to what remains a legal reasoning process. This is not to make assumptions about the views of jurors, who may be influenced, at least at the beginning of the trial, by television shows that create a fantasy world where all sorts of crimes can be detected using scientific evidence. To be sure, every situation is different, and the presence of a DNA trace in a hair left in passing, of semen after a rape, of a weapon used in a crime, or an object handled by several people – in other words the nature of the evidence and the place where it is found – do not carry the same weight. In any case, contrary to what was described in earlier periods (Lynch, 2013), the tendency to accept DNA as a "truth machine" does not prevent efforts to contextualize it.

Exoneration

The power of DNA evidence can operate in another way: sometimes DNA reveals a discrepancy, or mismatch, which helps to remove an individual from the category of suspect or to exonerate someone previously convicted. As a reminder, in the first criminal investigation analyzed by Alec Jeffreys in the United Kingdom, DNA helped to exonerate a suspect who had confessed to the crimes despite being innocent. This raises the question of how many such situations there are. There are no statistics on this subject, and it is difficult to assess how often they occur during criminal investigations. The best known and most widely publicized exculpations are those that occur after a conviction. This is particularly true in the United States, where the Innocence Project helped to exonerate 375 individuals on the basis of DNA between 1992 and 2021, 21 of whom were on death row.[2] The project's impact report reveals other very interesting facts. First, it shows the disproportionate number of unfounded convictions of African Americans in the United States: 60% of those wrongly convicted were "African American," 31% were "Caucasian," 8% were "Latinx." It also shows that prisoners officially exonerated on the basis of DNA evidence had spent an average of 14 years in prison, that their average age was 26.6 when they were convicted and 46 when they were exonerated. In around 12% of the cases, the individuals had pleaded guilty. Other statistics also help to clarify the reason for these unfounded convictions, where eyewitness misidentification is frequent: 69% of those convicted were misidentified by an eyewitness. Finally, these exonerations show how often individuals, particularly young people, make false confessions: suspects made false confessions in 29% of cases, and in 31% of these they were 18 or under. These trial reviews, and other cases, thus highlight the fallibility of convictions based on false confessions, inaccurate eyewitness testimony, and other forms of poorly supported evidence. Lynch (2013) also points out that DNA profiling acts as a lever for changes to certain legal regulations: both the statute of limitations, because in some jurisdictions limitation periods were set aside in cases where DNA evidence was available, and the attitude of courts toward psychologists' evidence about the fallibility of eyewitness testimony. In the same vein, Jasanoff (2006) recounts that in 2000 the then governor of the state of Illinois, hitherto a committed supporter of the death penalty, ordered a moratorium on executions: his view on justice had been profoundly shaken by a series of cases where convicted prisoners on death row were exonerated, some of them on the basis of DNA evidence.

Thus DNA analysis has become key to exonerating the innocent and furthering justice in criminal investigations. This argument was put forward in support of widening profiling to the entire French population, despite the crippling burden of social and legal problems this proposal would generate. For example, in 2003 a parliamentary deputy already cited in the introduction claimed in the National Assembly: "If the FNAEG was extended to the entire population, it would be a powerful mechanism for exonerating those who are wrongly suspected. That seems to me the most promising development."[3] On this point, those who oppose the use of large genetic databases argue that a database is not necessary to exonerate an innocent person, because the suspect's DNA can always be compared *directly* with that at the crime scene, without resorting to a database (Wallace, 2006).

The fallibility of DNA evidence

Notwithstanding the factors discussed here, and the important role it may play in some cases, DNA evidence is demonstrably not infallible. The main reasons that DNA evidence may be compromised are: mixtures of several different types of DNA; DNA that is too old and degraded; contamination of the sample by someone working on it; and human error. The first two lead to errors in interpretation; the latter two are due to mistakes in handling. In the former case, it must be pointed out that interpretation can be extremely technically difficult where DNA is mixed or partially degraded. If the sample contains the DNA of more than one person it can be difficult to deduce how many individuals contribute to it and to distinguish individual profiles. The smaller the sample, the higher the probability of incorrect genetic information appearing during the analysis, and the higher the likelihood that other existing genetic information is missing. Small peaks whose significance is hard to determine, making it difficult to say whether they really correspond to the presence of a repeated sequence, may appear in sequence images. Allele dropout is an artifact that means that one of the individual's genetic markers simply does not appear during the analysis because the quantity of DNA is too small. In other words, a biologist assessing a degraded mixture on the basis of a small quantity of DNA may see the genetic markers of a suspect in a certain number of loci but not see them in one or a number of sites. Thus working on small samples, or samples of partially degraded DNA, has an effect not only on the identification of the trace but also on the statistical proof. Moreover, French judges have not always been trained in these developments, as one geneticist notes:

> Today laboratories are increasingly providing what are called complex mixtures, but the judges have had no training whatsoever in that. So you give them things that are five or six times more complex than what you were giving them ten years ago, and people make absolutely no distinction between a complex mixture and a pure profile.
>
> *(Geneticist 4)*

Another approach that is debated by the professionals, and based on new, more effective sequencing techniques called next-generation sequencing, is increasingly being used but not yet on a mass scale. The geneticists justified it on two grounds: the possibility of increasing the number of traces that can be analyzed, such as touch traces with small quantities of often degraded DNA and/or several types of DNA; and the opportunity to examine a large number of genetic characteristics in a single analysis. These promises are based on the fact that next-generation sequencing not only provides information on the length of DNA markers but also reveals variations in base pairs (Hopman et al., 2023).

Some questions about the fallibility of DNA have recently re-emerged in public debate, particularly in the United States. One enlightening article on this subject is by US lawyer Bess Stiffelman (2019). The context is that in order to confer probative value on complex and/or incomplete mixtures of DNA, laboratories in the United States are increasingly turning to what are known as Likelihood Ratios (LR), based on computer programs that use complex algorithms. These likelihood ratios are supposed to express the probabilistic relationship between two hypotheses: for example, the hypothesis that the DNA of the suspect features in the sample compared to the hypothesis that it does not. In addition, these programs are supposed to take into account various uncertainties, evaluating the probability that the sample contains incomplete or incorrect information, as well as the difficulty of separating individual profiles when the sample contains DNA from more than one person. The final calculation appears to answer the question of whether the accused contributed to the DNA, but this is misleading because in reality it merely evaluates *the relative probability of two specific hypotheses* chosen by the laboratories. Stiffelman offers some telling examples that help to explain this.

She first imagines the following scenario: someone returns home to find their dog sitting next to a torn-up pillow, with feathers everywhere. This person might compare the hypothesis that their house has been burgled with the hypothesis that the pillows they had bought were designed to self-destruct after six months. After gathering various data, such as the fact that the door was still locked and nothing else had been damaged, they might come up with a Likelihood Ratio. Given the various factors in the situation, they might determine the likelihood ratio that it is 10,000 times more likely that the pillow fell to pieces than that the house was ransacked by burglars. The problem is that neither of these hypotheses provides the correct explanation. In fact, the dog had played with the pillow and torn it up. Thus although it is 10,000 times more likely that the pillow fell to pieces than that the house was burgled, this does not prove that the pillow fell apart on its own. This person presumed from the outset that their hypotheses were the only two possible explanations, but both were incorrect. This illustrates that the number produced by the calculation is the relative probability of two specific hypotheses, not the probability that one of the hypotheses is correct.

Stiffelman then describes an imaginary scenario closer to a real-life criminal investigation. A car with four men, all of Caribbean origin, is stopped by the police. The car is searched, and a gun is found in the trunk. The four men are arrested and the gun sent to the laboratory to be swabbed for DNA. The laboratory analyst reports finding a mixture of DNA on the gun but that no individual profile can be distinguished. He believes that the mixture contains the DNA of at least three individuals but also cannot state with certainty how many. However, he adds that the sample can be compared to the DNA of the suspects. A judge then orders samples to be taken from the four men. The laboratory begins the process of producing a number that is supposed to calculate a probability. The analyst proposes calculating the hypothesis that the DNA on the gun comes from three unrelated individuals in the car against the hypothesis that it comes from each of the men in turn plus two other unknown individuals. Not only are there a number of alternative hypotheses, but these two hypotheses could both be false. Does the hypothesis take into account the fact that the four men are of Caribbean origin and are more likely to share certain genetic markers? Is the hypothesis that some of the contributors might come from the same biological family taken into account? Is any account taken of the fact that one, two, three, or four of the individuals present in the car could have contributed to the DNA in the mixture, since the number of contributors is unknown? These parameters can have serious consequences. Stiffelman cites the case of an American exchange student who was convicted of the murder of her roommate in 2007 and then exonerated in 2015. When the forensic DNA analyst increased the proposed number of contributors to one sample by a single individual, the Likelihood Ratio produced was reduced by ten million.

On top of all this, the statistical and computer models used vary widely from one program to another. Consequently, the LR results for a given situation may also be very different, depending on the program. Opacity is added to complexity, since the algorithms used to determine LRs are often unknown or protected under confidentiality clauses by the companies that sell them. In other words, LR calculations conducted under these conditions only have the *appearance* of science. Moreover, judges, lawyers, and juries are increasingly less equipped to understand how these calculations, which are presented as evidence, are determined. Stiffelman concludes: "These statistics, posing as the likelihood of guilt or innocence, create a trial by mathematics – fundamentally inconsistent with the constitutional norms of the criminal justice system" (Stiffelman, 2019, p. 146).

With regard to errors in handling, as noted above, social science researchers point out that while geneticists are especially concerned about the probability of false matches, there are many other sources of error that the courts may not know about: the DNA may be contaminated or wrongly labeled (Lynch and McNally, 2009). In the United Kingdom, administrative errors, or reproduced errors in spelling, dates, or police codes, which may have serious consequences, have been reported. In the United States, a man was arrested in 2017 because DNA tests had identified a spot on his washing machine as the blood of a 75-year-old man who had been stabbed to death sixteen months earlier. According to a police report, the DNA almost certainly came from the victim, and a judge spoke of "incontestable evidence." However, in 2018 the public defender detected anomalies in the documents relating to DNA supplied by the forensic laboratory. Why did the exhibit filed under seal as number 19, corresponding to the lid of the washing machine, contain the victim's DNA when exhibit 16, from the knife used in the murder, did not? He formed a theory, based on the resemblance of the figures 6 and 9: had a laboratory analyst switched the two DNA samples? This theory was confirmed by an independent expert commissioned by the defense to retest the samples. The accused man was freed after three years in prison.[4]

One frequently heard argument is that those who have done nothing wrong have nothing to fear from their DNA profile being included in a database. If they are innocent of a crime, they will automatically be excluded from suspicion thanks to comparison of profiles. This argument is based on the hypothesis of absence of error in the comparison procedure, a hypothesis that is unattainable in any human activity. Lynch (2013) argues that the idea that genetic profiles are unique identifiers of an individual should not be confused with the idea that experts are capable of determining without error whether two genetic profiles match. This remark can be transposed to these new methods of studying genetic profiles. It is not insignificant that those whose profile is stored in a genetic database may, rightly or wrongly, be linked to offenses when a sample found at a crime scene matches their profile. This adds grist to the mill of Lynch and co-authors, who argue in *Truth Machine* that current DNA evidence does not represent "the end of the story," even if it has emerged from the controversy of the 1990s, and that analysis of the challenges it poses needs to continue (Lynch et al., 2008). Innovations in the field offer further indication of this, as I show in the following section.[5]

New uses of genetic evidence

Legal scholars remind us that the imperatives of judicial truth are not only of the scientific order; they are articulated with the protection of other interests that frame and guide the judicial process of seeking the truth, such as personal dignity and protection of privacy, public order, and the proper administration of justice. New areas of research into DNA evidence call for a reconsideration of the relationship between science and the law, and of the production of suspects.

Familial searching

Other approaches emerged in the early 2000s, in connection with genetic databases. These focused particularly on familial searching – the possibility, in the absence of a matching profile, of searching the genetic database for biologically related profiles with the aim of finding a partial match. This technique presupposes that a biological relative of an offender has already had dealings with the justice system and has had their own data recorded in the database. Familial searching thus makes it possible to identify "first-time suspects" or "first-time offenders" using the database, which was not the case previously, as it served purely for comparing genetic data with those of individuals known to the police.[6] It can also be used to identify unidentified bodies, on the basis of databases of DNA profiles voluntarily provided by people related to missing persons in order to facilitate their identification.

The technique was first used in Wales in 2001, to solve the murder of three little girls. It was imported into France in the case of Elodie Kulick, a young woman raped and murdered in the Somme département. After ten years of fruitless investigation between 2002 and 2012, familial searching revealed a partial match between sperm traces found at the crime scene and the genetic profile of a man serving a prison sentence for sexual assault. When compared with that of his partner, the DNA in the trace was shown to match that of one of their sons who had died in a road traffic accident in 2003; his body was exhumed for the purposes of the investigation. By the spring of 2018, this type of analysis, which had been approved without any parliamentary debate, under the extremely lengthy anti-terrorist law of 2016,[7] had been used around 60 times in France and had led to the identification of 6 individuals related to someone with a profile in the database. Under this law, the offenses for which familial searching may be used are those that fall within the scope of the FNAEG, which as I have noted is very broad. Currently in France, this approach is confined to direct-line relatives (ancestors and descendants), but in other countries such as the United States, where it is used in 10 states,[8] the circle of individuals concerned may widen to siblings, uncles and aunts, cousins, etc.

Individuals who have a profile in the database that is a partial match, and more particularly people related to them, then become the subject of a traditional police investigation. Recourse to the database for the purposes of familial searches thus raises sociological and legal questions about police investigations into both individuals included in the database who are related to a suspect but themselves have nothing to do with the crime (otherwise there would be a direct match) and into people related to them. These relatives are more at risk of being investigated by the police without their knowledge than people related to individuals whose profiles are not included in the database: this raises questions of invasion of privacy (Williams and Johnson, 2005; Cole and Prainsack, 2015). At a conference in France, a senior member of the Syndicat de la Magistrature (Judges' Union) raised these issues:

> In an investigation, a genetic trace will be identified [...], and all of those who are recorded in the database, plus potentially their relatives via familial searching, are automatically deemed suspects.
>
> *(Judge 3)*

In interview, a representative of the Ligue des Droits de l'Homme went further:

> DNA profiling is extended to the offender's entire family. So that poses a problem, because you [...] are not responsible for your brothers, your cousins, etc. [...] This is stigmatization of families that is absolutely unacceptable.
>
> *(Ligue des Droits de l'Homme 1)*

What is at issue is the *extension of suspicion to biological relatives* of individuals recorded in the database: police services have greater access to data, and this reconfigures the issue of suspicion to take in family relationships. In short, when familial searches are performed, it is as if relatives are partially profiled. This means that we need to re-evaluate the figures for the number of individual profiles in the FNAEG (3.3 million in 2020, discounting duplicates), representing around 5% of the French population. Clearly, if their ancestors and descendants are added in, the percentage of the population directly or indirectly profiled is much higher. Given an average of two children per family in France, the percentage of individuals whose data is at risk of being analyzed is multiplied by five (the person profiled but also their two parents and two children), amounting to around 25% of the population.

Familial searching reconfigures the question of the link between DNA and biological relationships, a question previously addressed in other contexts such as genetic diseases, parental relationships in civil law, and family reunification. I have pointed out that genetic information is both individual by nature and shared within family groups, making it more sensitive than other information. This was emphasized by the European Court of Human Rights in its Marper judgment, cited above:

> Familial searching might [...] lead to revealing previously unknown or concealed genetic relationships. [...] the use of the DNA data base in searching for relatives [is a] particularly sensitive [question].[9]

One example is that of a complex criminal investigation in Bergamo, in Italy, where this procedure revealed an affair between two people in a town where such affairs generally went unspoken (the perpetrator of the crime was the son of a woman and man who were married to other people).[10] Here it becomes clear that the parallel often drawn by professionals between physical fingerprints and genetic "fingerprints," suggesting that the latter are neutral in terms of the information they provide, is contradicted by familial searches: such a method could obviously not be applied to physical fingerprints, which do not provide the same familial information.

In light of these problems, sociologists Granja and Machado (2019) report that in the United Kingdom, a mechanism they describe as "regulating by exceptionality" is used to avoid public controversy in this domain. According to the British professionals involved, consensus is based on three conditions: that familial searching is restricted to serious crimes (rape, murder, serious sexual assault); that other possible criminal investigation methods have been explored as far as possible; and oversight by national bodies responsible for ensuring accountability. It should be noted in this regard that the United Kingdom regularly publishes accounts and transparent statistics on activity related to the National DNA Database, including on familial searching, which are available online. There is no equivalent in France, and data relating to the FNAEG or other genetic analysis used in criminal investigations are not accessible in this way.

Genealogical tests

Genealogical tests are an extension of familial searching, made possible by free or paid-for online services where users upload their genetic information in order to search for relatives, find out about their ancestors, and seek information on their health. These websites, which are particularly popular in the United States, constituted substantial databases that did not escape the notice of forensic scientists, US law enforcement, and biotechnology companies selling their services. They realized that they could draw on these private databanks, rather than on databases managed by police and judicial bodies, for the raw material to search for partial matches with the aim of identifying relatives of a suspect.

This method was practiced for the first time in the United States in the search for a particularly dangerous serial killer who had committed 13 murders, more than 50 rapes, and hundreds of burglaries, between 1976 and 1986 in California. Forensic scientists used a DNA sample found at the scene of a double murder in 1980 to create a false profile on GEDmatch, a free genealogical website with around 1.2 million profiles. Lists of probable relatives of the reference profile were obtained and used to deduce extensive family trees with the help of marriage certificates, death registers, etc. In line with the discussion above about revelation of the self, social media networks also constituted a valuable source of information that helped to establish family relationships. Branches of the family tree that individuals' ages and location indicated were not relevant were excluded in order to narrow down the group of probable suspects. Finally, the sample proved a partial match with the profiles of two first cousins of the perpetrator who were listed in the database, and he was arrested in 2018. Following this high-profile case, the method was used in several dozen more cases throughout the United States to identify suspects or unidentified bodies, with links being made to relatives as distant as fourth or fifth cousins. In 2020 Parabon NanoLabs, the leading company selling these genealogical services to the police, reported that it had been involved in this way in nearly 500 police investigations and the identification of 109 suspects. Initially reserved for rape and murder, the method began to be applied to less serious offenses and was used at least once in the case of a violent attack on an elderly woman. Subsequently, the owner of GEDmatch approved searches through its website without informing other users, leading to the arrest of a high school student.[11] It is thus possible that following their application to a particularly horrific first case that received a great deal of media attention these techniques are being used in other ways in less serious cases. On this note, a survey of over 1,500 adults in the United States showed that 91% of them approved genealogical tests for violent crimes but only 46% for non-violent offenses.[12]

Genealogical tests raise a number of questions, first and foremost in terms of regulation. As with other digital spaces, there is little regulation of the use of genetic databases by the authorities, so that today it is largely left to companies and their users to self-regulate. Some of these sites have taken measures to ensure users are not scared off by this unforeseen use of their data, which would in turn render them less useful to investigators. In 2019 GEDmatch revised its policy so that such searches were only permitted for the records of people who had explicitly agreed to be included. Nevertheless, after this decision, a police officer in Florida obtained a warrant from a judge authorizing him to search the entire database, including people who had not given their agreement. The officer explained his approach at the conference of the International Association of Chiefs of Police, sparking interest among his colleagues, who asked for a copy of the warrant so that they could apply the method in their own cases. Clearly, this situation creates a disturbing precedent with regard to the protection of personal data. Another website, Family Tree DNA, limited police use of these data to investigations into homicide, sexual assault, and kidnaping. It offered its clients an opt-out, so that they were deemed by default as having authorized use of their data by the police unless they had explicitly refused. In the same vein, seeking to reassure clients but probably only partly succeeding, the website of the major databank 23andMe states that staff will examine all requests from law enforcement and will comply with court rulings, summonses, and search warrants that they deem legally valid.[13]

Nevertheless, in view of the limited nature of such self-regulation, two US states, Maryland and Montana, have placed restrictions on the use of these genealogical tests for the first time. Since 2021, investigators in Maryland have had to have a judge's approval, may only use this technique for serious crimes (murder, sexual assault), and only draw on sites that have a strict policy on consent to such tests. Investigators in Montana must have a search warrant unless the user of the database has given their agreement.[14]

Secondly, and in line with the discussion in the previous chapter about genetic analysis used in the attempt to deduce suspect appearance, genealogical testing raises the question of privacy, how it is defined, and proportionality between ends and means. One important point is that the genetic markers revealed in these databases are incomparably more numerous (in the hundreds of thousands) than those recorded in police databases (around 20). Thus, the information they might reveal is also more complete (including information relating to health). Consequently, these new uses of DNA are a source of concern to legal scholars, users of genetic databases, and privacy campaigners, whose focus is not the privacy of criminals who do not upload their data to these sites but that of all users. Should the violence of the crimes outweigh concerns about the method used to obtain results? One view is that users of these easily consulted websites should not expect to retain control over the use of their data and that criminal investigations serve the public interest. A second viewpoint maintains that these users are the only ones with the capacity to decide how those of their genetic data that reveal personal information may be used. The lack of consensus around what is "good" (pursuing a suspect, protecting data) creates uncertainty. To paraphrase Ricœur (1991), the problem of justice then becomes that of how to prioritize goods that impinge on one another and each claim all of the space. One factor that makes it possible to decide between the two options is that the decision taken by those who provide data to these sites may be more or less well informed: in the case discussed above, the police searches were performed afterwards, and without their consent. Adding an opt-out clause, as some sites do, is not a convincing solution: it would be better to add in explicit agreement for use, rather than to presume agreement where there is no refusal.

Crucially, the user takes a decision not only for themselves but for their entire biological family, usually without consulting them, the singular feature of this process being that the details they share also provide information on the members of their current, past, and future family. As danah boyd (2012) notes, where the boundaries and connections between individuals are not clearly demarcated, the relevant unit of analysis in terms of privacy is no longer the individual but the group, community, or network. This is especially true for users of GEDmatch, who can upload files of genetic data from various other databases such as 23andMe, Ancestry, MyHeritage, Family Tree DNA, Living DNA, and tellmeGen. They can also obtain information from these databases, regardless of the DNA test used. Genetic data thus form a second network between various databases, in addition to the family network, and one that has conceptual implications to which I shall return in the conclusion. Reflecting on the challenges raised by the social networks popular with young people, danah boyd analyzes the implications of "networked privacy." While the information shared in genealogical databases is different from that shared online, in both cases the choice is not truly individual. Moreover, in this type of networked structure, data are more easily consulted and longer-lived than they would have been in the past. Given that data are shared in networks, and that it is not possible to control the collective mass of information held, boyd argues for better regulation of their use *by third parties*. This is the key consideration in the matter of DNA.

The third important issue raised by genealogical tests is that of their extent. An article in the journal *Science* sparked heated debate in the United States.[15] It showed that people living in the United States who were of European ancestry had a 60% chance of having a cousin or a relative registered in the MyHeritage database, which contains 1.28 million DNA profiles of individuals seeking information on their family history (those of sub-Saharan ancestry have a 40% chance). This means that such a search could potentially identify around 60% of residents with European ancestry on the basis of a DNA sample, even if they have never provided their DNA to an ancestry database. With the increase in the number of users and the range of databases, it is likely that today almost all people resident in the United States could be found via this process. Evidently, a sort of *continuum thus emerges between different types of suspects* (profiled suspects, closely related suspects, genealogical suspects) to the point that it incorporates the majority if not the entirety of the US population. It is no longer a matter of separating out individuals likely to commit offenses from others, as in the past, but a process that makes the division between groups less clear.

Fourth, as in other domains that touch on public safety, these developments testify to the issues raised by this kind of approach when public interest (security) intersects with private concerns (privacy). In 2019 the Californian company Verogen, which specializes in the sale of products and instruments used in human identification in forensic contexts, bought GEDmatch. GEDmatch was thus diverted away from its original aims, provoking the ire of some users of these databases that had been set up purely for family and genealogical purposes. Although GEDmatch is still marketed as a site offering free DNA uploads and analysis tools, here as elsewhere the commercialization of personal data continues.

Finally, genealogical tests raise questions about the globalization of data. In France genealogical tests, sometimes called commercial DNA tests for leisure purposes (genealogy, health), are banned. At the same time, however, the internet is by definition a global network, and many French clients are apparently seeking answers to their questions on US sites: the National Institute for Health and Medical Research (Institut national de la santé et de la recherche médicale, Inserm) estimates the number of people in France who have used one of these "leisure" tests bought from such sites, usually in the United States, at 100,000–200,000 annually.[16] In a television interview, a French gendarme from the IRCGN spoke of private databases that are widely accessible, which the French police can use to seek people related to an unidentified trace from a crime scene. Tellingly, GEDmatch's confidentiality policy includes a specific clause for residents of the European Union and the United Kingdom that reads:

> We [...] process your personal data when we believe it furthers our legitimate interests or those of third parties. [...] In some cases, we process personal data based on the consent you expressly grant to us at the time we collect such data. [...] From time to time we may also need to process personal data to comply with a legal obligation, if it is necessary to protect the vital interests of you or other data subjects, or if it is necessary for a task carried out in the public interest.
>
> *(Terms of service and privacy policy, GEDmatch, December 30 2021)*

In 2022, for the first time, a man who had allegedly committed five rapes in France between 1998 and 2008 was identified via this process, through collaboration with the FBI in the United States.[17] The issues raised are thus not confined to United States residents, now that the databases are located in a globalized space.

Covert sampling

When genealogical tests are used in the United States, law enforcement officers quite frequently test individuals' DNA surreptitiously, without always being in possession of a judge's warrant with its protections and constraints (judicial oversight). Police may follow suspects until they throw away objects containing their DNA, such as a napkin or soda can. They may also take and analyze trash left by the person they suspect in garbage cans (cigarette butts, cotton swabs, tissues, hair, water bottles, beer cans, etc.) and test the DNA on these objects to determine whether it matches the traces at the crime scene. Indeed, though the case did not involve genealogical tests, *The New York Times* reported that in 2018 police officers offered a soda to a 12-year-old boy as he was being interrogated at the precinct. They then took the straw, obtained his genetic profile, and added it to a local database. The child's family had to go to court to demand that it be removed from the database.[18]

Legal scholars explain that in most jurisdictions in the United States the police are not required to obtain a warrant or court order before surreptitiously taking DNA samples (Slobogin and Hazel, 2021). They note that state laws that place restrictions on surreptitious collection and analysis of genetic material without the consent of the individual concerned generally include exceptions for law enforcement. Moreover, with regard to the DNA of relatives of a suspect, as opposed to the suspect themselves, they add that while Department of Justice policy prohibits covert collection of DNA samples, guidelines may permit public prosecutors to bypass this restriction if they have "reasonable grounds to believe that [seeking informed consent] would compromise the integrity of the investigation," giving them wide leeway to approve it (Slobogin and Hazel, 2021). Those who support search and seizure without warrant draw on an argument that dates back several decades, which suggests that when a person leaves their garbage on the sidewalk they give up their right to privacy.[19] They assert that these individuals have no reasonable expectation of privacy with regard to their trash bags, and consequently no privacy interest to defend in regard of the DNA they leave on items they throw away. However, while it is possible to sort trash, it is not possible to avoid leaving DNA on items. The police could potentially create databanks of this covertly acquired information. Nevertheless, other authors argue that in most countries DNA recovered in this way cannot be integrated into databases (Cole and Prainsack, 2015).

In France the police may collect a suspect's toothbrush or cigarette butt and study evidence shed by the human body within the context of an investigation.

Under the Code of Penal Procedure, genetic profiles may be identified "on the basis of biological material naturally shed by the body of the person concerned."[20] A Ministry of Justice memorandum states still more precisely:

> When there is no possibility of taking a biological sample from a convicted or suspect individual, samples of biological materials shed from that individual's body may be analyzed for the purposes of identifying a genetic profile. These are biological traces left on objects, glasses, toothbrush, clothing, etc.[21]

Edmond Locard, a professor of forensic medicine who founded the world's first forensic police laboratory in Lyon in 1910, had a well-known adage: "Any individual who moves around a place leaves traces there, and conversely takes traces of that place with him." This remark can be extended to say that any individual leaves traces not only of their movement through a place but also irreducible traces of themselves. The question raised here is that of their (in) visibility and the attention focused on them, inviting new research into current practices. Covert collection of samples in public spaces turns our bodies into permanent trackers that cannot be controlled. More generally, following the 20th century, which was the "century of the gene" (Fox Keller, 2000), perhaps the 21st will be the century of the trace, with the development of new genetic and digital techniques that also leave traces that are hard to erase (Galinon-Mélénec et al., 2016).

Rapid analysis

One other new approach, being trialed by the FBI at the time of writing, is that of rapid DNA analysis. This term describes an entirely automated process of producing a DNA profile within one to two hours, which can be performed by police officers in precincts without recourse to a forensic laboratory and with no need for human interpretation.[22] Currently, the FBI plans to limit its use to the buccal DNA of arrestees and to exclude analysis of crime scene traces because rapid analysis requires a large amount of good-quality material. The aim is immediate analysis of the DNA of qualified arrestees against the national database so that the profile of each arrestee can be compared with traces from unsolved crimes while they are being held. Where there is a match, the various booking, arresting, and investigating agencies would immediately be notified. This new approach raises questions about the accreditation of police forces, and about misuse and leaking of data (Cole and Prainsack, 2015).

* * *

In the laboratory, in the institution that manages the database, at the police precinct, and in the courtroom, the forensic expert identifies, with a certain degree of probability, the bodies whose genetic sequences show matches with those of a trace left at a crime scene, backed by the authority of science. Within a few decades, the status of DNA analysis moved from being an emerging and sometimes contested scientific tool to that of indispensable resource in the quest to guarantee equitable decisions as to guilt and innocence in judicial procedures. Much progress has been made in standardizing and monitoring the quality of DNA analysis, and no one among those who take a close interest in these questions denies that DNA can offer important and very useful tools for resolving investigations. DNA evidence is often portrayed in the media as the "acme of evidence," but there is room for questioning whether it might not lose this status in complex cases. To begin with, as a number of professionals we interviewed pointed out, the place of DNA should not be overestimated: a more precise account of the situation would be that in many cases this molecule represents *a piece of evidence*. While tools for examining genetic evidence are becoming increasingly sensitive, and increasingly tiny quantities of DNA from a crime scene can be analyzed, this evidence is not sufficient in itself. Observers also argue that the new generation of genetic evidence using LR calculations of complex mixtures, which is being used particularly in the United States, is different from that of the preceding generation, and they question how much confidence should be placed in its capacity to establish the truth. Finally, various questions arise with respect to the broadening of DNA searches, such as the extension of the category of suspect to include all individuals linked to a crime scene by partial genetic matches, and the continuum being created between genetic suspects, family suspects, and members of the population interested in genealogical tests. Other questions that remain to be answered arise around police investigations of family members that find partial matches and the revelation of family histories. These questions are not preventing police investigators and courts in the United States from broadening database searches, in the absence of specific legal and procedural guarantees, in a way that should be of concern to any country where clients seek genealogical tests. In other words, the use of DNA evidence in the judicial system raises new challenges in relation to civil liberties and the "correct" articulation of science and the law.

Notes

1 Roubaud, J.-F. (2007, March 23). Antibes: le test d'ADN trompeur a failli coûter 30 ans de prison à un innocent. *Nice-Matin.*
2 See https://www.innocenceproject.org/cases/ (accessed January 17 2022).
3 National Assembly, Ordinary Session 2002–2003, 3rd sitting of Thursday January 1 2003. See https://www.assemblee-nationale.fr/12/cra/2002-2003/120.asp (accessed January 21 2021).
4 Murphy, H. (2020, June 26). A DNA mix-up involving a washing machine kept a man in jail for 3 years. *The New York Times.*
5 For a forensic science review of these recent techniques and their uses, see especially Butler, J. M. (2023). Recent advances in forensic biology and forensic DNA typing: INTERPOL Review 2019–2022. *Forensic Science International: Synergy, 6*, 100311.
6 This technique bears no relation to the potential search for a "criminality gene," alleged to influence behavior, which has never been shown to exist (Larregue, 2020). Here DNA is used only to trace identity and not to determine the cause of a behavior.

7 Article 706-56-1-1 of law no. 2016–731 of June 3 2016, "reinforcing the fight against organized crime and terrorism, and the funding of them, and improving the efficacy and protections of criminal justice procedure".
8 These states are: Arkansas, California, Colorado, Florida, Michigan, Texas, Utah, Virginia, Wisconsin, and Wyoming. See the FBI website https://www.fbi.gov/services/laboratory/biometric-analysis/codis/codis-and-ndis-fact-sheet (accessed January 5 2022).
9 Case of S. and Marper v. United Kingdom, Judgment of December 4 2008, p. 12.
10 Rérolle, R. (2019, August 7). Meurtre de la petite Yara: sur les traces de l'inconnu numéro un. *Le Monde*.
11 Aldhous, P. (2019, May 14). The arrest of a teen on an assault charge has sparked new privacy fears about DNA sleuthing. *BuzzFeed News*.
12 Guerrini, C. J. et al. (2018). Should police have access to genetic genealogy databases? Capturing the Golden State killer and other criminals using a controversial new forensic technique. *PLoS Biology*, 16(10), 42006906.
13 23andMe website, see https://customercare.23andme.com/hc/en-us/articles/212271048-How-23andMe-Responds-to-Law-Enforcement-Requests-for-Customer-Information (accessed October 20 2021).
14 Laws, V. (2021, May 31). Two new laws restrict police use of DNA search method. *The New York Times*.
15 Erlich, Y. et al. (2018). Identity inference of genomic data using long-range familial searches. *Science, 362(6415)*, 690–694.
16 Tests génétiques 'récréatifs': juste un jeu? *Inserm magazine, 42*, January 28 2019.
17 AFP (2022, December 16). Affaire du 'prédateur des bois': des analyses du FBI mènent à un sexagénaire, mis en examen et incarcéré pour des viols en série entre 1998 et 2008. *Le Monde*.
18 Sandoval, E. (2020, February 20). N.Y.P.D. to remove DNA profiles of non-criminals from database. *The New York Times*.
19 Ramirez, A. Police need a warrant to collect DNA we inevitably leave behind, March 10 2020, and American Civil Liberties Union website, https://www.aclu.org/news/privacy-technology/police-need-a-warrant-to-collect-dna-we-inevitably-leave-behind/ (accessed January 25 2022).
20 Article 706–56 of the Code of Penal Procedure.
21 Ministry of Justice memorandum of July 27 2004, CRIM. PJ no. 97–28.H5.
22 Guide to all things rapid DNA, January 27 2022: https://www.fbi.gov/file-repository/rapid-dna-guide-january-2022.pdf/view (accessed February 28 2022).

References

Aas, K. F. (2006). "The body does not lie": Identity, risk and trust in technoculture. *Crime, Media, Culture: An International Journal*, 2(2), 143–158. doi:10.1177/1741659006065401.

Aronson, J. D. (2007). *Genetic witness: Science, law, and controversy in the making of DNA profiling*. Rutgers University Press.

Bloor, D. (1983 [1976]). *Socio/logie de la logique ou les limites de l'épistémologie*. Pandore.

Bourdieu, P. (2004). *Science of science and reflexivity*, trans. Richard Nice. Polity.

boyd, d. (2012). Networked privacy. *Surveillance and Society*, 10(3/4), 348–350. doi:10.24908/ss.v10i3/4.4529.

Cole, S. A., & Prainsack, B. (2015). Genetics and forensics. In J. Wright (Ed.), *The international encyclopedia of the social and behavioral sciences*, 2nd edn (pp. 955–961). Elsevier.

Fassin, D., & d'Halluin, E. (2005). The truth from the body: Medical certificates as ultimate evidence for asylum seekers. *American Anthropologist*, 107(4), 597–608. doi:10.1525/aa.2005.107.4.597.

Foucault, M. (2001 [1994]). *Dits et écrits II, 1976–1988*. Gallimard.

Fox Keller, E. (2000). *The century of the gene*. Harvard University Press.

Galinon-Mélénec, B., Zlitni, S., & Liénard, F. (2016). *L'Homme trace: Inscriptions corporelles et techniques*. CNRS Éditions.

Granja, R., & Machado, H. (2019). Ethical controversies of familial searching: The views of stakeholders in the United Kingdom and in Poland. *Science, Technology & Human Values*, 44(6), 1068–1092. doi:10.1177/0162243919828219.

Hacking, I. (2000). *The social construction of what?* Harvard University Press.

Hopman, R., van Oorschot, I., & M'charek, A. (2023). From promise to practice: Anticipatory work and the adoption of massive parallel sequencing in forensics. In V. Toom, M. Wienroth, & A. M'charek (Eds.), *Law, practice and politics of forensic DNA profiling: Forensic genetics and their technolegal worlds* (pp. 93–110). Routledge.

Jasanoff, S. (2006). Just evidence: The limits of science in the legal process. *Journal of Law, Medicine & Ethics*, 34(2), 328–341. doi:10.1111/j.1748-720X.2006.00038.x.

Larregue, J. (2020). *Héréditaire: L'éternel retour des théories biologiques du crime*. Seuil.

Latour, B., & Woolgar, S. (1986 [1979]). *Laboratory life: The construction of scientific facts*. Princeton University Press.

Lloyd, G. (2003). Les concepts de vérité en Grèce et en Chine anciennes: Perspectives et implications comparatives. In J.-P. Changeux (Ed.), *La vérité dans les sciences* (pp. 49–60). Odile Jacob.

Lynch, M. (2013). Science, truth, and forensic cultures: The exceptional legal status of DNA evidence. *Studies in History and Philosophy of Biological and Biomedical Sciences*, 44, 60–70. doi:10.1016/j.shpsc.2012.09.008.

Lynch, M., Cole, S. A., McNally, R., & Jordan, K. (2008). *Truth machine: The contentious history of DNA fingerprinting*. University of Chicago Press.

Lynch, M., & McNally, R. (2009). Forensic DNA databases and biolegality: The coproduction of law, surveillance technology and suspects' bodies. In P. Atkinson, P. Glasner, & M. Lock (Eds.). *Handbook of genetics and society: Mapping the new genomic era* (pp. 283–301). Routledge.

Montel, N. (2004). L'administration de la preuve: Des sciences expérimentales à l'histoire des sciences. *Genèses*, 56, 148–162. doi:10.3917/gen.056.0148.

Pickering, A. (1992). *Science as practice and culture*. University of Chicago Press.

Ricœur, P. (1991). Qu'est-ce que la justice? Le juste entre le légal et le bon. *Esprit*, September 1991, 5–21.

Slobogin, C., & Hazel, J. W. (2021). A world of difference? Law enforcement, genetic data, and the Fourth Amendment. *Duke Law Journal*, 70(4), 705–774.

Stiffelman, B. (2019). No longer the gold standard: Probabilistic genotyping is changing the nature of DNA evidence in criminal trials. *Berkeley Journal of Criminal Law*, 24 (1), 110–146. doi:10.15779/Z384Q7QQ6X.

Vinck, D. (1995). *Sociologie des sciences*. Armand Colin.

Wallace, H. (2006). The UK National DNA Database: Balancing crime detection, human rights and privacy. *Embo Reports*, 7, S26–S30. doi:10.1038/sj.embor.7400727.

Williams, R., & Johnson, P. (2005). Inclusiveness, effectiveness and intrusiveness: Issues in the developing uses of DNA profiling in support of criminal investigations. *The Journal of Law, Medical & Ethics*, 33(3), 545–558. doi:10.1111/j.1748-720X.2005.tb00517.x.

6

TRACKING SUSPECTS THROUGH EUROPE

The owner of an auto repair shop is attacked by two hooded, armed men who beat him and tie him up with a belt before stealing jewelry and a little money. Three months later, during the course of the gendarmerie's investigation, a trace of DNA not recorded in the FNAEG is found on the belt that was used to tie up the victim. The investigation stalls for a further four months, until a match is established between the unidentified trace and a DNA profile located in Germany. Three weeks later, in response to a request from the French investigator under the terms of the European agreements known as the Prüm decision, Germany sends full information on the profile, which was obtained during the investigation of a burglary in Germany ten years earlier. The details supplied include the name [A], the date and place of birth, a photograph, and the fingerprints of the man concerned. The French investigator lodges a series of information requests with various bodies (the gendarmerie's central criminal intelligence service, the centralized visa application department, etc.) in an attempt to locate the man in France, but they turn up nothing. Unbeknownst to him, the man has been arrested in Germany in the meantime, under a false identity and with false documents. The investigator shows the photograph sent by his German counterparts to the victim, who recognizes him from having come across him at a rival garage. The investigator then shows the photo to the owner of this other garage, who recognizes him as a customer under another name [B], the name under which he is naturalized in France. The investigator finds his address under this Gallicized name and confirms that the photo in his naturalization file matches that sent by the German police. This is the moment when genetic identity and nominal identity are realigned. The man is arrested and sentenced to four years' imprisonment. In custody, he explains that he fled Russia with false documents to escape the war against Chechen separatists in the 2000s. After traveling through Italy and Germany under a false name [A],

DOI: 10.4324/9781003456056-10

he settled in France under his true Russian identity [C], before being naturalized under a Gallicized version of his Russian name [B]. While the investigator mentions other elements of evidence, particularly GPS tracking of the suspect's cell phone, which confirmed his presence at the time and in the area of the attack, he stresses the importance of DNA in his investigation: "It's thanks to the DNA trace that came back from Germany that we were able to find a trail," he concludes.

This case demonstrates how "primary," embodied identity (Jenkins, 2000), based on genetic markers, can be used first to find a genetic profile. Subsequently, the circulation of the photograph, hence the suspect's appearance (supported by Germany, where the genetic database is managed by the police), helps to attach the primary identity to a nominal identity that varies geographically. This is one example of the cases we were told about in detail during our interviews with professionals. It takes us straight to the heart of the question of the bioidentities of individuals suspected of crime in the European space; at the same time, it places those bioidentities in the political context of relations between the police and the judiciary. In this chapter, I return to some of the questions raised in earlier chapters in relation to the FNAEG, to examine how they emerge at European level. These questions can be formulated as follows: to what extent do the social practices of genetics in European law enforcement and judicial procedure alter the bioidentities (as defined above) attributed to those suspected of crime? What relations of power support these processes, and how do they reconfigure the articulation between data on the living being and the lived experience of individuals?

A thus far small number of social science studies analyze the exchanges of genetic data made possible by the Prüm decision, highlighting the contribution the system makes to solving certain crimes and, the authors claim, the empowerment that such elucidations can offer victims. However, these studies also emphasize the risks involved, particularly in terms of uncertainty about matches between genetic profiles (false positives), invasion of privacy, erosion of the presumption of innocence, and the extension of the European Union's governance via monitoring of crime (see, in particular, Prainsack and Toom, 2010; McCartney et al., 2011; Santos and Machado, 2017; Machado and Granja, 2019; Toom et al., 2019; Bellivier et al., 2021). Other studies have analyzed how criminologically genetic searches lead to the construction of categories of suspicion (Machado et al., 2020). However, the implications that systems for circulating genetic and nominal information for security purposes (whether automated or not) entail for bioidentity and related concepts have yet to be explored. To my knowledge, there has not yet been any field study of the discourses and practices of police investigators, despite the fact that such studies could offer a pertinent lens for examining the relationship between biological life (in the use of DNA) and social life (in the traditional police investigation; Vailly, 2023).

This chapter is organized around the three roles played by DNA in this context: identification, connection, and location. During interviews, we were given access to six anonymized criminal case files involving Prüm exchanges of DNA data. For the purposes of clarifying methodology and interpretation, I should point out that these files were selected by one of the senior national officers of the Judicial Police in charge of these matters, and that they are counted among the "successes" attributed to the Prüm system by institutional bodies, although, as I show below, evaluating its efficacy is a more complex matter (Toom et al., 2019).

Continent-wide identification of suspects

I focus first on the detail of protocols for exchange of information between European countries and also situations of "friction" (Cresswell, 2014) that may hamper such exchanges.

The aim of the Prüm decision is to facilitate the circulation of information between European police and justice services, by giving automated access to secure databases concerning individuals to third parties on a continent-wide scale.[1] This decision was consequent on the Prüm Convention, signed in 2005, following an agreement between seven European countries (Belgium, Germany, Spain, France, Luxembourg, the Netherlands, and Austria) that aimed to strengthen co-operation in the fight against terrorism, cross-border crime, and illegal migration. In 2008 the EU's Justice and Internal Affairs Council, which is made up of ministerial representatives from all the countries involved, transposed some parts of the Prüm Convention into the European Union acquis, the collection of legislation, regulations, and decisions that make up the body of law shared by member states.[2] Following the decision, data relating to DNA, physical fingerprints, and vehicle registration numbers were made available and consultable to each member of the European Union. With regard to DNA, countries were required to set up databases of genetic profiles if they did not already have them, and to gradually come into the Prüm system as their national database became operational. Nevertheless, the police officers we interviewed told us that exchanges of information about DNA under the Prüm agreement are more strictly regulated than other kinds of exchange: "Everything to do with DNA is totally locked down"; "We have no access. We lose all control" (Police officer 10). Although this protocol is not a matter of "genetic exceptionalism" (the idea that genetic information is by its very nature exceptional; Murray, 2019), it does indicate particular attention to the sensitive issue of such data because it means that politics is involved in establishing procedures that are not under the sole control of the professionals involved. Because social actors often describe these data as "private," their circulation is regulated. In other words, the bioidentity of suspects can only be determined at European level on condition that a protocol is scrupulously followed.

How do intra-European exchanges work in practice? In order to describe them, I draw on the concept of "forms of circulation" put forward by Arjun Appadurai (2010) in relation to the journeys of ideas and cultural goods in the era of globalization. According to Appadurai, these forms are characterized by the circuits they travel through, their scale, and the speed with which they spread; they sometimes involve disjunctures, differences, and negotiations. I propose here to extend this concept to the circulation of biometric and biographical information relating to suspects within the European space.

The first thing to note is that France's requests to third countries, which mainly concern unidentified DNA stains found at crime scenes, go through one or two stages.[3] In the first stage, step one, anonymized genetic profiles are sent in batches to the countries active in the Prüm network, to be compared with the national database in each country. The responses received are processed by FNAEG administrators, who decide whether or not there is a "match" or correspondence between profiles.[4] A match report is then sent to the investigating police officer or examining magistrate who recorded the profile in the database. The range of dissemination in step one has gradually broadened as more countries enter the Prüm system: by the end of 2021, 26 countries of the European Union, plus the United Kingdom, had signed up.[5] However, Prüm exchanges are not operational with all countries: for example, again at the end of 2021, France exchanged its data with 24 countries, Belgium with 22, and the United Kingdom with 13. Step one forms part of what we might term a "digital europeoscape," a sort of spatial extension, on the continental scale, of the digital cityscape, which Mimi Sheller (2014) describes as combining cities, the presence of bodies, physical mobilities, and multiscalar mediations through the operation of digital systems. With regard to timing, in France batches of genetic profiles are disseminated to the various European countries once every two months; matching itself is automatic and virtually instantaneous.[6]

The second stage, step two, involves a request for information about any person whose profile matches a profile from a third country. This request is made through "National Points of Contact", set up under the Prüm decision, who receive all the French requests to other countries. Many of the step one matches are not confirmed after checks or are not followed by step two (Toom, 2018); I shall come back to this point. In France, the point of contact for step two is a body known as the Prüm Co-ordination and Assistance Unit (Unité de Coordination et d'Assistance Prüm, UCAP), made up of three people, within the International Relations Division (DRI) of the Central Directorate of the Judicial Police. Located in the Paris region, it is the national police and gendarmerie's gateway to international co-operation. UCAP transmits the request for information from the investigator to the National Point of Contact in the country where the match was found. The information requested is usually personal data (family name and given name, any criminal record, the reason the sample was taken) and supplementary details (vehicle registration number, identity card, address, photographs, etc.). While comparisons in step one are made automatically, the extent and nature of the information supplied in step two depend on the goodwill of institutions, and the legislation in each country (albeit there is an obligation to respond).[7] The separation of the two stages, and the active involvement of the National Points of Contact, ensure that individual data are protected, as the legality of the request and the conditions under which anonymity of data may be lifted is subject to assessment in each country (Machado and Granja, 2019).[8]

With this context established, I now turn to consider the process whereby the bioidentity of the suspect is established through this exchange. Unlike step one, which centers on genetic data, step two is based on biographical data. To take up George Canguilhem's proposed distinction (1966), if the first stage relates to the living being (in the sense of the organization of matter), the second concerns lived experience (in the sense of human beings' experience). The two components, of living being and lived experience, seem to follow on from one another: the imperceptible trace of the body that leaves a molecular signature transformed into figures, then the lived experience of the person who is, in a more traditional way, distinguished by their name and personal history but today shaped by the international, standardized circulation of information. In other words, the circulation of information relates to an anonymous biological life in one case and an individual subject in the other, reconfiguring the articulation between biological and social life (Vailly et al., 2011).

A case study will help to illustrate how the two components of this process are linked. A couple is attacked at their home while they sleep. The woman, who only regains consciousness the following evening, finds her husband dead, killed by one or more violent blows to the head, which experts later report could have been made with a hammer. She has also been beaten and raped. Samples taken do not reveal any trace of sperm that could provide investigators with the suspect's DNA. However, they collect some incomplete DNA from an object in the house; this DNA contains a rare allele[9] carried by only 1% of people in the world, and which is not found in either the couple's DNA or that of their friends and family. Not far from the scene, on the same night, a man tried to enter a neighboring property but was chased off by the owner. On the route the criminal took as he fled, the investigators find an object with a trace of DNA, this time complete, that contains the same rare allele as that found at the house. The complete DNA profile from the second object is sent to the FNAEG and then, since there is no match in the French database, transmitted to the European databases in the Prüm system for comparison. A match is found with a man known to the police in an Eastern European country for rape, night-time burglaries, and attempted murder. From the information communicated by the point of contact in the country concerned, where the suspect is at that time in prison, French investigators establish not only that the suspect was present in the village that day but also that his criminal record matches the crime. He is interrogated in custody while he completes his prison sentence and then extradited to France. He is given a life sentence without remission, confirmed on appeal. The examining magistrate in charge of the case says:

> The complete DNA was found in the neighboring house, but the [name of the rare allele] was found at the crime scene, and the circumstances and criminal record meant that we were able to track him down. [...] Fortunately, there was that [the DNA], otherwise the case would not have been solved.
>
> *(Judge 12)*

In the absence of the suspect's complete DNA at the crime scene, here the probative power of the rare allele was sufficient to suggest a link between the two cases, and thus a reason for examining any complete DNA located in the neighborhood. This purely biological evidence was supplemented by information from the suspect's criminal record, and from the modus operandi. This illustrates how DNA operates as evidence not on its own but alongside other elements in the case file. These various pieces of biological and biographical information created a bundle of evidence that pointed toward the suspect: his bioidentity became that of a "reliable suspect," to use the term I proposed earlier. Going further, we can return to the concepts of sameness and selfhood discussed above. Sameness is articulated first when the partial DNA and the complete DNA found on the two objects are compared (the same rare allele is found in both cases), and again when the complete DNA found in the neighborhood and the DNA profiles in the FNAEG are compared (revealing no match in France), then a third time when the complete DNA found in the neighborhood is compared with profiles in the Prüm system (establishing a match). Selfhood is also invoked, in the form of the criminal characterization of the suspect, whose record is marked by crimes of the same type as those committed in France, using a similar modus operandi. In the absence of complete DNA at the crime scene, it was ultimately the combination of these two forms of bioidentity that led to him being identified as the culprit. The combination of the living being and lived experience enabled first the biological identification of the suspect, and subsequently the correlation of his criminal identity, his acts and gestures, the place where the DNA was recovered, and the circumstances of the crime.

The role of DNA identification in criminal investigations does not stop at this type of case, since it may also be used to search for co-perpetrators; for example, in some drug-trafficking cases, as this police officer suggests:

> All the same, the aim is to try and break up the network or the structure. You've got stains, you know you've got five different profiles in a case. You've got one that belongs to the guy who's been arrested; you know there are four at large who were also involved in the crime. This means you can identify them and also, once you've done that, have them arrested in another country. Or not – because sometimes it goes out the window.
>
> *(Police officer 11)*

Thus DNA can help to identify individuals involved in a "criminal association," or a gang robbery. I shall show below that it can play a much greater role in establishing the bioidentity of suspects where they work together.

The police's dominant role

In addition to the two-stage procedure described above, the bioidentity of individuals is also a function of the ease with which information on them is circulated, and the power relations revealed by this process. Two parameters may limit or even block the exchange of information in step two. First, the coverage of national databases varies from country to country, in a context where differences in legislation have long constituted a problem in the European space. Countries communicate information in step two only in relation to offenses that fall under their own database's coverage, rather than that of the requesting country. For example, various financial offenses (insider trading, tax fraud, misuse of corporate assets) and the offense of escaping custody do not fall under the coverage of the FNAEG. Consequently, France does not transmit information on an individual who has committed such crimes elsewhere to third countries, as an officer at the FNAEG explained:

> Germany keeps on demanding that UCAP provide information that we don't want to give them because it's outside our coverage. We spent nearly six months arguing with them, trying to explain that since escape doesn't fall under the coverage of the FNAEG, we can't comply with their request.
>
> *(Police officer 12)*

Nevertheless in Europe, almost all countries incorporated into the Prüm system include suspects in their databases and authorize step one comparisons involving suspects with third countries.[10] In this way, just as with national databases (Cole and Lynch, 2006), a suspect is a suspect not only in these countries; she/he is also a suspect each time her/his profile is compared with traces from other countries, provided the legislation in her/his country permits the transmission of information under step two. The extension of suspicion I have described in relation to France thus extends to European countries. Moreover, given the length of periods of retention of data in France, the suspect may remain a suspect over a long period, sometimes even longer in other European countries.[11] The bioidentity of suspects is *extended in both space and time*: it aligns with that of convicted offenders, whose profiles are compared in the same way.

The speed and quantity of responses from countries asked for information depends on their national judicial structure, and therefore the system – whether attached to the police or the judiciary – that manages the database. An officer at the FNAEG explained:

> There are countries [where] the database is managed by the judiciary, and others where it's the police. You notice that straight away, because the

> information they provide when it's the police, it's really mutual support, police co-operation, basically they give us everything. But when it's managed by the judiciary it's much more difficult.
>
> *(Police officer 12)*

The circulation of information from France to a third country is illuminating because this is a country where the genetic database is managed by the police. UCAP therefore does not ask third countries to apply to a magistrate and obtain an International Letter Rogatory; it passes the foreign request for information directly to the administrators at the FNAEG. Where the request concerns an individual, the FNAEG administrators send UCAP the name, date of birth, parents, place of birth, the case number, and the name of the investigator who recorded the identity of the suspect. Furthermore, the UCAP officer stated that they seek to provide the maximum possible information to third countries within a minimum number of communications. In order to complete the file, she searches for any past offense committed by the suspect in national databases such as the Traitement d'Antécédents Judiciaires (Criminal Records Database, TAJ), or seeks information from the investigator who recorded the profile in the database. She also consults the national database of prisoners, and that of persons of interest. She thus attempts to gather together all the material (the individual's photograph and fingerprints, the names of any accomplices and modus operandi) so as to "send a full response to the country," as she puts it. This illustrates how circulation of information is expanding among countries where databases are managed by the police, generating new modes of access to the social environments of offenders, and new forms of interaction between countries through the medium of DNA searches. There is thus a mobility of information not only in the register of sameness (digital connectivity, comparison of genetic profiles) but also more detailed exchanges in the register of selfhood (characterization of individuals via exchange of biographical information).

Conversely, when France requests information from other countries, some third countries (those where the database is managed by the police) send detailed information including family name, given name, address, fingerprints, photograph, and criminal record, while others (where the judiciary manages the database) send only the family name. Our interviewees cited four countries where Prüm information requests are handled by the judiciary: the Benelux countries (Belgium, the Netherlands, and Luxembourg) and Portugal. If there is a positive match, two of them (the Netherlands and Portugal) supply the family name, given name and date of birth of the individual, and the nature of the crime they committed, but any further details on the case (co-perpetrators, the precise date of the events, etc.) must be sought via a request for mutual assistance in criminal matters, and therefore through a judge. Portugal, which entered the system only shortly before I began my research, and Luxembourg require a request for mutual assistance in criminal matters. Another difference is that countries where requests are handled by the police respond within three days to three weeks, while those where requests are handled by the judiciary respond only after two to three months, or even "just half the time," according to a police officer I interviewed.

These observations can be usefully situated in the context of a theory of power relations between the police and the judiciary. With their distinct roles in the criminal justice system, these actors have different practices and apply different standards: police officers share more information than judges (Toom, 2018). The fact that the vast majority of European genetic databases are managed by the police generally facilitates circulation of information, and the constitution of continent-wide suspect bioidentities. This aligns with other observations I have made about power relations weighted in the police's favor, to the detriment of the judiciary in this domain in France; observation at the European level shows how the phenomenon extends over the continent.

Putting together substantial case files: from minor offense to major crime

DNA may play a more unexpected role in the case of minor offenses, when the bioidentity of suspects is used to shift the case from the arena of minor to that of major crime.

Connecting cases

While DNA may help to identify an individual, it is often not enough to justify pursuing an investigation in the case of the most frequent offenses, which are not sufficiently serious to warrant other modes of inquiry. An investigator whose work focuses mainly on theft, with or without breaking and entering, says:

> Generally [the suspects] live abroad, so police co-operation for crimes like [theft]... It's not big stakes. [...] It's true, an individual's identity, if he lives in Romania or Germany, well yeah ... so what? [...] It's always people who are passing through, generally they have a base in another country, it's because they move around all the time. [...] We've identified the perpetrator and that's the end of it. There's no response from criminal justice. There's no follow-up.
>
> *(Police officer 13)*

This officer has not encountered any case where the investigation was relaunched thanks to the Prüm system, and he thinks that the system is of no great use in this type of crime. He cites a case where DNA found at the scene of a burglary was matched with a profile in Spain through Prüm. The Spanish authorities provided the corresponding identity, but there had been no trace of the man in the preceding ten years, and his address was unknown. Other evidence, such as phone records, could be useful, but the costs would become "excessive," he says, compared to the losses from the burglary. He adds that he has come to a dead end and will have to close the case file unsolved in six months unless new evidence emerges. The problem raised here is the proportionality between requests for additional information and the harm suffered, particularly when, as in some countries, the request has to go via a judge, which may discourage officers from making applications. It also relates to the fact that reopening a case file may be too complex (I shall return to this) unless it concerns a particularly serious offense. The investigator may simply decide that the procedure is too troublesome to implement: one Dutch study showed that, for the Netherlands in 2010, only 6% of step one matches between DNA stains in unsolved cases and European genetic databases were followed up by a step two request (Taverne and Broeders, 2015).

Some investigators nevertheless manage to overcome the difficulty of locating individuals whose offenses do not merit a request for international co-operation. In these cases, DNA serves not (only) to identify individuals but, as these officers put it, to "put together substantial case files" on property crimes, making connections between cases. To this end, three investigators in one of the gendarmerie's Research Departments worked together for six months on different cases. The head of this small team emphasized the crucial role played, at one point or another in the investigation, by DNA matches, combined with telephone records, in showing that the same type of theft with the same DNA (whether identified or not) was observed in several countries. DNA was described as the "glue that holds the whole file together," the link between the various crimes that adds weight to the case. Then it is no longer a question of minor offenses such as the theft of a few copper cables or the motor from a boat but of the theft of tons of copper or hundreds of motors. Moreover, according to the professionals we interviewed, these matches show that the case might concern not isolated individuals but organized crime. And organized group theft, unlike gang robbery, falls under the umbrella of major rather than minor crime.[12] A gendarme explains:

> DNA, when I can put different cases together, [...] it's one of the elements that doesn't establish the offense, [but] it goes to the fact that we're looking at an organized group. [...] DNA, when you reopen the cases together, you say: look, given the number of cases we're putting together, given the crime, given the stuff they're going for, now, let's say for example shoplifting, given the amount of stuff stolen, there's a network for receiving the stuff behind them, we're certainly looking at an organized gang. What sometimes allows me to say that, to put those cases together, is DNA. Not always. There's DNA and telephone records, those are the two factors.
>
> *(Gendarme 5)*

This gendarme describes the organized gang as a "clan" structure, in which one family dominates others in a city but organizes thefts abroad. He cites the example of a case that rested on several Prüm matches with Sweden, Spain, and Germany and led to the imprisonment of 16 individuals, all from the same neighborhood. From a legal point of view, the organized gang presupposes that offenses are premeditated, and (in contrast to a conspiracy to commit crime) assumes a structured, hierarchical organization of its members. Knowledge of genetic identities generates social identities that move into the register of serious crime, and thus bring into being "groups" and "group leaders." In addition, DNA that recurs in several cases is detected by molecular comparison, in the register of sameness, but also characterizes offenders, who move from the status of perpetrators of minor offenses to serious criminals, in the register of selfhood.

The professionals we interviewed described two types of such cases. The first relates to theft of specific, targeted goods, such as satnavs, boat motors, or farm tractors, stolen using the same method and then sold on by networks. The second relates to theft of everyday consumer products (games consoles, clothing, disposable razors, etc.). The perpetrators of thefts of specific material, such as copper from one region's railroad depots, were sentenced to six or seven years' imprisonment, despite the fact that the thefts were committed without violence or forced entry: the repetition of the offenses (according to the case files, between 20 and 150 cases spread across different locations and regions of France) considerably increased the consequent penalty. This leads me to the issue of relations between the police and courts in this type of case.

Negotiation of resources between the police and judiciary

While in most countries the possibility of an exchange of information under the Prüm decision depends on the police authorities, the subsequent processing of criminal cases necessarily involves co-operation between the police and the judiciary.

Under French law, the judicial police's exercise of its mission of seeking the perpetrators of offenses and gathering evidence is subject to the oversight of judges. To put it more precisely, the criminal investigation is placed under the oversight of a public prosecutor (inquiry phase) or an examining magistrate (preliminary legal investigation or legal examination phase). The initial inquiry is a police investigation opened at the initiative of the police force or under instruction from the public prosecutor (or under certain conditions, when a complaint has been lodged). When the initiative comes from the police or gendarmerie, the police officer in charge of the inquiry must inform the public prosecutor if there is evidence against a particular individual, giving the public prosecutor the information necessary to decide whether she/he should pursue the case. Following this phase of police or gendarmerie inquiry, which may be quite long, the preliminary legal investigation (compulsory for major crimes, not compulsory for minor offenses) takes place if the public prosecutor decides to send the case to the examining magistrate. If need be the examining magistrate proceeds to investigate, in order to gather and assess the evidence. By issuing a warrant, she/he may also delegate some aspects of the investigation to a police officer or another judge: taking a statement, conducting a search or a seizure, putting telephone taps in place, questioning individuals, and so on. It should also be pointed out that offenses that fall under the category of major and organized crime give police and judicial investigators access to more resources, either in the form of reinforcement of traditional inquiry methods or through the use of specific prerogatives: bugging buildings or vehicles, undercover operations, interception of phone calls, particular conditions for custody and for searches, national surveillance, and so on.

According to the gendarmes quoted above, being able to "put together substantial files" and connect cases helps them explain to senior officers, and particularly to judges, why it might be worth opening a property crime case in relation to offenses that are relatively minor taken in isolation. While they do not have to negotiate with the judges for investigation resources for crimes involving violence against the person (murder, rape, etc.), particularly where DNA identifies a suspect, for minor offenses they have to persuade judges to allocate the resources, enabling them to pursue their investigation. Connecting cases provides them with arguments to justify opening a preliminary legal investigation, giving them access to certain legal tools (warrants, etc.) and additional resources (telephone records, witness statements, etc.):

> In that case, [...] DNA was what enabled us to go and see a judge and say: 'Give us the judicial resources to work on this, a warrant and everything, let us work on it because we're up against a team where we've found matches between the DNA in seven or eight offenses.' Afterwards, when we were given permission to work on it, with other elements as well as DNA, [...] afterwards we used phone records, witness statements, that stuff, we connected a total of 65 cases.
>
> *(Gendarme 5)*

In this example, DNA serves not only as a link between cases but also as a tool of negotiation in the power relations between the courts and the police. The aim is to delay the judge's closing of the case file because while DNA is an important factor in reopening cases of violence against the person, it can be difficult to request reopening of a file on property crime once a decision has been made and the case is closed. In the view of this police officer:

> The most important thing is to have the result [on the DNA] while an investigation is ongoing. That's the thing that makes the biggest difference. It gives us more motivation, and we have the judge's support for continuing to investigate. When the case is no longer open, when it's been closed and ruled on, the judges aren't interested any more, unless there really is new evidence or a serious crime that hasn't been solved.
>
> *(Police officer 10)*

While in local police investigation of a minor offense a request for international information will be blocked unless several local cases can be connected, "putting together a substantial file" makes possible a change of scale. The case thus moves from the local or regional level to the national and international level, using an approach rooted in DNA analysis. I have discussed previously the power relations weighted in the police's favor, resulting from institutional decisions about how national databases are to be managed; these power relations *operate alongside* exchanges of information under Prüm. Here by contrast the power relations *operate directly through* DNA and are modified by the circulation of genetic knowledge: it is the recurrent DNA stain that serves as the point of negotiation for police officers.

These questions of power need to be addressed in conjunction with those of the legitimacy of these practices and their use in law. These issues raise, among others, the question of efficacy. Efficacy can be only one aspect of the debate in democratic societies, to be considered alongside the issues of proportionality, false positives, costs, etc. As other authors note (Prainsack and Toom, 2010; Toom, 2018), though not wishing to underestimate the importance of this tool in identifying perpetrators of serious crimes such as the often extremely violent offenses interviewees recounted to us, it is difficult to discuss these practices without being accused of seeking to block the development of policies for protecting society. All the same, it can be pointed out that such accusations do not help to assess the overall efficacy of information exchanges resulting from this process. As our interviewees confirmed, there are currently no statistics that would make it possible to estimate the proportion of matches that involve individuals who were not already identified as suspects during the investigation. Similarly, there is not really any possibility of assessing the role played by use of DNA in the conduct of the investigation, and its use as evidence in court, or its true influence on the outcome of cases where a match was made. As noted above, this is also the case with regard to the FNAEG. The only available indication comes from the Dutch study cited above, which shows that in the Netherlands in 2010, "2% of all [Prüm] matches is brought to court" (Taverne and Broeders, 2015, p. 52). It is worth pointing out that the police officers responsible for managing the FNAEG get little feedback from investigators about the cases on which they have requested information. The same is true in the United States, where the FBI is not informed of the outcome of a case when the national database produces a match. It is therefore not possible to estimate the number and kind of cases resolved that can be genuinely imputed to the Prüm system, despite the constant evaluation fostered by "audit culture" (Strathern, 2000) in European and North American societies.

Locating individuals: mobility and alterity

As well as demonstrating another, more peripheral role of DNA in the sphere of criminal justice, in this section I also want to look in further detail at the bioidentity generated by the Prüm system, to grasp one of the particular features that distinguishes it from national uses of DNA.

Biolocation when mobility is interrupted

Often, identifying an individual through their DNA is not sufficient to locate them. There are, however, times when it does become possible, revealing another of DNA's potential roles, albeit one less frequently used. One example is a case involving the armed robbery of around sixty cell phones. During the investigation, the DNA stain found at the crime scenes was matched with the genetic profile of the perpetrator of a theft in a supermarket in another French town, but the man identified could not be located. Rather than following the usual practice when a stain has been identified, and deleting the stain from the unsolved case from the FNAEG, the investigators left this "unresolved" trace in the database, and it therefore continued to be compared with profiles from countries in the Prüm system. Four months later, the profile in the stain was matched with DNA found in Austria. A request for urgent police co-operation was made, under the procedure for individual cases. The Austrians confirmed that the genetic profiles matched and sent the French investigators a range of information: name, date and place of birth, names of parents, aliases, fingerprints, a photograph, and a list of offenses he had been convicted of, followed by sentences – all details that completed the description of the suspect. Another important piece of information was that the man had been in prison in Austria for two months. Once his sentence was completed, he was extradited to France, where he was sentenced to seven years' imprisonment. Clearly, then, other clues need to be taken into consideration, such as those left in transitional spaces where movement is interrupted or slowed down: borders, airports, toll roads, and so on but also, as in this case, prisons (Sheller, 2014). In short, DNA helped first to establish the bioidentity of the individual in relation to another offense committed in France and then, in a new development, helped to determine the *biolocation* of the body (using DNA) of a man who moves around (drawing in his criminal record).

A mobile Other

For police officers, locating suspects becomes particularly important when they are mobile, in a context where the international mobility of persons, information, and objects is more dynamic, complex, and traceable than ever before (Sheller, 2014). Officers comment that genetic profiles recorded in the FNAEG may sometimes be matched with one, two, three, or four countries; for example, Germany, Spain, Austria, and Belgium (countries that have a large number of DNA-based Prüm exchanges with France). In their view, this is the sign of an "itinerant criminality." One senior officer at the FNAEG cited the case of 24 identical French traces that matched 16 Spanish traces, indicating that the alleged perpetrator had committed offenses on both sides of the border. In the view of one senior officer in charge of handling these issues, serial burglaries are committed by highly mobile teams that are "known" (in other words to the police) in other European countries. According to the people we interviewed, these practices are part of a "major trend" that has arisen in the last 15 years. A gendarme told us that prior to this period, in terms of property crime he only had to deal with local or regional criminality, except in the case of armed robbery. But today, he said, there was a criminality "that isn't rooted anywhere" and "rampages through France looting." The police officers we interviewed describe *mobile* suspects, not only because the Prüm system by definition focuses on people who have come from other countries or who commit offenses in other countries but also because, they claim, the individuals targeted are moving around much more than before.

In one third of the interviews we conducted on the subject of the Prüm decision – and with almost all the police officers interviewed, except those working near the Spanish border in the fight against drug trafficking from Spain – criminality coming from Eastern European countries was the issue. In the six cases selected by UCAP for our research, all the perpetrators came from Eastern Europe. For example, one gendarme told us:

> Where I'm seeing a huge change – it's not a small change, it's huge – is in property crime. Ten or 15 years ago, I didn't have any cases that involved people from Eastern countries [...]: Moldavia, Albania, former Yugoslavia so Serbians and Croatians, Romanians – the Romanians it's mainly Roma – [...] Lithuanians, Georgians, Ukrainians, that's more or less the range of people who've been coming to France, as organized gangs, for the last 15 years. They don't come as individuals or in groups of two or three to commit a few thefts, they come as an organized gang.
>
> *(Gendarme 5)*

This view is supported by the report of the investigative police's Information Service for Intelligence and Strategic Analysis on Organized Crime (Service d'information de renseignement et d'analyse stratégique sur la criminalité organisée, SIRASCO), which states that criminal organizations from the Balkans, the Caucasus, and Russia have come to add to those long established in France.[13] Another gendarme working in criminal identification added: "The burglaries we're seeing, that are plundering France, it's Eastern Europe. They stay six months in France, they commit all possible and imaginable crimes" (Gendarme 6). But when we told him that traces stored in the FNAEG are automatically compared with those in other databases in the Prüm system, he was surprised that he does not get more matches (around two each year), given what he sees as the large number of burglaries committed by people from Eastern Europe. In 2021, statistics for matches between an unknown stain found in France and a person from another European country showed that the percentage from the 11 Central and Eastern European countries taken together was only 8%. The highest percentage of matches was with the United Kingdom (55%), followed by Germany (10.7%), Spain (6.5%), the Netherlands (5.6%), and Austria (3.9%).[14] More generally, during the period of our research this "exponential" criminality was not manifested in a massive increase in the number of matches our interviewees found with Prüm system countries (between zero and six per year, often only one or two over an entire career). Furthermore, the ratio of "Prüm matches" to "national matches" was only 3% in France in 2015 (Santos and Machado, 2017). This figure is supported by statistics from the Ministry of Justice, which show that for all offenses taken together, including immigration offenses, the vast majority of those convicted (85%) were of French nationality (the 15% remaining being therefore of other nationalities).[15]

It is not possible from my research to fully decipher the reasons for the discrepancy between these figures and our interviewees' remarks.[16] What can be stated at this stage is first that the Prüm system tends to magnify the focus on crime that is both itinerant (by definition) and involves offenses that are minor and frequent (such as theft), or serious and draw major media attention.[17] This was confirmed by one senior officer at UCAP: "We have a lot of burglaries. That's the majority of the cases we deal with. [...] We get them from a lot of police stations. Just individual police stations, it's not that there's some big duty of reporting" (Police officer 14). Three main factors explain this phenomenon.

The first is that, in France as elsewhere, property crime (theft, burglary, etc.) is much more common than attacks on the person (murder, rape, etc.) (Vailly and Krikorian, 2018). Secondly, it depends on the kind of offenses non-nationals are involved in: 99.2% of convictions of non-nationals are not for serious crimes but for minor offenses, one quarter of them in the category "theft, receiving stolen goods."[18] Finally, it is due to a particularity of DNA, which provides a clue when investigators have not identified any suspect by traditional methods – something that is, they report, quite common in the case of burglary, although the clear-up rate is low. This point was already discussed in Chapter 1, so I shall not develop it further here.

Whatever the case may be, the implicit bioidentity of the suspects who emerge from the accounts given by our interviewees is that of a highly mobile subject, often coming from Eastern Europe, who can be identified thanks to stains left at the crime scene (for other studies on this theme, drawn from national points of contact in various European countries, see Machado et al., 2020). Here Rabinow's insight (1996, p. 103) that "older forms of cultural classification will be joined by a vast array of new ones that will cross-cut, partially supersede and eventually redefine the older categories" comes into play. More specifically, it appears that in some cases the traditional category of Eastern European countries expands when substantial files on organized gangs are assembled. In other cases, there is a disconnection between investigators' experience of Prüm matches, limited to a few cases over the course of their career, and their discourse. In other words, as well as manifesting a "geneticization"[19] (Lippman, 1992) of these investigation practices, in the discourse of our interviewees the older cultural classifications, assumptions, and contradictory experience in terms of frequency are rearticulated or attached to the bioidentities of suspects.

* * *

Advances in science and technology, combined with European-level decisions, have led to the growth of international exchanges of information on genetic profiles and individuals suspected of crime. Examining the meeting between European policy and actors involved in the constitution of bioidentities from within the field, I have studied how these provisions are put into practice and into discourse by social actors (police officers and gendarmes). These methods result in a continent-wide extension of suspects' bioidentities because the individual remains a suspect not only over time but also across the broader space of countries that include suspects in their databases. With the two stages of step one and step two, bioidentity is located, even more clearly than in the FNAEG, at the point where sameness and selfhood converge, where the Other is constituted both as a unique individual (by means of a DNA comparison that demonstrates their uniqueness, in the register of sameness, in step one) and as a member of a collective (of profiled perpetrators and suspects, in the register of selfhood, in step two). Three remarks may be drawn from this.

Firstly, some studies reduce the use of biometrics to corporeal data that serve as the sole "truth guarantee" as to the identity of individuals, established when they cross international borders (Aas, 2011). In this study, however, it becomes clear that biography and lived experience (criminal record, modus operandi, movements, etc.) are incorporated within a biological and social existence, over and above the data used to identify bodies. More generally, to paraphrase Didier Fassin (2018), life itself, revealed in step one, and life as such, which emerges in step two, create life spaces that are at their most interesting when they intersect and give the concept of life back all of its density. In our context, while DNA plays an important role in some cases, it is one element among others (biography, criminal history, etc.) in the case file. This confirms the need to correct the sometimes overstated value of biomedical knowledge in constituting subjects in the era of genetics (Nelkin and Lindee, 1994; Fox Keller, 2000). Old categories and assumptions about people from Eastern Europe are overlaid on or interwoven with those of "genetic suspects" (Hindmarsh and Prainsack, 2010), which in no way obscure them; rather they reinforce these categories and assumptions when DNA serves as a vector for accounts depicting "organized gangs" or "clans" coming from the East.

Secondly, bioidentity draws in issues that are political in the true sense: the Other is identified as such in a network of knowledge/power, a fact that is sometimes underestimated by research in this field, as Thomas Lemke points out (2015). Once again, this enables us to take a step back from the first accepted sense of bioidentity, associated with individuals voluntarily adhering to a group of patients, and to move toward the constitution of a bioidentity that in this case is formed within a network of power relations on multiple geographical scales (Glick Schiller and Salazar, 2013).

Finally, the fact that the same dynamic produces both circulation of information and sometimes obstacles to that circulation shows how securitarian flows are changing in the era of transnational spaces. Approaching the subject from the point of view of regimes of mobility allows us to consider how mobility and immobility are interwoven in the case of data that is relatively sensitive (being linked to DNA), despite the fact that, overall, mobility of information is the dominant paradigm. This invites comparison of this situation with those that do not involve genetic data (fingerprints, facial recognition, etc.), at a time when automatic exchange of other biometric data, such as facial recognition, within the EU, is being discussed institutionally,[20] and where the use of biometrics at border control for non-European citizens is rapidly growing (Schindel, 2019 [2018]).

Notes

1 In France, this decision was formalized by Decree no. 2009–785 of June 23 2009.
2 For the history of the process of this decision, see McCartney et al. (2011).
3 Exceptionally, individuals' profiles or unidentified stains may be sent urgently, as individual cases (known as article 3 consignments).
4 Decree no. 2009–931 of July 29 2009.
5 Council of the European Union, 2022. Statistics and reports on automated data exchange for 2021, see eu-council-prum-statistics-2021-5436-22.pdf (accessed June 24 2022).
6 Roughly every two months France sends all of its step one data to the various countries in turn. Other countries have chosen to send data more frequently, and to all countries at once.
7 Step two is in fact not technically part of the Prüm decision but rather a matter of traditional international co-operation.
8 Conversely, when other European countries consult the Prüm database, step one and step two are also implemented: France responds automatically whether a match exists or not, and, if it does, the third country may lodge a request with the French National Point of Contact, who will consult the FNAEG to obtain the additional information. With regard to step two, in 2016 417 requests were sent by France, and 1,340 were received from third countries (plus 152 article 3 applications, which involve individual requests relating to single cases).
9 An allele is one of the possible versions of a DNA sequence.
10 See General Secretariat of the Council, 2022. Implementation of the Provisions on Information Exchange of the Prüm Decisions, available at eu-council-prum-notifications-declarations-5183–22-rev2.pdf (accessed June 24 2022).
11 Santos et al. (2013) note that Estonia and Lithuania erase suspects' profiles ten years after their death (or one hundred years after they were first entered, in the case of Lithuania).
12 The relevant offenses in French law are "vol en bande organisée" (organized group theft) and "vol en réunion" (gang robbery) [translator].
13 Borredon, L., & Piel, S. (2013, December 14). Gangs des cités ou d'Europe de l'Est: Le nouveau visage du crime organisé. *Le Monde*.
14 Council of the European Union (2022). Statistics and reports on automated data exchange for 2021, see eu-council-prum-statistics-2021-5436-22.pdf (accessed June 24 2022).
15 Ministry of Justice (2020a). Statistiques des condamnations en 2018, https://bit.ly/3knqBon (accessed October 12 2020).

16 One obvious point is that some of the countries mentioned by the gendarme quoted are not in the Prüm system (Moldavia, Albania, Georgia, Ukraine, some countries of former Yugoslavia).

17 De Cossette, P. (2011). Un crime en Espagne résolu en France. *Europe 1*, https://www.europe1.fr/faits-divers/Un-crime-en-Espagne-resolu-en-France-339836 (accessed November 20 2020).

18 Ministry of Justice (2020b). Tableaux sur les condamnations selon les types d'infraction, la nature de l'infraction, la nature de la peine et les caractéristiques des condamnés, de 2006 à 2018 (provisoire), https://bit.ly/3knqBon (accessed October 12 2020).

19 For a discussion of this term in relation to medical practices, see Weiner et al. (2017).

20 Policy Department for Citizens' Rights and Constitutional Affairs 2020. Police Information Exchange. The future developments regarding Prüm and the API Directive. Directorate-General for Internal Policies. PE 658.542 – September 2020.

References

Aas, K. F. (2011). "Crimmigrant" bodies and bona fide travelers: Surveillance, citizenship and global governance. *Theoretical Criminology*, 15(3), 331–346. doi:10.1177/1362480610396643.

Appadurai, A. (2010). How histories make geographies: Circulation and context in a global perspective. *Journal of Transcultural Studies*, 1(1), 4–13. doi:10.11588/ts.2010.1.6129.

Bellivier, F., Krikorian, G., & Noiville, C. (2021). La coopération pénale en Europe entre souveraineté des États et disponibilité de l'information génétique: Promesses et faiblesses du système Prüm. In J. Vailly (Ed.), *Sur la trace des suspects: L'incorporation de la preuve et de l'indice à l'ère de la génétique* (pp. 205–223). Éditions de la Maison des sciences de l'homme.

Canguilhem, G. (1966). Le concept et la vie. *Revue philosophique de Louvain*, 64(82), 193–223. doi: 10.3406/phlou.1966.5347.

Cole, S. A., & Lynch, M. (2006). The social and legal construction of suspects. *Annual Review of Law and Social Science*, 2, 39–60. doi:10.1146/annurev.lawsocsci.2.081805.110001.

Cresswell, T. (2014). Friction. In P. Adey, D. Bissell, K. Hannam, P. Merriman, & M. Sheller (Eds.), *The Routledge handbook of mobilities* (pp. 107–115). Routledge.

Fassin, D. (2018). *Life: A critical user's manual.* Polity.

Fox Keller, E. (2000). *The century of the gene.* Harvard University Press.

Glick Schiller, N., & Salazar, N. B. (2013). Regimes of mobility across the globe. *Journal of Ethnic and Migration Studies*, 39(2), 183–200. doi:10.1080/1369183X.2013.723253.

Hindmarsh, R., & Prainsack, B. (Eds.). (2010). *Genetic suspects: Global governance of forensic DNA profiling and databasing.* Cambridge University Press.

Jenkins, R. (2000). Categorization: Identity, social process and epistemology. *Current Sociology*, 48(3), 7–25. doi:10.1177/0011392100048003003.

Lemke, T. (2015). Patient organizations as biosocial communities? Conceptual clarifications and critical remarks. In P. Wehling, W. Viehöver, & S. Koenen (Eds.), *The public shaping of medical research: Patient associations, health movements and biomedicine* (pp. 191–206). Routledge.

Lippman, A. (1992). Led (astray) by genetic maps: The cartography of the human genome and health care. *Social Science & Medicine*, 35(12), 1469–1476. doi:10.1016/0277-9536(92)90049-V.

Machado, H., & Granja, R. (2019). Risks and benefits of transnational exchange of forensic DNA data in the EU: The views of professionals operating the Prüm system. *Journal of Forensic and Legal Medicine*, 68, 1–7. doi:10.1016/j.jflm.2019.101872.

Machado, H., Granja, R., & Amelung, N. (2020). Constructing suspicion through forensic DNA databases in the EU: The views of the Prüm professionals. *British Journal of Criminology*, 60, 141–159. doi:10.1093/bjc/azz057.

McCartney, C. I., Wilson, T. J., & Williams, R. (2011). Transnational exchange of forensic DNA: Viability, legitimacy, and acceptability. *European Journal on Criminal policy and Research*, 17(4), 305–322.

Murray, T. (2019). Is genetic exceptionalism past its sell-by-date? On genomic diaries, context and content. *American Journal of Bioethics*, 19(1), 13–15. doi:10.1080/15265161.2018.1552038.

Nelkin, D., & Lindee, S. (1994). *The DNA mystique: The gene as cultural icon*. W. H. Freeman & Co Ltd.

Prainsack, B., & Toom, V. (2010). The Prüm régime: Situated dis/empowerment in transnational DNA profile exchange. *British Journal of Criminology*, 50(6), 1117–1135. doi:10.1093/bjc/azq055.

Rabinow, P. (1996). Artificiality and enlightenment: From sociobiology to biosociality. In P. Rabinow (Ed.), *Essays on the anthropology of reason* (pp. 91–112). Princeton University Press.

Santos, F., & Machado, H. (2017). Patterns of exchange of forensic DNA data in the European Union through the Prüm system. *Science and Justice*, 57(4), 307–313. doi:10.1016/j.scijus.2017.04.001.

Santos, F., Machado, H., & Silva, S. (2013). Forensic DNA databases in European countries: Is size linked to performance? *Life Sciences, Society and Policy*, 9, 1–13. doi:10.1186/2195-7819-9-12.

Schindel, E. (2019 [2018]). Biométrie, normalisation des corps et contrôle des frontières dans l'Union Européenne. *Politika*. doi:10.26095/s5vg-9p34.

Sheller, M. (2014). The new mobilities paradigm for a live sociology. *Current Sociology Review*, 62(6), 789–811. doi:10.1177/0011392114533211.

Strathern, M. (Ed.). (2000). *Audit culture: Anthropological studies in accountability, ethics and the academy*. Routledge.

Taverne, M. D., & Broeders, T. (2015). *The light's at the end of the funnel! Evaluating the effectiveness of the transnational exchange of DNA profiles between the Netherlands and other Prüm Countries*. Legal Publishers.

Toom, V. (2018). *Cross-border exchange and comparison of forensic DNA data in the context of the Prüm decision*. Brussels, Report for Directorate general for internal policies, Policy department for citizen's rights and constitutional affairs, Civil liberties, justice and home affairs, June 2018.

Toom, V., Granja, R., & Ludvig, A. (2019). The Prüm decisions as an aspirational regime: Reviewing a decade of cross-border exchange and comparison of forensic DNA data. *Forensic Science International: Genetics*, 41, 50–57. doi:10.1016/j.fsigen.2019.03.023.

Vailly, J. (2023). Identifier, connecter, localiser: La bio-identité des suspects génétiques en Europe. *L'Homme - Revue française d'anthropologie*, 245, 23–54. doi:10.4000/lhomme.45046.

Vailly, J., Kehr, J., & Niewöhner, J. (Eds.). (2011). *De la vie biologique à la vie sociale: Approches sociologiques et anthropologiques*. La Découverte.

Vailly, J., & Krikorian, G. (2018). Durabilité et extension du soupçon: Catégorisations et usages policiers du fichier d'empreintes génétiques en France. *Revue française de sociologie*, 59(4), 707–733. doi:10.3917/rfs.594.0707.

Weiner, K., Martin, P., Richards, M., & Tutton, R. (2017). Have we seen the geneticisation of society? Expectations and evidence. *Sociology of Health & Illness*, 39(7), 989–1004. doi:10.1111/1467-9566.12551.

CONCLUSION

This book offers a contribution to analysis of the body of the contemporary suspect, or more precisely of that body as witness to scientific and legal truths deemed the marker of past offenses and of present and future risks to society. On that basis, it examines how definitions and delineations of criminality, individual rights, and concepts of identity and difference are transformed by the development of biological knowledge and techniques concerning the human. Reflecting on a series of scientific, legal, and political developments that have transformed the use of DNA, it analyzes the contemporary practices emerging from these in the spheres of policing, the justice system, and science. It also offers a broader reflection on what Foucault calls the "government" of security in the era of genetics and biometrics.

In addressing these questions, which are at once vast and embedded in social micropractices, a social sciences approach makes it possible to study how public policies and innovations that bring changes to the law are deployed on the ground, and to grasp discourses and practices at the level of actors in the field. We therefore conducted in-depth interviews with individuals who implement policies, those who propose new technical and scientific approaches, and those who contest them: officers of the forensic police, judges and lawyers, police investigators, gendarmes, senior civil servants, heads of biotechnology companies, and opponents of the way the FNAEG is currently used. We observed trials of individuals who refused to provide a DNA sample and gatherings of professionals (conferences, a session of the French National Consultative Committee on Human Rights, and others). A number of criminal cases were analyzed, some of them illustrating the major contribution made by DNA to identifying the perpetrators of crime and establishing judicial proof, notwithstanding the fact that no overall evaluation of these policies is available. In the view of some actors, current limits on genetic profiling are as they should be.

DOI: 10.4324/9781003456056-11

Others believe they are too restrictive, while still others see them as too broad. However that may be, in democratic societies the question of the appropriateness, the scope, and the use of databases cannot be reduced purely to their efficacy. My aim here is rather to show what is produced when actors on the ground appropriate categories defined in law and the rationales that come into play with the proliferation and expansion of databases.

The question of how the suspect body and the government of security have changed in the era of genetics is articulated around three themes: (1) how the relationship between respect for individual rights and the security of populations is discussed in society and put into practice, which addresses the relationship between penal policy, security policy, and civil liberties; (2) the new issues uses of DNA by the police and the justice system, such as phenotyping, bring into play, which concerns the articulation between the biological and the social in the construction of identities and alterities; (3) the new boundaries of DNA evidence and circulation of data among European states. This final theme raises two questions, first concerning the place of science in the production and administration of judicial truth, and second about the relations between the national and international in the circulation of data and people. Rather than returning to each of these three themes, my conclusion attempts to draw out the social meaning of these developments.

A number of remarks are called for, each offering the potential for further discussion in the future. New uses of DNA have ushered in a new era, succeeding the 20th-century period of databases confined to sex offenders, because the expansion of DNA databases and its most recent manifestation is a matter not only of techniques applied to individuals but also of the government of populations. It is striking that this expansion is occurring in increasing numbers of countries where genetic profiling has been introduced. The question of transparency also needs to be addressed because in France data relating to the FNAEG or other genetic analyses used in criminal cases are not as accessible as in, for example, the United Kingdom, which publishes reports on the subject. The increasingly broad range of individuals from whom DNA samples are taken, and of types of offense for which DNA data are retained, sometimes described as "functional drift" (Hindmarsh and Prainsack, 2010, p. 28), makes it all the more urgent to grasp the arguments and reasoning of the professionals.

Securitarian justice, police-based security

The police are almost unanimous in wishing for the largest database permitted by the law, in order to increase the statistical probability of matches between profiles and to meet the demand of victims who want the perpetrators of crimes identified. This view converges with the legislators' choice to extend the field of application of the FNAEG, making it quite natural for the police to make the greatest possible use of a tool that technically can help advance their investigations. Within this general perspective, those who promote such uses of DNA take two types of approach, which sometimes overlap.

The first of these is to extend profiling to all of those who might commit offenses, in order to identify the group that could represent a potential danger. In this sense, it is a matter of not only identifying but also making a selection, in order to distinguish categories of individuals who constitute a risk. While this is a quite conventional approach in security practice, contemporary techniques bring qualitative changes in terms of speed of execution and lasting application, scientific grounding, and digital classification (Gros, 2019 [2012]). What could be described as "genetic transparency" enables the police to define the profiles of offenders or potential offenders, in the same way as it allows medical practitioners to define the profiles of patients or potential patients.

The classification of groups and individuals, based not only on their actions but also the possibility that they might commit them, is enshrined in the text of the law. At the same time, it appears to *exceed* the law in seeking to anticipate and prevent the risk of crime, and to identify future perpetrators. To understand the tension between this internalization and externalization of the law, it may be aligned with an important, broader change in the criminal law, whereby individuals are maintained under its jurisdiction by virtue not only of the acts they commit but also of the potential for future acts (Delmas-Marty, 2010). Independently of genetic databases, the 2008 French law on preventative detention authorizes preventative measures in anticipation of potential behavior, for the purpose of prevention and precaution. This was initially applied to sex offenders but since 2015 has also been applied in cases of terrorism. The individual thus remains subject to penal jurisdiction not only on the basis of her/his actions but also, once she/he has served her/his sentence, on the basis of the *risk* that she/he will commit a crime. Legal scholar Mireille Delmas-Marty points out that this creates a doubling of the penal system, supplementing the traditional "responsibility/punishment" binary with a new pairing of "dangerousness/preventative measure." Retaining the majority of suspect profiles in a database ultimately fits well in a penal framework that is attempting to establish a form of predictive, securitarian justice.

The second approach supported by professionals, which is in some sense an extension of the first, is to move to a generalized expansion that would basically mean that all citizens were potential criminals. This approach is sometimes formulated explicitly, with the ambition of profiling the entire population of a country, and sometimes in a more roundabout, indirect way, put into practice through searches for partial genetic matches among increasingly larger groups. In both cases, taking the risk of including a smaller proportion of people in the database so that some suspects pass through the net appears to be no longer acceptable to the majority of actors. As a senior judge we interviewed said:

> There's no longer that kind of acceptance of the risk that there might have been 20 or 30 years ago. When we said, well yes, not everyone is in the database, but that's the price you pay for individual freedom, so that you don't have a Leviathan or an omniscient state that knows everything about

> everybody. That's the price you pay, so there are criminals who aren't in the databases. Now, you see it a lot with terrorism, people are not happy to pay that price anymore.
>
> *(Judge 13)*

This situation has become established in the context of changing relations of power between the police and the justice system. The regulatory committees for both the courts and the police, and the legal guarantees that frame the security apparatus, offer some pledges as to the balance between the penal state, the securitarian state, and collective freedoms. Despite this, it seems that the power relation in the matter of databases puts the justice system and the appellant at a disadvantage compared to the police (profiling of those questioned under caution, responsibility for entering records into the FNAEG resting with the police, etc.). The same observation can be made about the Prüm system, given the large number of countries where management of DNA databases rests with the police. In terms of the different senses of the term "security" discussed in the introduction, this supports a development that reinforces police-based security to the detriment of judicial security, which was historically primary (Gros, 2019 [2012]).

One of the questions raised by this shift is whether the FNAEG can still be considered a judicial database; in other words, a database whose aim is to contribute to the production of DNA evidence in order to establish judicial truth (as when it was set up), or whether it is a database for flagging potential suspects whose prior behavior suggests that they might be clients for the police. Overall, DNA databases clearly constitute not only a tool of identification under the jurisdiction of a judge but also a tool of investigation in the hands of the police. While originally DNA comparisons aimed to identify or to exonerate suspects found by other investigation methods, through a one-time comparison of their DNA with biological material found at a crime scene, the large DNA databases are also mechanisms for actively maintaining individuals in the status of suspect. In this respect, it is worth remembering that DNA can also reveal the absence of a match, helping to exonerate an individual and hence remove her/him from this category, and sometimes take her/him off death row, as shown by dozens of cases in the United States. Nevertheless, there is a much larger shift toward the profiles of millions of individuals, including minors, being held in the database for years although they have not been convicted. This process is amplified by familial searching, extending suspicion to those biologically related to people included in the database, not to mention the developing technology of genealogical searching, which indirectly affects a large proportion of the United States population and users of consumer websites. Added to these are the individuals in Europe who become suspects throughout the entire continent, provided that it is permitted by the principle of sovereignty, according to which the criminal law in each state imposes restrictions on what data may be exchanged. As I suggested above, a sort of continuum becomes established between different kinds of suspects (profiled suspects, familial suspects, genealogical suspects, European continent-wide suspects).

Moreover, in relation to phenotyping, I have shown how crucial questions relating to how the racialization of individuals is deproblematized and how professionals and the public perceive the inscription of difference in bodies. I have pointed out that new appearance tests and focusing on the visible make origin tests acceptable and routine, without the combination of DNA, crime, and origin being as controversial, even explosive, as it was ten years earlier in France.

In short, we have moved from a rationale of targeted identification of individuals to one of profiling based on suspicion or the provision of data on one part of the population. The expansion of databases, tests on extended circles of relatives, and increasingly advanced methods of analyzing DNA stains raise the question of whether the "truth machine" is running out of control.

No opposition from the majority of the population

The various developments I have summed up here overall engender little public reaction in France or other countries. The lack of public debate does not necessarily indicate that the majority are in favor. However, the comments of opponents are illuminating because by their own admission they find it difficult to gain a hearing for their cause and to mobilize public opinion in France. This is also the case when they try to make their argument in the media, indicating that the absence of debate cannot entirely be interpreted as citizens or residents simply failing to recognize the facts. It indicates rather a tolerance, whether this can be ascribed to indifference as to the current conditions of use of the FNAEG or to consent from the majority of the French population. It seems that professional practice resonates with concerns in the public space and political discourse, for the emotions aroused by horrific crimes or terrorism create a climate that is fed by debates around security. The police and gendarmerie are concerned with promoting, through the use of advanced technologies, a principle of security applied to entire populations who broadly tolerate it, and purportedly seek to limit a danger that is expressed in bodily form. However this may be, these methods cannot simply be seen as an imposition from on high. Molecular knowledge of the human body has become not only a securitarian instrument driven by the state but also an essential argument in victims' demands, as well as a symbol of the indifference or assent of the majority of the population. Thus "government," as typically defined, is exercised not only from the top of the state downward but also sometimes from the base toward the top. In this sense, I would add that we may talk not only of government but also of govern/mentality.

More generally, we have thus moved from a period of hostility toward personal databases and databanks (Piazza, 2009) to a form of indifference or support, in a broader context where resistance to the now systematic use of biometrics in identity documents, and the processing of these data, has become relatively marginal. An opinion issued by the National Consultative Committee on Ethics with regard to biometric data states:

> We are seeing a sort of consensual confiscation of freedom. In the name of the security paradigm, our society is quietly becoming accustomed to the use of these biometric markers, and everyone ultimately, and even with some indifference, accepts being registered, observed, noticed, traced, often without even being aware of it.
>
> *(2007, p. 16)*[1]

Some writers have highlighted the growing demand for security among the public and institutions in European and North American societies, both before 9/11 and even more since then (Castel, 2003; Delmas-Marty, 2010; Marx, 2015). For example, Robert Castel (2003, p. 6) remarks:

> Modern insecurity is not the absence of protections, but rather their opposite, the shadow they cast over a social world that is organized around a ceaseless quest for protection and a desperate search for security.

For these diverse reasons, the French population's majority tolerance of the FNAEG prompts reflection on situations that cannot be reduced to imposed surveillance. Many academic research studies emphasize the effects of hierarchical imposition of practices of surveillance and social monitoring but fail to explain why some tools are adopted and even supported by individuals or communities who are also affected by them. Some of these studies focus on an almost imperceptible "creeping surveillance" marked by subtle and invisible forms of social monitoring (Nelkin and Andrews, 1999). They often omit to mention that modern forms of surveillance in democratic countries are more participatory than they were in the past (Gros, 2019 [2012]). A new culture appears to call for ever more protection and security, without any sense of the efficacy of the measures taken. Yet the growing possibilities of access to identification on the basis of surreptitious traces raise questions about the disappearance of anonymity and the absence of safeguards against a potential totalitarian regime.

From surveillance to capture

Further to these reflections, it may be added that it is hard to see the police's use of genealogical databases in terms of Orwellian "Big Brother" surveillance. The notion of "capture," proposed in the 1990s by the philosopher of information and communication technologies Philip Agre (1994), seems to better reflect what is played out in this case. Capture refers to the act of transferring human activities, translated into data, via the intermediary of a human operator or an electronic device, in a context of growing integration of computers into everyday practices. It involves, for example, the reorganization of work activities "captured" by computers and retranscribed by artificial intelligence. In the context under discussion, it is genetic data that are captured: a database like GEDmatch captures the data of all users who upload information from other databases.

There are a number of points to be made in accounting for this process in more depth. First, as I have shown, with genealogical tests the issue is no longer one of distinguishing groups classified differently according to dangerousness and risk category, as suggested in many studies of surveillance (Lyon, 2018) but rather of targeting at least the majority of the population of a country like the United States, and beyond that the population of other countries. Second, the capture model presupposes that the information captured is directed in many different ways, to many different ends. While the surveillance model rested for a long time on the idea that masses of data were gathered and stored in a central location, the capture model is not a unitary phenomenon. On the contrary, each domain of activity in which private databases are concerned – in this case genealogy for family research, the study of "predisposition" to disease, criminal investigation – has its own logic, its own history, its own repertoire of actions, and its own social relations. Agre also argues that this model is different from the surveillance model in the sense that the organization is decentralized. In our context, there is a whole series of genealogical databases, some of them networked together. Moreover, while the surveillance model originated in the political sphere of state action, even if it was later modified by the study of digital tools (Aïm, 2020), the capture model has deep roots in the practical application of information systems. In our context, the capture of genetic data has a dual origin, with both the state and private websites. Finally, the capture model helps to explain the repercussions of gathering information on private life and the restructuring of the work of the police and forensic experts, in a process where the individual whose genetic data are compared is not under permanent observation. It thus seems that the capture model can usefully complement analysis of these developments in genetics.

Toward a new role for judges?

Given the various new approaches I have described (searching for partial matches in DNA databases, phenotyping, the Prüm system), the tendency is toward diversification of technical approaches, each of which taps into social, political, moral, and legal issues. It is striking that reference is made to privacy in the context of all these techniques, whether the FNAEG, with the debate on non-coding DNA (by opponents of current uses of the database), kinship and genealogical testing (by critical judges, website users, legal scholars, etc.), and phenotyping (particularly by judges and geneticists). Such reference does not influence their development in a broader context where public demands for privacy have fallen away. This is remarkable in a country like France, where historically the protection of the right to private life has been strong (Halpérin, 2015). If we extend Bernard Harcourt's remark (2015, p. 168) on the commercial logic of the internet to issues of security, it seems that "privacy fared a lot better when it was seen as an integral part of our human essence," in the mid-20th century, than since it has been used for the alleged purpose of increasing our security.

I focus particularly on the notion of privacy because it has been debated in the European Court of Human Rights (ECHR) from the point of view of proportionality, which the majority of the professional actors we encountered during our research do not address. A relatively contained resistance to the new developments is evident in the appeals made to the ECHR by individuals convicted of refusing to provide a DNA sample; the Court ultimately ruled against France on the FNAEG. Through these opponents of the use of the FNAEG, the dual nature of the "arm of the law", mobilized by those who wish to criticize this public policy and its application, is revealed (Israël, 2020). It is first defensive, as it relies on the courts to become a platform for expression and a stage of contestation. It is also offensive, in that it appeals to justice in the name of higher principles recognized by international agreements. Finally, it extends beyond geographical boundaries, and it is by turning the tools of the legal sphere back on itself that it seems to produce the greatest effect. Thus the role of the ECHR helps to reveal some of the tensions at work on the European rather than the national level. This is especially true since the European Convention on Human Rights, signed in 1948 in Paris after 60 sessions of debate, would be difficult to renegotiate if an individual government wished to do so, given the large number of countries involved.[2] Notwithstanding its limitations, the law, in recent times, seems to have at least partially regained some of the ground dominated by police rationales, via a detour through international bodies. Time will tell how this manifests at national level.

What emerges at the current time is a society that seems divided into two types of subject: a large majority who say they have nothing to hide and feel protected by police databases (consenting subjects), and a minority who feel they are under surveillance and fear being targeted (opposing subjects). This division is set in a context where new advances in science and technology will continue to foster not only the targeted identification of individuals but also the profiling of groups, who will no doubt produce new suspects. In this sense, what I argue here is that DNA is not just a tracker of suspicion but constitutes a marker of contemporary social developments, both around consent to the transfer of bodily and personal data and around the vain pursuit of a world free of risk and crime.

Notes

1 Comité consultatif national d'éthique (2007). Avis no. 98: "Biométrie, données identifiantes et droits de l'homme."

2 François Héran, lectures at the Collège de France, 2017–2018, and https://www.college-de-france.fr/site/francois-heran/Francois-Heran-Video-de-presentation-du-cours-de-l-annee.htm (accessed March 17 2022).

References

Agre, P. E. (1994). Surveillance and capture: Two models of privacy. *Information Society*, 10(2), 101–127. doi:10.1080/01972243.1994.9960162.

Aïm, O. (2020). *Les théories de la surveillance: Du panoptique aux* Surveillance Studies. Armand Colin.

Castel, R. (2003). *L'insécurité sociale: Qu'est-ce qu'être protégé?* Seuil.

Delmas-Marty, M. (2010). *Libertés et sûreté dans un monde dangereux*. Seuil.

Gros, F. (2019 [2012]). *The security principle: From serenity to regulation*, trans. David Broder. Verso.

Halpérin, J.-L. (2015). Protection de la vie privée et privacy: Deux traditions juridiques différentes? *Nouveaux Cahiers du Conseil constitutionnel*, 48, 59–68. doi:10.3917/nccc1.048.0059.

Harcourt, B. (2015). *Exposed: Desire and disobedience in the digital age*. Harvard University Press.

Hindmarsh, R., & Prainsack, B. (Eds.). (2010). *Genetic suspects: Global governance of forensic DNA profiling and databasing*. Cambridge University Press.

Israël, L. (2020). *L'arme du droit*, 2nd edn. Presses de Sciences Po.

Lyon, D. (2018). *The culture of surveillance*. Polity.

Marx, G. T. (2015). Surveillance studies. *International encyclopedia of the social and behavioral sciences*, 23, 733–741. doi:10.1016/B978-0-08-097086-8.64025-4.

Nelkin, D., & Andrews, L. (1999). DNA identification and surveillance creep. *Sociology of Health & Illness*, 21(5), 689–706. doi:10.1111/1467-9566.00179.

Piazza, P. (2009). Edvige et les résistances au fichage policier. *Hermès, La Revue*, 53, 75–78. doi:10.4267/2042/31479.

INDEX

References to tables are in **bold**.

For Product Safety Concerns and Information please contact our EU representative GPSR@taylorandfrancis.com
Taylor & Francis Verlag GmbH, Kaufingerstraße 24, 80331 München, Germany

www.ingramcontent.com/pod-product-compliance
Ingram Content Group UK Ltd.
Pitfield, Milton Keynes, MK11 3LW, UK
UKHW020005200926
475702UK00015B/2486
* 9 7 8 1 0 3 2 5 8 8 8 8 9 *